Covering the Shi`a

Covering the Shi`a

English Press Representation of the Lebanese Shi`a 1975–1985

Robert Tomlinson

LEXINGTON BOOKS
Lanham • Boulder • New York • London

Published by Lexington Books
An imprint of The Rowman & Littlefield Publishing Group, Inc.
4501 Forbes Boulevard, Suite 200, Lanham, Maryland 20706
www.rowman.com

6 Tinworth Street, London SE11 5AL

Copyright © 2018 by The Rowman & Littlefield Publishing Group, Inc.

All rights reserved. No part of this book may be reproduced in any form or by any electronic or mechanical means, including information storage and retrieval systems, without written permission from the publisher, except by a reviewer who may quote passages in a review.

British Library Cataloguing in Publication Information Available

Library of Congress Cataloging-in-Publication Data Available

ISBN 978-1-4985-6547-9 (cloth : alk. paper)
ISBN 978-1-4985-6548-6 (electronic)

∞™ The paper used in this publication meets the minimum requirements of American National Standard for Information Sciences Permanence of Paper for Printed Library Materials, ANSI/NISO Z39.48-1992.

Printed in the United States of America

Dedication

To the 241 Americans who lost their lives at the Marine Battalion Landing Team (BLT) headquarters in Beirut on October 23, 1983. May they always be remembered.

Contents

A Note on Transliteration		ix
Acknowledgments		xi
Introduction		xiii
1	Musa al-Sadr and the Shi`i Narratives in Lebanon, 1975–1985:	1
2	The Shi`a Expulsion from Nab`a: Nab`a and the Shi`a Influence	37
3	The Effects of the Iranian Revolution on the Lebanese Shi`a	57
4	The Israeli Invasion of Lebanon 1982	89
5	Epilogue	121
Conclusion		129
Bibliography		137
Index		143
About the Author		151

A Note on Transliteration

Throughout this work I have attempted to standardize the transliteration of Arabic terms. In a number of cases where authors quote or use reports directly from correspondence and media outlets, their spellings of the terms appear. The intent is to give the reader a better understanding of the difficulty obtaining an accurate representation of what was happening in Lebanon to the Shi`a during the years of this study. In most other cases, I have applied generally accepted transliteration of Arabic and Persian words, as noted by the *International Journal of Middle East Studies*.

In support of the reader's experience, the following conventions have been adopted for referencing Shi`i Islam:

Shi`i* – adjective and singular noun (referring to an individual within *Shi`ism)
Shi`a – plural noun, a collective reference to the community in general

Map of Lebanon *Source:* CIA World Factbook

Acknowledgments

Most individuals reading this book will skip over this page in order to get to the meat of the text. However, in many ways this is the most important page in the book. Few authors are able to invest the enormous amount of time and effort in crafting a book without the help and encouragement of others. For my part, I had a number of people help sustain my efforts and offer advice and encouragement along the way. It is my goal to publically acknowledge their efforts and to thank those who helped bring this book to fruition. First, to Joseph Parry, Bryndee Ryan, and the other editorial folks at Lexington Press, I appreciate your help in the book production process. Next, to my dissertation committee at Claremont Graduate University, Professors Arash Khazeni, Janet Farrell Brodie and Hamid Mavani these individuals encouraged me to pursue the topic of this book and were also my first call once I received the book contract. I am enormously grateful for your support and your sage advice along the way. Thank you to my academic colleagues from the School of Advanced Military Studies (SAMS) in Ft. Leavenworth, Kansas or, as I affectionately refer to them, members of the Hayloft. During my first foray into the academic realm these Hayloft members constructed an outstanding atmosphere where a fledgling academic could exchange ideas and grow. Dr. G. Steve (Viper) Lauer, Dr. Chris (Trunk Monkey) Marsh, Dr. Rick (The Pope) Herrera, Dr. Misha (Xena) Blocksome, Dr. Jeff (Kubster) Kubiak, and Dr. Tony (Shaggy) Carlson you are the best. Also, honorary members of the Hayloft, Dr. Robert Davis and Dr. Steve Bourque I appreciate your constant support and friendship. To my partner in crime here at the Naval War College, Dr. Jon Czarnecki, thanks for being a great sounding board for the different ideas and thoughts I had while working on this project. A big shout out and word of thanks also go to Dr. Donald Stoker. Don you are a great author and historian and I thank you for challenging me to write this book and encouraging me along the way.

The people who were the closest to me during this process were my family. I particularly wish to acknowledge my children Katrina, Rob Jr., Troy, and Tiffany who are always an inspiration, and Nichole who inevitably offered humor along the journey. To my brother and sisters, Arthur, Carolyn, and Donna thank you for your constant support. To my parents; my mother Doris Tomlinson, who is no longer with us but inspires me spiritually every day and to my father, Arthur Tomlinson, who has always been a source of strength and inspiration I thank you. Finally, to the most important person in this process who has been through the ups and down and the pain and joy of this project my wife, Dr. Katherine Yvette Tomlinson. Thank you for your outstanding critiques of my work during this process. You have my eternal gratitude and, as always, my love.

Introduction

October 16, 1983—on an autumn day in South Lebanon, a nineteen-year-old young man, Soheil Hammoura, waited with thousands of other Shi`a men and women to see the procession coming down the main street.[1] The procession, in the town of Nabatiyah, commemorated Ashura, one of the defining events in the Shi`i religion.[2] This event (which highlights a key episode in the schism between the Shi`i and the Sunni sects of Islam) is as important symbolically to the Shi`a as the crucifixion is to Christianity.[3] On this day, the passion and sacrifice of Imam Husayn, the son of Imam Ali and grandson of the Seal of Prophets, Muhammad (the most revered religious leader in Islamic history), was reenacted.[4]

More than a thousand years before this day, Imam Husayn stood on the plains outside of present day Kerbala, Iraq, and courageously faced imminent death, unflinching with total faith and commitment to Allah (God) and to the Islamic principle that a man must "forbid the evil" and do what is right. Facing enormous odds, Husayn and his small band of followers were willing to make the point that they would not submit to an unjust, illegitimate, and corrupt ruler and that they would do God's will no matter the outcome. That outcome was certain: although they fought courageously against the Army of Yazid I—the Islamic leader (caliphate) whom Husayn viewed as illegitimate and corrupt—death came to Husayn and his followers.[5]

Husayn's sacrifice represented an even larger theme within the Shi`i religious tradition. Theologically, the Shi`a believe in "an absolute and irrevocable necessity of justice as a condition of rulership."[6] The notion of justice, whether it is religious, social, or economic, resonates within the community. Husayn's stand at Kerbala embodied the overall ideal that this community of the faithful would seek justice and fairness no matter the odds.

Throughout Shi'i Islam Husayn's ordeal at Kerbala is noted in rituals of remembrance. Many of these rituals include memorial services and recitations. However, there are other commemorations that are less accepted within the Shi'i mainstream. One such commemoration is enigmatic to most outsiders because Shi'a men cut themselves on the forehead to induce bleeding; it involves self-flagellation, chanting, and the beating of chests. The purpose of this ritual is to induce in the participants and observers the passion and sense of self-sacrifice experienced by Husayn and his followers so many years ago.[7] Though a pious occasion, this is not a ceremony that every leader supports. Many eschew the ceremony as being base and not representative of the true Shi'i religion, but in this instance, when the Shi'i community had been under intense pressure from the Lebanese Civil War and the recent Israeli invasion, commemorating this seminal event in their religion seemed even more important and appropriate.[8]

Soheil Hammoura had traveled from Beirut to witness the procession. In the midst of the procession, with thousands of people in the streets and passions running high, a convoy of Israeli military vehicles attempted to proceed through the ceremony. The participants were angered by the Israelis' total disregard of their religious observance and their homeland. The Israeli soldiers, part of the army that had invaded Lebanon less than a year before, at this point faced an incensed and frenzied crowd throwing stones at them. The soldiers reacted with force: using automatic weapons, they killed two worshippers and wounded another seven as they attempted to extract themselves from the angry throng.[9] Among the dead was Soheil Hammoura. Hammoura, who had not been particularly religious, was then transformed into a symbol of martyrdom for the Shi'a. The reaction from the Shi'i community was almost immediate. Shams al-Din, leader of the powerful "Higher Islamic Shi'ite Council of Lebanon" issued a religious decree (*fatwa*) stating that no Shi'a could deal with the Israelis.[10] As a result, resistance to the Israelis was now a religious obligation for the Shi'a in Lebanon. Amal, the most prominent Shi'i militia group of that time also condemned the Israeli attack on the worshippers and was forced to take a more active role in fighting against the Israeli Defense Force (IDF), lest it be discredited in the eyes of the Shi'i community.[11] For the Shi'a of Lebanon, this one act by the Israeli forces was deemed sacrilegious and became the rallying point of their resistance to the Israeli occupation of Lebanon.[12]

Other segments of Lebanese society voiced their disapprobation of the Israeli operation. Shafiq al-Wazzan, the Lebanese prime minister, condemned the Israeli action, stating, "The Israeli occupation cannot possibly be perpetuated. . . . The Lebanese must take pride in the national uprising staged by our sons in An-Nabatiyah."[13] The Lebanese press decried the incident vehemently, but the *New York Times* and most American media, as well as the *Times* (London) and the majority of British media, represented the incident differently.

Seven days after the incident in Nabatiyah, a truck laden with explosives drove through a sentry point and detonated underneath the United States Marine Battalion Landing Team (BLT) headquarters. Two hundred forty-one Americans were killed that morning. The culprit for the attack was a radical Shi`i group from Baalbek, Lebanon.[14] The American press asked, "Why, how could this happen?"[15] Had the Lebanese Shi`a narrative been accurately reported and understood, perhaps such an occurrence could have been anticipated, if not avoided.

How did the English-language press and media represent the Lebanese Shi`a from 1975 to 1985?[16] English-language media often ignored the plight of the Shi`a, conflated their civil rights movement in Lebanon with other Arab independence movements, and failed to understand and report the nature of the transnational networks that supported the Shi`i community in Lebanon. This book focuses particular attention on the *New York Times,* the *Times* (London), and the *Guardian* (Manchester). During this period, the *New York Times,* the *Times*, and the *Guardian* were among the most influential institutions in shaping the information and stories in the realm of international affairs for the English-language market.[17]

The *New York Times,* the *Times* (London), and the *Guardian* (Manchester) were the preferred papers of the English-language foreign policy making apparatus and the business community.[18] Information from these papers informed and educated these groups about events within Lebanon. The lack of understanding of the role of the Shi`a within Lebanese society by members of the English-language foreign policy making apparatus and the business community can in no small part be linked to the dearth of information, and distortions of the Shi`a represented in these papers.[19]

This book also highlights that although the American and British media misrepresented the Lebanese Shi`a, discernible differences existed in the coverage offered by the two media outlets. Oftentimes from 1975 to 1985, the American press and media, in particular the *New York Times,* constructed a representation of the Lebanese Shi`a different from what appeared in the British press and media. While the American press[20] often ignored the Lebanese Shi`a, or erroneously conflated their movement with other Arab independence groups or the Shi`a revolution in Iran, the British prestige press and media, particularly the *Times* and the *Guardian*, were able to discern some of these differences and gave their readers a more nuanced picture of the events in Lebanon.

Underlying the American and British media representation of the Lebanese Shi`a, is narrative—a contested concept within academia and the subject of a great deal of debate. In order to give the reader a solid framework with which to examine the Lebanese Shi`a, this book narrowly defines *narrative* as the historically grounded story that reflects a community's self-identity and experience—or explains its hopes, aspirations, and concerns.[21] The construction of a "news narrative" is accomplished in a larger discourse, as documented by broadcast or print journalists.[22]

Modern technology, the use of computers and social media has had a profound effect on the construction of narrative. Groups such as the Islamic State in the Levant (ISIL) have been able to construct their own narrative through the use of images, personal testimonies, and storylines in a professional, relatively inexpensive manner. This narrative is then disseminated to millions worldwide through the internet. That technology, however, was unavailable during the timeframe covered in this book. Ultimately, the American and British press constructed for their Western audiences a narrative representation of the Lebanese Shi`a that did not coincide with that group's putative representation of itself. Once ascertained, it is clear that the predominant Lebanese Shi`a narratives from 1975 to 1985 contrast with the representations in American and British media.

This book would be remiss if it did not mention, albeit briefly, the theory of political communications. Political communications theory seeks to explain the transmission of narrative to policymakers using strategic dissemination to influence public knowledge, beliefs, and actions on political matters. Political communications theory emphasizes the strategic nature of communication, highlighting the role of persuasion in political discourse.[23] Certainly, policymakers used information garnered from news sources to inform decisions and actions with regard to Lebanon. Although this work is focused on how the English language press and media represented the Lebanese Shi`a, political communications theory is an understated part of this story. The messages created by the press and media directly affected how policymakers supported the legitimacy of their decision making, or shaped a new narrative to fit their desired policy goals.

ORGANIZATION AND METHODOLOGY

This book is organized into an introduction and four chapters, each chapter exploring one of four critical events that shaped a dominant narrative within the Shi`i community between 1975 and 1985.[24] The first chapter explores Musa al-Sadr and his role in transforming the Shi`a into a more activist community, one that demanded civil rights within Lebanese society and legitimized the use of force in the community's defense. The second chapter centers on the expulsion of the Shi`a from the town of Nab`a and explains how that event shaped their notion of armed resistance to violence and injustice perpetrated against the Lebanese Shi`i community. Chapter 3 covers the effects of the Iranian Revolution on the Lebanese Shi`a and exposes the transnational nature of the Shi`i community. Chapter 4 covers the Israeli invasion of 1982 and its solidifying effect on the civil rights and armed resistance movements for the Lebanese Shi`a. Each chapter also highlights the coverage of the English-language press and media of the respective events that shaped the Shi`i narratives in Lebanon. The conclusion of the book offers an explanation as to why the representation by English-language press and media was so at odds with the narratives of the Lebanese Shi`a. The inability of journalists and correspondents to uncover and interpret the dominant narrative of the Lebanese Shi`a afforded the media little chance to properly decode and represent the Lebanese Shi`a's actions.

Throughout, this book references and uses Edward Said's concept of Orientalism to uncover a specific tendency of American and British reporters in representing the Shi`a of Lebanon. In his seminal work called *Orientalism* (1978), Said uncovered how Western writers and chroniclers of the Middle East used words and images to depict an inferior society and culture. His contention was that

> without examining Orientalism [the basis for Western dominance and intolerance of non-Westerns] as a discourse one cannot possibly understand the enormously systematic discipline by which European culture was able to manage—and even produce—the Orient politically, sociologically, militarily, ideologically, scientifically, and imaginatively during the post-Enlightenment period.[25]

In essence, one who practices Orientalism devalues and disregards cultures other than the Occident. Douglas Little's work *American Orientalism: The United States in the Middle East Since 1945* (2002) reinforces this concept of Orientalism. Little discusses America's manifestation of Said's notion, stating that Americans were "influenced by potent racial and cultural stereotypes, some imported and some homegrown, that depicted the Muslim world as a decadent and inferior . . . tend[ing] to dismiss Arab aspirations for self-determination as politically primitive, economically suspect, and ideologically absurd."[26]

Patrick Porter's book *Military Orientalism: Eastern War through Western Eyes* (2009) offers a contemporary example of the importance of understanding the media's constructed representations of Lebanese Shi`a.[27] Patrick examined the Israeli military's stumbling into a disastrous war with Hezbullah (a Lebanese Shi`a resistance group) in the summer of 2006. Prior to the confrontation, the Israelis conflated their Hezbullah adversaries with the Palestinian irregulars they had been fighting in the West Bank and Gaza, noting that "Israeli forces shared the same mindset that confuses one Arab society for another; at a visceral level, it is one of the conceptual errors that led the IDF into a trap in 2006."[28] The fighters of Hezbullah overcame the ethnocultural fictions created by a Western press and media and fought back, crafting a new image grudgingly accepted in the West. In the end, such Orientalist constructions of the Lebanese Shi`a can have long-lasting and disastrous results if not exposed.

Another critical touchstone is Edward Said's *Covering Islam*.[29] In this work, Said admonished the American press for its coverage of the Islamic world and the Iranian Revolution (a Shi`i-inspired liberation movement) in particular. He blamed the press for not contextualizing the revolutionary struggle in Iran and framing the revolution strictly as a battle between Western modernity and Islamic reactionary forces.[30] *Covering the Shi`a* demonstrates that Lebanese Shi`a had their own representations, which were often misunderstood or not reported by Western sources.

Forty years after the publication of his iconic work, *Orientalism,* Said still resonates with scholars and intellectuals covering the Middle East. "[I]n Orientalism, Said unleashed our tongue and unsheathed the sword of our critical thinking."[31] In fact, Said's theories are vitally important to historians who must constantly examine their research and how they reconstruct narratives and represent those subalterns in history whose stories were important but somehow not recorded in mainstream accounts. The title of this book, *Covering the Shi`a,* is a direct homage to Said's iconic work on the Western media coverage of an Islamic movement.

This book uses extensive primary and secondary sourcing in constructing a narrative of the Lebanese Shi`a in the English-language prestige press. The period covered in this study, 1975–1985, was a decade of dramatic change for Lebanese Shi`a. The issues and the trauma experienced by the Shi`i community in this period had a profound impact on the geopolitical situation in the Levant today.[32] A great deal of information about the plight and concerns of the Shi`a was available to American and British journalists and media representatives. Shi`i leaders made oral statements and wrote about their situation in Lebanon. Shi`i groups were producing leaflets and posters representing their plight in Lebanon. However, the English-language press and media often failed to interpret correctly these representations and ignored many of them. This holds particularly true for the *New York Times* and other American media outlets. This occurred to a lesser extent in the British media, particularly the *Guardian*. By documenting these occurrences in a narrative form, this work contributes to scholarship on Lebanese Shi`a and uncovers important elements used in the Western media construction of Shi`a representation.

This book is a qualitative study that uses metanarrative to assess the media representation of the Lebanese Shi`a.[33] Essentially, it is a story about a story that ascertains how a critical population in Lebanon was misrepresented. Accordingly, a number of references to visual material such as photos, posters, and pictorial representations in papers and magazines are included. The purpose for inserting these visual materials is to give the reader a broader perspective on how representations are constructed from images as well as words. Images are vitally important to historical studies because they give a richer context to the story. Images lend themselves to interpretation and analysis. In this book the images and the explanations presented help to firmly situate the story of the Shi`a and contrast that to how the English-language press understood and interpreted these images.

An analysis of the documents, visual images, and media reports provides information sufficient for drawing conclusions about the coverage of the Lebanese Shi`a. While this book does not attempt to assert that a monolithic media constructed one representation of Lebanese Shi`a, the presentation of prominent stories and images will reveal the dominant news narrative constructed in the English-language press and media.

HISTORICAL BACKGROUND

Before covering the four critical events that shaped a dominant narrative of the Lebanese Shi`a between 1975 and 1985, it is important to situate the Lebanese Shi`a in history. Historian Kamal Salibi noted that "since its origin as a state in 1920 Christian and Muslim Lebanese have been in fundamental disagreement over the historicity of their country."[34] In the country of Lebanon, composed of different religious and ethnic communities, all laid claim to their unique narrative and its importance to the society. The Lebanese Shi`a were but one of these communities; however, due to their growing population and a changed self-identity, by the beginning of 1975 they were poised to become the most important religious group within Lebanon.

Historically, Lebanese Shi`ism can be traced back to the earliest formation of Islam and one of the most prominent companions of the Prophet Muhammad, Abu Dharr al-Ghifari. The companions are revered in Islam because they represent the earliest converts to the religion. The great schism in Islam, the causal factor for the split between the Sunni and the Shi`i, was a direct result of a crisis of succession. Abu Dharr al-Ghifari played a key role in supporting a faction opposed to naming a new leader (Abu Bakr) to guide the fledgling religion.

After the death of the Prophet, a critical point developed among the leadership of the new religion to determine who would lead members of the Islamic faith (*umma*). Members of the Sunni sect of Islam believed that, prior to his death, the Prophet had not formally designated his replacement. For the Shi`i sect, it was clear that Muhammad had designated his son-in-law, Ali, to lead the *umma* after his death. Abu Dharr al-Ghifari supported installing Ali to succeed Muhammad. Not only was Ali the Prophet's son-in law—he held two other distinctions that elevated his status within the early Islamic community. Ali was Muhammad's cousin, the son of Abu Talib, the protector uncle that Muhammad relied on after his mother's death. Additionally, Ali was one of the most trusted confidants of the Prophet, acting as his secretary and his deputy during their time in Medina.[35] Yet, after his death, a council of the Prophet's companions selected Abu Bakr to succeed the Prophet as leader (caliph) of the *umma*. Throughout Abu Bakr's reign and those of subsequent caliphs, al-Ghifari maintained the notion that Ali and the people of the house of Muhammad (*ahl-ul-bayt*) were the rightful leaders of the *umma*.[36] Under the reign of the third caliphate, Uthman, Al-Ghifari was banished from the caliphate's capital and sent to Damascus in exile. Mu'awiya (a cousin of Uthman and a strong opponent of Ali) used his power as governor of Syria to ban al-Ghifari from Damascus and sent him to Jabal Amil (present-day South Lebanon), where he preached the precepts of Shi`i Islam. In fact, Jabal Amil was among the first regions in the Middle East to convert to Shi`ism.[37]

The fortunes of the Shi`a in Lebanon declined for several centuries. As a minority within the larger Islamic world, they were continually persecuted and weakened. As an example, when the Sunni-dominated Egyptian Mamluks (an Egyptian empire led by members from the former military slave regiments) invaded the region in the middle of the thirteenth century, they forcefully displaced Shi`i Muslims in the Kisrawan region North of Beirut.[38] This was a mountain community overlooking the coastal roads and the trade route into the interior of the Levant and Damascus. The Sunni Mamluks distrusted the Shi`a sitting astride such a strategic road network. They forced this Shi`a population to convert to Sunni Islam or moved them to the Bekaa or South Lebanon.[39]

With only brief spates of prominence, under the Isma`ili sect of Shi`ism in the tenth century and the introduction of Lebanese Shi`i scholars to the Safavid dynasty in Persia in the sixteenth century, the Shi`a survived on the margins of society, particularly in Lebanon.[40] Despite their marginalization and persecution under Sunni regimes for hundreds of years, Shi`i scholars traveled between the religious places of learning in Iran and Lebanon, exchanging ideas and spreading new religious concepts and doctrine. They would often stop in the Shi`i centers of learning in Kerbala and Najaf, in modern Iraq.[41] Although governing entities changed throughout this region, the clerical class (*ulama*) in Shi`i Islam continued to be linked through their travel to these religious institutions. This transnationalism, described by historian Roschanack Shaery-Eisenlohr's as "the interconnectedness in human relations across . . . borders," was one of the early tendencies of the Twelver Shi`a that persists today.[42] Yet, despite the connectivity of Shi`i networks, they were persecuted throughout the Middle Eastern and North African region, particularly in Lebanon.

In 1516 the Ottoman Turkish sultan Salim I defeated the Egyptian Mamluk rulers of the Levant. During the campaign, Salim conquered Damascus and the area that is now Syria, Lebanon, Jordan, and Israel.[43] Salim was also paranoid about the threat the Shi`a posed to the Ottomans; he purportedly drew up a list of every known Shi`i in his realm, massacred up to forty thousand of them, and deported and imprisoned large numbers of the rest.[44] For years the Ottomans ruled the area using local strongmen and tribal chiefs to implement their policies and collect taxes. When needed, the Ottoman Sultans would send military expeditions to the region to thwart any ambition for complete independence by these powerful local leaders. For the Ottomans, this area became known as Greater Syria or *Bilad al-Sham*. Throughout Greater Syria the Ottomans ruled through administrative areas called *vilayets*. By the nineteenth century, the *vilayet* of Beirut incorporated most of the coastal region that is present-day Lebanon.

The Beirut *vilayet* became a very important commercial center, not only for the Ottoman Empire but for European powers wishing to access the trade routes from Damascus and the Syrian hinterland.[45] As the Ottoman Empire began its decline, ethnic and religious tensions between the various groups weakened the hold that the Ottoman state had on the area. Eventually, fighting between these groups spurred intervention into the region by European powers, particularly France, which supported the Christian groups in the Mount Lebanon region and the Shuf Mountains east of Beirut. The Ottoman Empire was forced to make concessions to the French over sovereignty in the region to forestall a major military confrontation and to retain its commercial benefits in the area.[46] This arrangement between the Ottoman Empire and France ensured European involvement in the region economically and politically even prior to World War I.

At the conclusion of World War I the European powers carved up the remnants of the Ottoman Empire. France's habitual relationship in Greater Syria was a leading factor in its acquisition of the territory under a mandate from the League of Nations. However, in 1920 France split the mandate into two regions of control, one representing present-day Syria and the other Lebanon. Lebanon, as historian Fawwaz Traboulsi wrote, "in frontiers defined on 1 September 1920, had never existed before in history. It was a product of the Franco-British colonial partition of the Middle East."[47] Incorporated in this Lebanese mandate was the largely Christian area of Mount Lebanon, the coastal and mixed area of greater Beirut, the largely Druze region of the Shuf Mountains, and the predominantly Shi`i areas of the Bekaa Valley and South Lebanon. France held on to the mandate until 1943. Weakened from initial defeat by the Germans in World War II, France no longer had the strength or capacity to retain its empire.

When Lebanon officially gained independence from France in 1943, the country was composed of three distinct religious groups. The Christians of the Mount Lebanon area composed the dominant sect, followed by the Sunni Muslims and the Shi`a. In a verbal pact between the sect leaders in Lebanon at that time, government power was divided along religious lines. This "confessional system" (named for the religious groups who confessed to different religious traditions) was the major feature of the Lebanese political system. At the time of the "pact," the Christians boasted the largest population in Lebanon, and they also had the backing of the French government. Under the confessional system, the Christians held the dominant political position (the presidency), a Sunni Muslim filled the prime minister position, and a Shi`i Muslim held the appointment of speaker of the house.[48] Despite the political structure, a great deal of power in Lebanon resided with the old-time political, tribal, and clan leaders (*zuama*), who ensured that they retained their influence and looked after their constituencies.[49] Among these *zuama* was the leader of the Druze, a small and very powerful Islamic sect in the Shouf Mountains overlooking Beirut. The Druze comprised only 6 percent of the Lebanese population and clung fiercely to their traditional homeland in the Shouf.

Each of the confessional groups had its coterie of *zuama*, but the Shi`a occupied the lowest political position within the Lebanese government and rested on the lowest rung on the Lebanese social strata.[50] This was the Shi`i situation from the formation of the Lebanese state in 1943 until the 1960s. Their interests within Lebanese society were predominantly represented by Ahmad Bey al Assad in the 1940s and 1950s, and his son Kamel in the 1960s.[51] Ahmad Bey and his son had no interest in improving the conditions for their fellow Shi`a; they sought to maintain their own power base.[52] Kamel would eventually become one of the biggest opponents of Imam Musa al-Sadr, the most prominent Shi`i leader in Lebanon and the driving force behind a reform movement in Lebanon.[53]

In the early 1960s, the Shi`a of Lebanon began to emerge from their political acquiescence to the power of the *zuama*. Initially, leftist political parties drew their attention, but by the beginning of 1975 Musa al-Sadr had inspired Shi`i empowerment and a civil rights movement in Lebanon. This movement, and the rest of the major events in the Shi`i narratives outlined in this work would soon be affected by a major civil conflict within Lebanon.

THE LEBANESE CIVIL WAR

From the spring of 1975 until the signing of a peace treaty called the Taif Accord in 1989, a civil war raged in Lebanon. Numerous cease-fires punctuated the conflict, but for fifteen years civil unrest and violence pervaded Lebanon. The beginning of this conflict can be traced to an incident between the Palestinians and the Phalange, a Christian militia group, in April 1975.[54] Yet the origins of the conflict constitute a case for historical debate and involve the arrival of the Palestinians in Lebanon.

At the conclusion of the first Arab–Israeli war in 1948, 120,000 Palestinians fled the newly formed state of Israel and inserted themselves into refugee camps within Lebanon. Most of these Palestinians were Sunni Muslims, yet many Shi`a identified with the Palestinian position of disenfranchisement from their homeland and their new community in Lebanon. Lebanese Shi`a believed they were in a similar position.[55]

From the initial entry of the Palestinians into Lebanon, the majority of the Lebanese Maronite Christians opposed the Palestinians and their activities in the country. Their presence served to change the religious demographic in the country. Additionally, when the Lebanese government signed the Cairo Agreement of 1969, it gave Palestinian officials the right to control their refugee camps in Lebanon and sanctioned the right of Palestinian fighters to attack Israel from Lebanese territory.[56] Violence between Lebanon and Israel remained at a low level prior to 1970, but in September 1970, actions by the Palestinians in Jordan changed that dramatically.

A clash in the neighboring country of Jordan between Palestinian fighters and Jordan's army dramatically shifted the focal point of Palestinian activities against Israel. The attempt by members of the Palestinian Liberation Organization (PLO) to act autonomously from the Jordanian government, and their call for the overthrow of the country's ruler, King Hussein, forced the hand of Hussein. He ordered his military to act against the leadership and military infrastructure of the PLO within his country. Over three thousand Palestinians died, and eleven thousand were wounded in the clash with Jordanian troops.[57] This incident, known to many Palestinians as Black September, spurred the migration of many Palestinians and their leadership into Lebanon. By 1971, there were almost three hundred thousand Palestinians in Lebanon. The arrival of a large number of Palestinians into Lebanon in the early 1970s destabilized the country's domestic politics and became problematic for the entire Lebanese society. Initially, the Muslim community in Lebanon (particularly the Shi`a) shared sympathy for the plight of the Palestinians. However, Lebanon then became the central front for the Palestinian's military actions against Israel, and South Lebanon (where most of the Shi`a lived) became the battleground.

Edgar O'Ballance, former freelance journalist and historian, wrote that "a dispute between mainly poor Shi`a fishermen in Sidon and a company backed by the Lebanese government was the powder that caused the explosion of the civil war in April 1975."[58] The government granted exclusive fishing rights to its Christian clientele, exposing a rift between the Christian-dominated government and the predominantly poor Muslim population. This incident, in February 1975, resulted in the government's use of military force to put down the demonstrations by the Shi`i fishermen. Palestinian militiamen intervened on the side of the fishermen, signaling to the Christian-dominated government that they would not stand idly by while force was used against their fellow Muslims. There were deaths on both sides. In April 1975, when a confrontation occurred between Christian Phalangist militia and Palestinians outside the Christian district in Rumaniyeh, the animosity exploded into a full-fledged civil war.

Historian Fawwaz Traboulsi has contended that the conflict's origins were based upon the newly arrived Palestinian commandos' ability to break the monopoly of violence once held by Christian militia groups.[59] At the same time, other confessional and political groups within Lebanon believed the time was appropriate to challenge the status quo of the governmental structure. Historian Itamar Rabinovich, places the onus for the civil war on the persistent pressures of rival internal and external forces.[60] The civil war in Lebanon was never a binary affair of political left against right, or of Christian against Muslim. Throughout the decade of fighting in Lebanon, forces internally and externally switched sides in an effort to gain the most advantageous outcomes. Yet it was the Shi`i community in Lebanon that was affected most dramatically by the decade of civil war. The disappearance of Imam Musa al-Sadr, the fighting and expulsion of Shi`a from Nab`a, the Iranian Revolution, and the Israeli invasion in 1982 all occurred in the midst of this civil war.

In conclusion, from 1975 to 1985 the Lebanese Shi`a transformed themselves from a quietist group into one of the most influential groups in the Levant, but the English-language prestige press constructed a faulty representation of the Lebanese Shi`a by refusing to cover the details of their civil rights movement, failing to comprehend the transnational networks that supported their community, and linking their plight with other Arab independence movements. This news narrative was at odds with the dominant Lebanese Shi`i narrative, which demanded equal rights within Lebanese society and supported the idea of armed resistance to violence and injustice. The following chapters will trace the formation of the Lebanese narrative by covering the four major events that shaped that narrative. The rise of Musa al-Sadr, the battle of Nab`a, the Iranian revolution, and the Israeli invasion of Lebanon were all major events in the narrative of the Shi`a—but of those four events, the most important was the rise and disappearance of Imam Musa al-Sadr.

NOTES

1. Robert Fisk, "Gunshot Victims Belie Israeli Claims after Nabatiya Rioting," *Times* (London), October 18, 1983.
2. Andrew Rippin, *Muslims: Their Religious Beliefs and Practices* (New York: Routledge, 2001), 125.
3. There is no attempt to correlate the redemptive nature of Christ's crucifixion with the martyrdom of Husayn. Shi`i Islam has no such theological equivalency to the crucifixion and its power to redeem believers.

4. For a detailed description of the Ashura ceremony, refer to Moojan Momen, *An Introduction to Shi`i Islam: The History and Doctrines of Twelver Shi`ism* (New Haven, CT: Yale University Press, 1985), 241–43; and Vali Nasr, *The Shia Revival: How Conflicts within Islam Will Shape the Future* (New York: W. W. Norton, 2006), 46–49.

5. Rippin, *Muslims*, 125.

6. Hamid Enayat, *Modern Islamic Political Thought* (Austin: University of Texas Press, 1982), 5.

7. Lara Deeb, *An Enchanted Modern: Gender and Public Piety in Shi`i Lebanon* (Princeton, NJ: Princeton University Press, 2006), 152.

8. Jamal Sankari, *Fadlallah: The Making of a Radical Shi'ite Leader* (London: SAQI, 2005), 46.

9. Robert Fisk, *Pity the Nation: The Abduction of Lebanon* (New York: Thunder Mountain Press, 1990), 557.

10. "Shi'ite Leader Declares Resistance to Israel," trans. Foreign Broadcast Information Service (Lebanon), October 16, 1983.

11. Augustus Richard Norton, *Amal and the Shi`a: Struggle for the Soul of Lebanon* (Austin: University of Texas Press, 1987), 114.

12. Ibid., 113.

13. "Al-Wazzan Praises An Nabatiyah Uprising," trans. Foreign Broadcast Information Service (Lebanon), October 18, 1983.

14. Timothy J. Geraghty, *Peacekeepers at War: Beirut 1983, The Marine Commander Tells His Story* (Washington, DC: Potomac Books, 2009), 181. Colonel Geraghty provides the most comprehensive review of evidence against Islamic Amal for the bombing at the BLT, which includes a National Security Agency–intercepted cable from Iran instructing the group to take spectacular action against the Marines.

15. Lawrence Pintak, *Seeds of Hate: How America's Flawed Middle East Policy Ignited Jihad* (London: Pluto Press, 2003), xii.

16. The Shi`a compose approximately 10 to 15 percent of the worldwide Muslim population. Within the Shi`i community are a number of other communities who draw their heritage from a religious schism in Islam in the late seventh century. The focus of this study is the Twelver Shi`a, who recognize the first twelve Imams and whose members predominate in Lebanon.

17. Russ Braley, *Bad News: The Foreign Policy of the* New York Times (Chicago: Regnery Gateway, 1984), 570.

18. Martin Walker, *Powers of the Press: Twelve of the World's Influential Newspapers* (New York: The Pilgrim Press, 1983), 2.

19. A review of the minutes of the Reagan administration's National Security Policy Group (NSPG) meetings and National Security Council (NSC) meetings on Lebanon demonstrated a clear lack of understanding of the Shi`a in Lebanon. Minutes of these meetings were accessed through the Reagan Presidential Library archives.

20. G. H. Stempel, a media analyst and professor, established the category and term *prestige press* during his reporting of newspaper coverage of the 1960 presidential election. He put fifteen newspapers in this category; the *New York Times* was among the most prominent.

21. For a good, albeit dated, article on the construction of narrative, see Jerome Bruner, "The Narrative Construction of Reality," *Critical Inquiry* 18, no. 1 (Autumn 1991): 1–21.

22. For a discussion of the importance of narrative and news narrative, see Hayden White, *The Content of the Form: Narrative Discourse and Historical Representation* (Baltimore: Johns Hopkins Press, 1987), 1; and Yahya R. Kamalipour, *The U.S. Media and the Middle East: Image and Perception* (London: Praeger, 1995), 28.

23. Wikipedia contributors, "Political communication," Wikipedia, The Free Encyclopedia, https.//enwikipedia.org/w/index.php?title=Political_communication&oldid=832699456 (accessed May 19, 2018).

24. Professor Richard August Norton of Boston University; Rodger Shanahan, fellow at the Lowy Institute of International Policy; and other scholars and journalists who have written on the Lebanese Shi`a agree that Musa al-Sadr's rise and disappearance, the Iranian Revolution, and the Israeli invasion in 1982 had a most profound effect on the Shi`a. I have added the

expulsion from Nab'a to this for its larger dislocation of the Shi'i population around Beirut and for its effect on one of the most prominent Lebanese Shi'i thinkers during this period, Sayyid Fadlallah. *Dominant narrative* refers to the dominant ideology of a group or society, or what most people believe is true.

25. Edward Said, *Orientalism* (New York: Vintage Books, 1979), 3.

26. Douglas Little, *American Orientalism: The United States and the Middle East since 1985* (Chapel Hill: University of North Carolina Press, 2004), 11.

27. Patrick Porter, *Military Orientalism: Eastern War through Western Eyes* (New York: Columbia University Press, 2009).

28. Ibid., 22, 179.

29. Edward W. Said, *Covering Islam: How the Media and the Experts Determine How We See the Rest of the World* (New York: Vintage Books, 1997).

30. Ibid., 7.

31. Hamid Dabashi "Edward Said's *Orientalism*: Forty Years Later," Al Jazeera https://www.aljazeera.com/indepth/opinion/edward-orientalism-forty-... (accessed May 3, 2018).

32. The Levant is the geographical region that incorporates present day Lebanon, Syria, Israel, and portions of Jordan. From the French word for rising, the term was generally used to describe a rising plateau east of the Mediterranean Sea to the Jordan Rift Valley and northeast of the Sinai Desert. The rise of and prominence of Hezbollah within Lebanon today has a direct linkage to the experience of the Shi'a during the period covered in this chapter.

33. *Metanarrative* is defined in postmodernist literary theory as a narrative about a narrative or narratives.

34. Kamal Salibi, *A House of Many Mansions: The History of Lebanon Reconsidered* (Berkeley: University of California Press, 1988), 3.

35. Momen, *An Introduction to Shi'i Islam*, 11, 13.

36. Majed Halawi, *A Lebanon Defied: Musa al-Sadr and the Shi'a Community* (Boulder, CO: Westview Press, 1992), 21.

37. Ibid., 29.

38. Kamal Salibi, *A House of Many Mansions*, 14.

39. Rodger Shanahan, *The Shi'a of Lebanon: Clans, Parties, and Clerics* (London: I. B. Tauris, 2005), 15.

40. Ibid., 14–15.

41. For an extensive look at the early connections and travel of Shi'i scholars between Lebanon, Iraq, and Iran, reference H. E. Chehabi and Hassan I. Mneineh's article "Five Centuries of Lebanese-Iranian Encounters," in Chehabi, *Distant Relations: Iran and Lebanon in the Last 500 Years* (London: I.B. Tauris, 2006).

42. Roschananck Shaery-Einsenlohr, *Shi'ite Lebanon: Transnational Religion and the Making of National Identities* (New York: Columbia University Press, 2008), xv.

43. Thomas Collelo, *Lebanon: A Country Study* (Washington, DC: United States Government, 1989), 12.

44. Momen, *An Introduction to Shi'i Islam*, 106.

45. Fawwaz Traboulsi, *A History of Modern Lebanon* (London: Pluto Press, 2007), 52.

46. William Cleveland, *A History of the Modern Middle East* (Boulder, CO: Westview Press, 2000), 213.

47. Traboulsi, *A History of Modern Lebanon*, 75.

48. Salibi, *A House of Many Mansions*, 185–86.

49. Sandra Makey, *Lebanon: A House Divided* (New York: W. W. Norton, 1989), 95.

50. Norton, *Amal and the Shi'a*, 17–18.

51. Fouad Ajami, *The Vanished Imam: Musa al-Sadr and the Shia of Lebanon* (Ithaca, NY: Cornell University Press, 1986), 70.

52. Ibid.

53. "Politicians Bicker While South Suffers," *Daily Star*, February 3, 1975.

54. The Phalange is a right-wing Lebanese nationalist party essentially made up of Maronite Christians. It was founded in 1936 by Pierre Gemayel, who was inspired by the Hitler Youth during the 1936 Olympic Games in Munich. The group attempted to mimic the Nazi group's discipline and martial attitude.

55. Traboulsi, *A History of Modern Lebanon*, 113.
56. Charles D. Smith, *Palestine and the Arab–Israeli Conflict: A History with Documents* (Boston: Bedford/St. Martin's, 2007), 315.
57. Ibid., 321.
58. Edgar O'Ballance, *Civil War in Lebanon, 1975–92* (New York: St. Martin's Press, 1998), 4–5.
59. Traboulsi, *A History of Modern Lebanon*, 176.
60. Itamar Rabinovich, *The War for Lebanon, 1970–1985* (Ithaca: Cornell University Press, 1984), 43.

Chapter One

Musa al-Sadr and the Shi`i Narratives in Lebanon, 1975–1985

THE RISE OF MUSA AL-SADR IN LEBANON

In 1959 a charismatic Imam[1] from Qom, Iran, arrived in Lebanon and started a transformational movement of the Lebanese Shi`a. His name was Musa al-Sadr. Born to a prominent Shi`i scholar, al-Sadr did not plan a religious career. His training and early education in Iran was secular. He attended Tehran's College of Faculty of Law, and Political Economy.[2] It was his father who finally persuaded a young al-Sadr that his talents were needed in the Shi`i "ulama." Al-Sadr completed his initial religious education in Qom, and a year after his father's death in 1953 he traveled to Najaf, Iraq, to study advanced Shi`i jurisprudence (*fiqh*) under one of the most prominent Shi`i scholars at the time, Sayyid Muhsin al-Hakim.[3] Invited to Lebanon after the death of the prominent Shi`i scholar and activist Sayyid Abdul Hussein, al-Sadr came to Lebanon with one of the most scholarly and clerical backgrounds within Shi`i Islam.[4] He assumed Hussein's mantle of activism and helped to redefine the role and the identity of the Shi`a within Lebanon.

This chapter examines the importance of Musa al-Sadr to the Shi`i narrative. It assesses how he helped transform the Shi`a into a more activist community, one that demanded civil rights within the Lebanese society and legitimized the use of force in the community's defense. The chapter also outlines the focus of Western news coverage in Lebanon, and how it ignored the plight of Musa al-Sadr and the violence surrounding the Lebanese Shi`a. Musa al-Sadr had a profound impact on the Shi`a, and his passion for improving the lives of the members of the Shi`i community was unequaled. Uncovering the narratives of the Lebanese Shi`a required a detailed understanding of al-Sadr's role in Lebanon.

Two of the most prominent chronicles of the life and times of Musa al-Sadr are Fouad Ajami's *The Vanished Imam* (1986) and Majed Halawi's *A Lebanon Defied: Musa al-Sadr and the Shi`a Community* (1992). Both books outline the incredible impact al-Sadr had on the Shi`i community. Reviewers of Ajami's book stated that his goal in writing about al-Sadr was to paint a different picture of the role of Shi`i clerics in Islam as a contrast to the dour, stern, and inflexible image of Ayatollah Khomeini projected in the Western media.[5] Khomeini's revolution in Iran in 1979 left an unfavorable impression of the Shi`a in the minds of most Westerners. In representing al-Sadr, Ajami sees a luminary, a person capable of lifting the Shi`i community past the excesses of violence displayed in Iran. Musa al-Sadr was a complex man capable of talking to and working with adversaries to achieve gains for his community. However, he was also capable of fiercely defending his community with military force if he felt threatened. Ajami only briefly touches on that facet, saying of Musa al-Sadr:

> Like a chameleon, he was different things to different people. The patricians among his followers saw him as a man of moderate politics, a reformer. For others, Musa al-Sadr was to become a great avenger, his tale and memory a warrant for daring deeds and uncompromising politics. His legacy was there to be claimed by men of means and caution and by young suicide drivers.[6]

Ajami preferred to view al-Sadr in the image given to him by a young Lebanese historian. The image was of Icarus, the tragic Greek mythological creature who was given wings by the gods to escape his captivity but flew too close to the sun and tragically plunged into the sea when his wings were burned. For Ajami, Musa al-Sadr embodied Icarus, and the sun reflected the old Shi`i traditions with their penchant for sorrow and violence.[7] Here Ajami falls into an Orientalist trap—first of defining al-Sadr in the occidental terms of Greek tragedy and then assuming that it was the Shi`i legacy and traditions that led to al-Sadr's ultimate demise. There were other forces outside of Shi`i Islam that also confronted and plagued Musa al-Sadr and undoubtedly were more responsible for his demise.

Halawi's book on Musa al-Sadr focused on the dynamics of the Shi`i community in Lebanon and highlighted that al-Sadr's rise to political prominence in Lebanon did not occur in a vacuum.[8] For Halawi, al-Sadr's success in Lebanon must be viewed in light of a larger Shi`i discourse, where Shi`i myth and praxis were used to articulate a new, more activist community internationally. He criticized Fouad Ajami's reductionist rendition of the history of Lebanese Shi`a, one that painted the community as submissive.[9] Halawi discussed other social dynamics at work in Lebanon prior to al-Sadr's transformational movement. This included the growing urbanization of the Shi`a and the increasing wealth within the community, as Shi`i merchants moved to West Africa and repatriated some of their wealth back to Lebanon.[10] Although Halawi recognized al-Sadr's greatness, unlike Ajami he viewed al-Sadr as a man who appeared at the right time in Lebanese Shi`a history rather than as the catalyst for change. Neither author focused on how the Western media viewed this important figure, although both authors would agree that the significance of his personality and influence would be impossible to miss within Lebanese society.

It was not unusual that a Shi`i cleric from Iran would make his way to Lebanon to lead a community of the faithful.[11] Years of Shi`i history demonstrated how easily Shi`i scholars and *ulama* moved between the places of Shi`i learning. Musa al-Sadr had an even greater reason to make the move to Lebanon. He traced his ancestral heritage back to South Lebanon, where oppression from Ottoman rulers forced his relatives to flee to Iraqi and later move to Iran.[12] In 1959, Musa al-Sadr arrived in Tyre, Lebanon, to lead the local Shi`i community. Even with his heavily Persian-accented Arabic, it did not take long for those around him to understand that Musa al-Sadr was a man of exceptional talent and drive. As Fouad Ajami explained in his biography of al-Sadr, "the turf in Tyre which was enough for his predecessor was only for him a beginning."[13] His Iranian origins did not hinder his meteoric rise to prominence within the Lebanese Shi`i community.

In her book *Shi`ite Lebanon: Transnational Religion and the Making of National Identities*, Roschanack Shaery-Eisenlohr expounded that al-Sadr understood that, though belief in God was the common denominator among groups in Lebanon, to be Lebanese required a strong identity with one's confessional group.[14] As a cleric and activist, Musa al-Sadr defined his role as "protecting the interest of his flock."[15] Al-Sadr's flock was the Shi`a of Lebanon, whose contact with the Iranians spanned antiquity.

Musa al-Sadr's magnetic personality and his populist message resonated with the downtrodden Shi`i community.[16] A tall, handsome man with seemingly boundless energy, al-Sadr's appearance was always well kept, and he had a gift for engaging all kinds of people within Lebanese society.[17] A poster of Musa al-Sadr shows a smiling, genial cleric with a black turban signifying him as a descendant of the Prophet Muhammad. In the upper right corner of the poster is the symbol for Amal, the Shi`i militia group that al-Sadr founded (see figure 1.1).

As an Imam, al-Sadr defined his role differently than did many of the traditional religious leaders in Lebanon. He claimed that his role was to be generous toward his community and that he would not confine himself just to religious matters but address the wider political goals of the Shi`a within Lebanese society.[18] Al-Sadr was persistent in his goal of elevating the Shi`i community. One of his most significant acts in that regard was the formation and the recognition of the Higher Islamic Shi`i Council (HISC) of Lebanon. The council brought together prominent Shi`i leaders from both the business

Figure 1.1. Poster of Imam Musa al-Sadr. Reproduced by permission of American University of Beirut Libraries, Archives and Special Collections.

and religious communities to represent the concerns of the Shi`a to the Lebanese government. Al-Sadr influenced the Lebanese government to pass a law enabling the Shi`a in Lebanon to act and express themselves in accordance with the religious dictates (*fatwas*) of the worldwide Shi`i community.[19] This reinforced the transnational nature of Lebanese Shi`ism so that religious dictates from outside of the country were then able to be enacted within the Shi`i community in Lebanon. In May 1970, the Lebanese government recognized the HISC of Lebanon and disbursed ten million dollars in aid to the group. As the elected president of the HISC of Lebanon, al-Sadr had a new and powerful platform from which to conduct his campaign for economic reform, social justice, and protection for the Shi`a in Lebanon.

It would be difficult to overestimate the growing importance of Musa al-Sadr in the Lebanese Shi`i community by the early 1970s. Lebanese historian Fawwaz Traboulsi stated that "Musa al-Sadr's short residence in Lebanon was to stamp Lebanon's Shi`a for a whole period of their history."[20] His efforts to secure civil rights and economic justice for the Shi`a in Lebanon were chronicled in many contemporary histories of Lebanon. Both Ajami and Halawi document al-Sadr's early trend of securing better conditions for his "flock." Through the use of charities, government social services, and bank loans, al-Sadr was able to establish social institutions for orphans and the destitute. He also established a home to teach Shi`i girls sewing and other domestic skills necessary for work and survival in the poverty-stricken environment in which most found themselves.[21] Historian Augustus Richard Norton wrote about al-Sadr's early success in establishing a Shi`i technical institute in 1964 in the southern town of Burj al-Shimali. This was to become one of the most important educational institutions for the Shi`a. Al-Sadr accomplished this by utilizing money collected from Shi`i benefactors.[22] Increasingly, however, al-Sadr became disheartened by the pace of Lebanese government support for the Shi`i community. There were large pockets of poverty where the Shi`a received no government aid and support. The Shi`a were also victims of violence in South Lebanon, from Israeli attacks on suspected Palestinian guerrillas encampments. The Lebanese government made little effort to protect these communities from the Israelis.

Seeking international support for the Lebanese Shi`i cause, as early as 1971 Musa al-Sadr asked a prominent Iranian scholar to pressure the shah of Iran to seek US support to stop Israeli attacks on South Lebanon.[23] These attacks were causing considerable damage to Shi`a in the region. Musa al-Sadr made statements in support of the Palestinians up until the 1970s, and he had been quoted as saying, "The Palestinian resistance and Lebanese sovereignty are compatible."[24] However, his initial support for the Palestinians in Lebanon waned as their fighters took over Shi`i farms and forcibly recruited Shi`i men into their militias.[25] Ultimately, Lebanon became the target of Israeli punitive raids against the Palestinians. In an April 1974 State

Department dispatch from Beirut, American officials stated that al-Sadr believed that Shi`a sympathies no longer extended to Palestinian actions that brought misery and deprivation to them.[26] Al-Sadr grew impatient with the Palestinian resistance groups because Israeli retaliatory attacks were killing many innocent Shi`a.[27] His outreach to the Iranians and the Americans to stop the violence in South Lebanon is just one example of his ability to work and deal with foreign entities and leaders in order to further the cause of the Lebanese Shi`a.

None of the scholarship on Musa al-Sadr gives a specific date or time when his dealings with the international community or the Lebanese government turned more strident, advocating a more forceful approach to gaining and maintaining Shi`i civil rights. H. E. Chehabi wrote in his book *Distant Relations: Iran and Lebanon in the Last 500 Years* that al-Sadr's relationship with the Iranian government and the shah began to cool after the 1973 Arab–Israeli War. He began to speak publicly against the shah's policies and accused him of weakening an Arab oil boycott against Israel and the West by continuing the sale of oil after the war.[28] It was feasible that al-Sadr viewed the close affiliation between the shah's regime, the Christian-dominated government in Lebanon, and the Israelis together as a bulwark against Shi`i progress in Lebanon. This affiliation policy of the shah was well known, as he hoped to forge an alliance with the Lebanese and the Israelis to counter what he perceived was an Arab, leftist threat in the region.[29] Al-Sadr, in contrast, began to court the heads of Arab states to ask for help in building and supporting the Shi`i community in Lebanon. In that regard, one of al-Sadr's most important political moves was to recognize the `Alawi sect of Islam as part of the Twelver Shi`i sect. The `Alawites were a small sect that predominated in Syria. The country's newly established leader, Hafez al-Assad, was a member of this minority sect and sought religious legitimacy in Islam to stave off opposition from the more numerous Sunni Muslims in Syria. Many Sunnis considered the `Alawites a heretical religion.[30] Since he was the leader of the HISC, al-Sadr's legitimation of the religion allowed him to curry favor with Assad and receive support from Syria. However, al-Sadr's ultimate goal was to change the conditions and the treatment of the Shi`a in Lebanon.

There seemed no noticeable improvement within Lebanon for the Shi`a. Dialogue with the government produced no results except deprivation, neglect, and continued confessional discrimination.[31] Caught between growing Palestinian military pressures, Israeli attacks, and an ineffectual government, al-Sadr talked of revolution and weapons.[32] In a famous speech in the Bekaa Valley in February 1974, he told his followers:

> We do not want to clash with the regime, with those who neglect us. Today, we shout out loud the wrongs against us, that cloud of injustice that has

followed us since the beginning of our history. Starting from today we will no longer complain nor cry. Our name is not *mitwali* [a name for Shi`a that has taken on a derogatory connotation]; our name is men of refusal . . . men of vengeance, men who revolt against all tyranny.[33]

In March 1974, at a massive rally in Baalbek, Lebanon, al-Sadr announced the formation of *Harakat al Mahrumin* (Movement of the Deprived).[34] This newly formed party was to become the voice of the Shi`i community throughout the Lebanese political process.[35] During his impassioned speech in Baalbek, Musa al-Sadr chided the Lebanese government for its neglect of the Shi`a. Disheartened that his words had not been effective in changing government actions in supporting and protecting the community, he stated "arms are an adornment of men."[36] He asked all those in attendance to join him in a vow to seize their rights or face martyrdom in the attempt.[37] Al-Sadr also realized that the Shi`i political organization was insufficient in their current environment. Due to the lack of government protection, it was necessary to defend his flock militarily from outside threats. The Shi`a fell prey not only to Israeli military actions but also to Palestinian militias and Christian clans in Lebanon. It would be over a year after al-Sadr's plea that the formation of a Shi`i militia group, to work in concert with *Harakat al Mahrumin*, would come to the attention of the press. *Amal* was the name of the militia group, and if the Lebanese government was unwilling or incapable of protecting its Shi`i citizens, al-Sadr's new militia would find a way to do it.

MUSA AL-SADR ON THE EVE OF THE CIVIL WAR 1975

There was no cessation to the violence or the deleterious effects it was having on the Lebanese Shi`a at the beginning of 1975. The Lebanese media offered clear insight into the toll that Israeli military attacks in South Lebanon took on Shi`i families. On January 3, 1975, a report in the Lebanese *Daily Star*, the leading English-language daily in the country, chronicled the death of four Lebanese civilians and one Lebanese soldier during an Israeli raid. The paper quoted a source within the town attacked by the Israelis as saying, "Ali Sharafuddin and his two sons went down fighting as the Israelis attempted to blow up their home."[38] The paper prominently displayed pictures of the three Shi`i men who had been killed in the raid. Additionally, the paper displayed pictures from the southern Lebanese town of Nabatiyah, where people burned tires in protest against the repeated Israeli raids. As he had many times before, Musa al-Sadr toured the area of conflict in South Lebanon, offering his condolences to the families victimized by the Israeli attacks.[39] His picture appeared on the front page of the *Daily Star* and its companion Arabic language newspaper *Al-Hayat*. Such raids by the Israeli forces were commonplace in early 1975, as they attempted to respond to the incursions of Palestinian fighters into Israel. Unfortunately for the Israelis and the Shi`a, these attacks did not always succeed in targeting the culprits of the incursions. The Shi`a who inhabited the region of South Lebanon were often the victims of these mistaken attacks. Al-Sadr could ignore neither the heavy toll the Israelis inflicted on his community nor the actions of the PLO, who put his "flock" in harm's way.

This proved to be an incredibly difficult time for al-Sadr. As stated by Fouad Ajami, "Musa al-Sadr walked between raindrops; he was an agile man. But it was too grim a time and place for anyone really to direct events."[40] Al-Sadr was certain that a major conflagration would embrace Lebanon. He warned religious leaders and politicians in Lebanon to work and solve many of the social and economic inequities in the country before these conditions led to violence.[41] As he attempted to forestall the coming disaster, al-Sadr was mindful not only of his Shi`i community but of Lebanese society at large.[42] By 1975, he had secured a prominent position throughout Lebanese society, but he was truly a man caught in the middle. In his role as spiritual leader of the Shi`a, Musa al-Sadr always attempted to maintain a delicate balance in his support and criticism of the Maronite and Palestinian communities in Lebanon.[43] Each community held an important key to elevating the status of the Shi`a within Lebanese society. The Maronites controlled the political power in the country, while the Palestinians maintained the dominant military force in the country. The Maronites increasingly looked upon al-Sadr with suspicion because of his Islamic religion, and the Palestinians looked at him with suspicion because of his Iranian background.[44] Yet al-Sadr was capable of insightful acts of unity. Just prior to the Lebanese Civil War, as a gesture of religious reconciliation, he visited a Catholic church to deliver a Lenten sermon early in 1975.[45] His message of uplifting the weak and selfless service to God resonated in the church among both Christians and Muslims, yet his attempt at reconciliation did not forestall the violence and sectarian conflict that would take place early that spring and summer in Lebanon.

While Shi`i men and women were caught between the military actions of the Israelis and the Palestinians, in the beginning of 1975, a larger, more devastating conflict brewed in Lebanon. Tensions between the Palestinians and the Maronite Christian militias in Lebanon sparked a violent conflict that would last more than fifteen years. Although Musa al-Sadr and the Shi`a were not the main protagonists in the civil war that commenced in April 1975, their community suffered egregiously in the ensuing battles.[46]

At the start of the Lebanese Civil War, al-Sadr was taken aback by the level of violence. His stature within Lebanese society allowed him to communicate with Palestinian leadership and that of the Christian militias. From the beginning of the conflict, al-Sadr was involved as a mediator in search of a political settlement to the crisis. Because he met with leaders of the opposing sides, his picture was often on the front page of Lebanese newspapers.[47] With the endorsement of Lebanese government officials, al-Sadr submitted peace proposals to the warring parties in an attempt to end the fighting.[48] Although al-Sadr's desires for peace were real, he had his own equities in the outcome of the fighting. Al-Sadr saw an opportunity to regain his political clout as a mediator between the Palestinians and the Maronites and gain more political power for the Shi`i community. Musa al-Sadr was mindful of the weakened position of the Shi`i community during the spring of 1975. His militia was not yet strong enough to support and protect his community, and there were competing demands for Shi`i manpower; however, the civil war was changing that dynamic.

Rodger Shanahan notes in his book *The Shi`a of Lebanon: Clans, Parties, and Clerics* (2005) that the civil war forced a consolidation of Shi`i groups and parties.[49] The violence of the civil war closed off many of the political avenues previously open to Shi`a. For years before the civil war, socialist and communist ideologies infiltrated a number of the Palestinian and Druze militia groups in Lebanon.[50] These leftist militias within Lebanon heavily recruited Shi`i men, many of whom held no particular ideological penchant for the organization. They were, however, in desperate need of employment.[51] Yet, as the civil war intensified, affiliation with one's communal group became increasingly important.

Richard Augustus Norton offers another explanation of the civil war's effects on al-Sadr's militia and the Lebanese Shi`a. Norton says that even during the height of the war al-Sadr controlled only a fraction of his "co-religionists."[52] A number of Shi`i men did operate in militias under the banner of the Lebanese National Movement (LNM). However, al-Sadr opposed the group's vision of a nonsecular Lebanon. He was also concerned that Shi`i men were strengthening the hand of Palestinian organizations and the Druze's Progressive Socialist Party (PSP) against the Christian sects. Despite al-Sadr's issues with the Christian sects, he firmly believed the Shi`a could fare better under the Lebanese confessional system than under the leftist state envisioned by Kamal Junblatt (leader of PSP and spiritual head of the Druze community). However, it took time to move the Lebanese Shi`a from these militia groups. Much of the data supports Norton's claim that in the early years Amal made little progress in weaning the Shi`a away from these rival militias.[53]

Despite al-Sadr's aversion to the politics of the LNM, practical issues demanded al-Sadr take a more nuanced approach to the group. Christian militias threatened the Chiyah district in Beirut, home to a number of Shi`i families.[54] Al-Sadr needed LNM forces to protect that community while he found an opportune time to strengthen his own militia. Once again, al-Sadr found himself in the middle, trying to extricate Shi`i men from these leftist militias but needing the militiamen to protect his community in the Chiyah.

For al-Sadr, advocating a peaceful settlement to the crisis was the only way forward.[55]

Sadr's attempts were among many seeking an end to the fighting and the civil war. However, when his initial efforts failed, new violence commenced in Lebanon. The renewed fighting precipitated a crisis within the Lebanese government. In June 1975, the prime minister and most of the cabinet resigned in protest of the violence and left the president unable to form a government. Al-Sadr now needed a "grand gesture" to halt the violence and cement his image as a peacemaker and reconciler.

On a morning in late June, Musa al-Sadr went to a Beirut mosque. "Violence," he said, "had defiled the country: I have come to the house of God, and my sustenance is the book of God (the Quran) and a few drops of water. I will stay here until death, or until the country is saved."[56] This was the "grand gesture" needed for the political and sectarian leaders to take notice and to find some form of accommodation. After several days, pictures on the front page of a Lebanese daily showed a gaunt Musa al-Sadr reclining on a mat in the mosque as he undertook his fast.[57] Other groups mobilized in support of al-Sadr and his call for national reconciliation. A group of Shi`i women from the southern slums of Beirut came to the mosque, saying they would stay with the Imam until his fast was over. Other Christian and Islamic clergy expressed support for al-Sadr and his efforts to end the violence in the country. Al-Sadr's image as a "Man of God" enhanced his stature and enabled him to facilitate an end to the fighting, yet it was his influence over the growing power of the Shi`a that drove Yasir Arafat (chairman of the PLO), groups of Christian clergymen, and the foreign minister of Syria to urge him to end his fast.[58] The newly designated Lebanese prime minister, Rashid Karami, persuaded al-Sadr to break his fast five days after he began, assuring him that he and his new cabinet would succeed in ending the violence where previous government officials had failed.[59] Upon ending his fast, al-Sadr spoke to a gathering in a mosque, stating, "Our brothers in the Bekaa Valley and elsewhere wanted to come to Beirut with their weapons. We refused. Enough destruction and enough ruin have befallen this country. . . . All I want is Allah's blessing and I know that His blessing comes from serving you."[60] Al-Sadr had personal charisma and held sway over a growing activist group of Shi`a who were not only willing to stand behind him in protest but prepared to defend themselves by force of arms. The quietist culture of the Shi`a silently enduring their deprivation was forever changed.

Five days after ending his fast and calling for a cessation of violence, the pragmatic side of Musa al-Sadr and the Shi`a came to light. The military wing of al-Sadr's movement, which had formed over a year before, was revealed on July 7, when he announced to the Lebanese press the formation of a new "resistance group" that he dubbed *Amal*.[61] Amal established a military complement to his "Movement of the Deprived," which he had announced in March 1974. In a press release announcing the formation of his resistance group *Afwaj al-Muqawama al-Lubnaniya* (better known by its initials, *Amal*, which means "hope" in Arabic[62]), al-Sadr acknowledged that a tragic accident had hastened his unveiling of the organization.[63] The accident in the Bekaa Valley occurred when a mine malfunctioned during a training session with a Palestinian instructor. The accident killed twenty-six members of the organization and wounded another forty-three. It was the first time any press organization had reported on the group, although it had been in existence for a year. Al-Sadr told his followers that Amal was being trained to go to South Lebanon and fight against Israeli incursions.[64] However, the security realities in Lebanon mandated that Amal assume a greater task. The protection of the Shi`i population from the exploitation of Palestinian *Feda'iyin* (fighters) in the South and protection of Shi`i communities around Beirut from Christian militias were both roles for his militia.[65]

Sadr was no great military leader, but he was a practical man.[66] The conflict that his fast was directed to end resumed not long after his announcement of the formation of Amal. This time, Christian militias threatened Shi`i slums in Western Beirut. In touring the Chiyah district of Beirut, al-Sadr said that the people of the area "received not a single service from the government and in the end they looked for only one—protection from armed gangs."[67] If the government would not protect his people, then Amal would do so. Ironically, a little more than a year later, al-Sadr's inability to protect a larger Shi`i community in northeast Beirut from the Christian militia would considerably weaken his power and prestige among the Shi`i population.[68] However, al-Sadr had put the rest of the confessional communities in Lebanon on notice that it would not be business as usual in dealing with the Shi`a. The Shi`i community had moved toward a more activist and assertive posture.

At the end of 1975, Musa al-Sadr emerged as "the most compelling voice in Lebanon."[69] As the de facto leader of the Shi`a, he moved them toward the goals of self-empowerment and activism. Also troubled by the increasing violence, al-Sadr and the HISC of Lebanon actively worked to secure a cease-fire and implement reform within the Lebanese government on behalf of all Lebanese people. Despite his efforts, brutal and intense fighting between militia groups and their supporters interrupted cease-fires and truces in Lebanon.

On December 31, 1975, al-Sadr participated in a religious forum in an effort to seek a solution to the violence. Shaykh Hassan Khaled, the grand mufti and leader of the Lebanese Sunni community, hosted this Islamic summit of Lebanese Muslim leaders. In attendance were the prime minister of Lebanon, Rashid Karami, and Yasir Arafat, the chairman of the Palestinian Liberation Organization (PLO). These Islamic leaders attempted to seek common ground for a diplomatic solution to the crisis in Lebanon. At the conclusion of the summit, the mufti issued a joint statement saying that all participants, while wanting to improve the Lebanese political, economic, and social conditions, were eager to safeguard Lebanese interests as a whole.[70] The message they conveyed to the Christian patriarch of Lebanon and to the rest of the warring factions was that the Muslims were committed to maintaining the integrity of the Lebanese state. Al-Sadr and members of the HISC of Lebanon were tied to the concept of preserving the Lebanese state and its unique confessional character. The Christian leadership for the Maronites, however, especially the Phalange, was adamant about maintaining the status quo. Supporting the confessional system was fine, but anything that altered the Christians' domination of the political and economic life of Lebanon would not be tolerated. This convinced al-Sadr that the Shi`a needed to continue on their path of self-empowerment, as changing the status quo would not come with the willing acceptance of the Maronites. Despite the Islamic summit's deliberations, compromise between the Christian and Islamic religious sects remained elusive. In the late spring of 1976, the Lebanese Civil War continued unabated.

For the Shi`a, new fighting brought new challenges. As president of the HISC of Lebanon, Musa al-Sadr participated in another Islamic summit on May 13, 1976. This time, the members of the summit charged him to travel to Syria in an effort to garner support to quell the fighting. A report in another Lebanese daily paper, *An-Nahar*, paints a comprehensive picture of his role. *An-Nahar* reported that "the clarity of understanding of the Syrian position that Sadr brought back from his meeting with Syrian President Assad could help to end the conflict and stabilize the situation within Lebanon."[71] The report quoted al-Sadr as saying he considered the mission one of the most successful in his life.[72] A month after his meeting with Assad, events in Lebanon would take a disastrous turn for the Shi`a. Syrian help would mean more violence in Lebanon, and Shi`i families suffered grievously.

Although al-Sadr proved skillful in his ability to negotiate with Arab heads of state, he remained naive regarding the ramifications of his bid for cooperation with Syria. Musa al-Sadr and the HISC of Lebanon had invested a great deal of effort and prestige in obtaining Syrian cooperation to calm the fighting in Lebanon. For Syria, cooperation meant attending to its own agenda in Lebanon by using a large number of troops.[73] The introduction of regular Syrian army units precipitated heavier fighting and a backlash against al-Sadr and the Shi`a in his organization. The Syrians were not honest brokers in the fighting, as their forces went after formations of the PLO and the Lebanese National Movement (LNM).[74] In a radio broadcast on June 8, 1976, al-Sadr appealed to Syrian president Hafez al-Assad to issue orders to Syrian forces to cease fire in Lebanon. Al-Sadr's plea stated, "everything is now being threatened and that the dearest things we possess are exposed to serious danger, that the Palestinian resistance, the Lebanese national will, and even the Syrian dignity are in a great danger."[75] Al-Sadr's concluding statement from that broadcast highlighted the fact that silence from the United States and the Soviet Union on the Syrian intervention indicated a developing international plot taking place "without exception."[76] Although *plot* may seem too dramatic a word for it, the United States was well aware of the Syrian military intervention and tacitly gave its support to ensure that the Christian militias would not be defeated.[77]

The leadership of the PLO viewed Musa al-Sadr's continued involvement and negotiation with the Syrians as a conspiracy against their organization.[78] On June 18, Lebanese radio reported that members of the PLO had surrounded the headquarters of the HISC and disarmed the guards.[79] The report stated that the PLO and its allies were attempting to force the leaders of the HISC to sign statements condemning the entry of the Syrian peacekeeping forces in Lebanon.[80] On June 28, the radio station for Beirut Domestic Service reported that Palestinians and their supporters had shelled the headquarters of the HISC and the home of Musa al-Sadr.[81] Al-Sadr's rift with the PLO was becoming more acute.

Despite al-Sadr and the Shi`i community's rift with the Palestinians, a bigger threat would appear from another sector of the Lebanese political spectrum. The Shi`a's biggest trauma in the civil war would come in August 1976, not from the Palestinians but from the Christian militias. Al-Sadr's activism and drive for self-empowerment could do nothing to stop the tragedy that would unfold in Nab`a. This tragedy and al-Sadr's role in it will be covered in detail in chapter 2. However, the calamity in Nab`a fueled al-Sadr's discontent.

In the spring of 1977, al-Sadr's growing frustration with the Lebanese government was palpable. In an April 9 meeting with the Lebanese president, Ilyas Sarkis, al-Sadr expressed his concerns about the continued fighting in South Lebanon and its effect on the Shi`a. Al-Sadr was careful to mention that the Shi`a would not accept any authority in the region except that of the Lebanese government. Neither the Christian militias nor the Palestinian organizations were acceptable to al-Sadr as the legitimate authority in the south. He also related to Sarkis that the Israelis exploited the tensions and the differences in the region to their own advantage.[82] However, the Lebanese government's inability to protect Shi`i civilians from ongoing Christian militia attacks continued to alienate Shi`a from the government.

The conflict between Christian, Israeli, and Palestinian fighters was changing the entire social fabric of the region.[83] Groups such as the Cultural Council for South Lebanon, a predominately Shi`i organization, attempted to represent their anguish in writings and posters (see figure 1.2). The theme for these posters centered on national resistance and liberation.[84]

In March 1978, a bungled Palestinian raid into Israel by Fatah fighters resulted in the death of thirty-three Israeli civilians on the Haifa-Tel Aviv Highway. The Lebanese government, powerless either to respond to the Pal-

Figure 1.2. Cultural Council for South Lebanon liberation poster "(We are) forever resisting for (on behalf of) the South, March 1978–1981." The Cultural Council for South Lebanon. Trans. Nathan Toronto. Reproduced by permission of American University of Beirut Libraries, Archives and Special Collections.

estinian provocation or to resist any action by the Israelis, stood by while the new Israeli prime minister, Menachem Begin, acted swiftly to mount a full-scale invasion of South Lebanon. The goal of Begin's invasion was to destroy PLO military camps and infrastructure in South Lebanon to prevent future attacks. Despite Israeli attempts to limit collateral damage, many civilians fell victim to the massive attacks, including Shi`i families.[85] In one of the most compelling stories affecting the Shi`a, Christian militiamen who had been fighting Palestinian guerrillas in South Lebanon forced a large group of Shi`i men, women, and children into a mosque in the village of Khiam and, under the eyes of Israeli officers, machine-gunned all of them to death.[86] Unfortunately, such tragedies were all too common for Shi`a in Lebanon.

The Israeli invasion reenergized the Shi`i community in Lebanon toward self-empowerment. Musa al-Sadr was more determined than ever to use the tragedy as an opportunity to forge a new relationship with the Palestinians and seek a stronger alliance with other Arab nations to oppose Israeli acts of aggression against the Shi`a in the south. In an interview in *Ad-Dustur* (a prominent Arabic-language daily), though less optimistic about an Israeli withdrawal and accommodation in South Lebanon, Imam Musa al-Sadr expressed hope for an eventual Palestinian–Lebanese reconciliation.[87] As he had in the past, al-Sadr attempted to leverage his influence in Arab capitals throughout the Middle East toward a changed dynamic in Lebanon. In the spring and summer of 1978, al-Sadr departed Beirut and traveled to Saudi Arabia, Jordan, and Algeria. It was during his stop in Algeria that he was advised by an official to travel to Libya to meet with Colonel Muammar el Qaddafi.[88] Qaddafi possessed money and a degree of influence with the Palestinians, which made him a valuable asset to al-Sadr's cause. Al-Sadr's audience with Qaddafi occurred on the thirty-first of August, after which he and two of his companions were never seen or heard from again.

Six days passed before members of the HISC in Lebanon inquired to the Libyan embassy in Lebanon regarding the whereabouts of Imam al-Sadr. In a radio statement in Lebanon on September 11, 1978, the HISC issued a statement that the Libyan embassy had notified the Lebanese government that Musa al-Sadr had left Libya for Rome aboard an Alitalia plane of August 31.[89] Yet he and his companions never arrived.

It is difficult to represent the depth of anguish and consternation al-Sadr's disappearance had on the Lebanese Shi`i community. The HISC continued to press the issue with the Libyans and the Lebanese government to no avail. The Italian government and Interpol followed the incident and sought information regarding al-Sadr's whereabouts. Additionally, an official delegation from the HISC in Lebanon traveled to Libya to conduct an independent investigation of al-Sadr's disappearance. Every formal inquiry uncovered no viable leads. By mid-September, rumors about al-Sadr's fate abounded in Lebanon. There were local reports that he was detained in a Libyan prison and never made it to his meeting with Qaddafi.[90] Other reports had al-Sadr in Damascus accompanied by PLO chairman Yasir Arafat.[91] The HISC cautioned the Lebanese to disregard all rumors and reports about al-Sadr unless they originated with the Shi`i council.[92] However, many Lebanese clung to the notion that their "Imam" might still be found safe and sound.

Additionally Islamic leaders in Lebanon directly requested American help to determine the whereabouts of al-Sadr. Beirut radio reported on a meeting between Mufti Hasan Khalid and United States ambassador Richard Parker in which the matter of Imam al-Sadr's fate was raised.[93] The mufti solicited the ambassador's assistance in determining the whereabouts of al-Sadr. However, there was no help forthcoming from the Americans.

On September 19, Muslim scholars, shaykhs, and other officials staged religious demonstrations in a number of Beirut's mosques as a sign of unity and protest against the dearth of information regarding the fate of Musa al-Sadr.[94] Reminiscent of the civil rights protests in the United States in the 1960s, the sit-ins were peaceful and pervaded by prayer invoking God's help for al-Sadr's peaceful return. Later that week, a delegation of Lebanese Shi`i leaders traveled to the Syrian–Lebanese border to present a note to Arab leaders who were holding a summit in Damascus.[95] Among the conference leaders in attendance was Libyan president Qaddafi. In his book, *The Vanished Imam*, Fouad Ajami states that two hundred thousand Shi`a accompanied the delegation to the Syrian capital demanding to know the whereabouts of al-Sadr.[96] Qaddafi agreed to a meeting with the clerics, and although he offered no resolution to the problem of the missing imam, the Lebanese Shi`a had put the world on notice. They would not remain quiet while their leaders and people suffered adverse actions.

No longer content to be associated with Pan-Arab nationalist ideas, or to blindly follow the Palestinian cause, the Shi`a's move toward self-empowerment and greater political clout had a new rallying symbol in the form of the missing Imam Musa al-Sadr. As a result, his image was posted everywhere in Shi`i communities. A typical poster, such as shown in figure 1.3, had the image of Musa al-Sadr flanked by the symbol for Amal, the militia group that he started. The poster employs a green background, the symbolic color of Islam.

Those displays provided a visual manifestation of the changing social climate in Lebanon. The themes of oppression, struggle, and martyrdom were all part of al-Sadr's discourse within the Shi`i community and were incorporated in the posters that appeared in Shi`i neighborhoods.[97] The community would no longer follow the quietist interpretation of their religion; Musa al-Sadr had shown them a new way. They would confront what they considered to be injustice and evil. This was in keeping with the tradition and foundation of Shi`ism, as demonstrated by Imam Husayn thousands of years earlier on the plains of Kerbala.

From his Iranian origins in Qum, Iran, Musa al-Sadr managed to make an indelible imprint on the Lebanese Shi`a. If the Shi`a were to be part of the Lebanese state, al-Sadr preached, they had to hold fast to their religious identity.[98] For al-Sadr, being Lebanese meant having a close affiliation to a religious (confessional) group. Yet he would no longer accept the Lebanese Shi`a being on the bottom rung of society. His efforts at redefining what it meant to be Shi`i in Lebanon significantly changed the narrative of the community. When the violence against the Shi`a continued unabated, al-Sadr proffered the use of force as an available, legitimate means of protecting themselves and securing their rights. The Shi`a would cajole, scrape, and fight for their civil rights within Lebanon. Al-Sadr's ability to connect with the wider transnational network of Shi`i activists also shaped the Shi`a narrative within Lebanon. As Roschanack Shaery-Eisenlor concludes in her book *Shi`ite Lebanon: Transnational Religion and the Making of National Identities*, al-Sadr's transnational discourse between Shi`i groups and leaders in Iran, Syria, and Iraq helped to shape debates of identity and narrative in

Figure 1.3. Poster of Musa al-Sadr Symbols: Amal, or "hope." Translation: "My place is amongst you, my throne is your (collective) heart, my power is your hands, my guard is your eyes, my glory is in assembling (reuniting) with you." Trans. Nathan Toronto. Reproduced by permission of American University of Beirut Libraries, Archives and Special Collections.

Lebanon.[99] Despite al-Sadr's initial support for the Palestinian cause and the strong support the cause received from other Shi`i international networks, al-Sadr's focus was on the Lebanese Shi`i civil rights movement. In the end, al-Sadr's disappearance not only imprinted itself on the Lebanese Shi`i narrative but gave the community a tangible symbol around which to rally. However, the English-language prestige press and media offered a different representation of al-Sadr's importance to Lebanon and his function within the Shi`i community.

THE INFLUENCE OF ENGLISH-LANGUAGE PRESS AND MEDIA

The United States and Great Britain dominated the English-language market for news media in 1975.[100] The largest distribution of international news, which had the greatest impact on Americans, came from a half-dozen television and radio networks and newspapers.[101] Among the most prominent of these daily sources was the *New York Times*. This paper, one of the most quoted periodicals in the Western world, was viewed as the journal of record for America and a major source of information for policymakers in the US government.[102] Every day, the words, images and representations of the *New York Times* shaped American perceptions and representations of people and situations around the globe. The *Times* (London), one of the longest-established newspapers in Great Britain also had considerable influence and exposure internationally.[103] Like the position of the *New York Times* in the United States, the *Times* (London) has long been considered the paper of record for the United Kingdom.[104] *The Manchester Guardian*, a left-of-center daily, also had considerable clout internationally and was widely read in the English-language market. Other media outlets in the United States and Great Britain covered Lebanon and the Shi`a from 1975 through 1985. However, this section focuses on how these three prominent papers covered violence against the Shi`a in Lebanon and represented Musa al-Sadr.

Although the *New York Times* was the paper of record for international news in the United States, academics criticized its reporting, particularly its coverage of the Middle East. A reading guide produced by the progressive nonprofit Middle East Research and Information Project (MERIP) in May 1974 warned readers that they must take caution when reading Western press reports on the Middle East. The guide stated that the wire services and the individual newspapers offered erratic coverage. Regarding the *New York Times* specifically, the guide stated that the paper was useful in its coverage but that one should be wary of the reports by reporter Juan de Onis.[105] His reports typified the erratic coverage of events in the Middle East. The *New York Times* coverage of the situation in Lebanon in early 1975 clearly justifies that admonition, especially as it applied to the Shi`i community in South Lebanon. Juan de Onis was responsible for covering events in Lebanon for the *New York Times* in January 1975, but, as MERIP had reported, his coverage was sometimes unreliable—especially when reporting on violence against the Shi`a.[106]

Prior to 1975, scant coverage of the Lebanese Shi`a and Musa al-Sadr appeared in the *New York Times* and the *Times* (London) however; one paper, the *Guardian*, paid attention to the plight of the Lebanese Shi`a as early as May 1970. At that time, reporter David Hirst reported on a strike organized by Musa al-Sadr, "the spiritual head of the Shi`ite Muslim community," to protest the attacks by the Israelis on Shi`i villagers in the South of Lebanon.[107] In an April 1974 article, the *Guardian* covered a rally by Musa al-Sadr in Baalbek. The paper stated that over one hundred thousand people attended the rally, the biggest gathering Lebanon had ever seen.[108] As if a precursor to the next decade, Hirst stated in his article that "the Shi`ites of Lebanon are on the move. They are determined to secure what in the light of Lebanon's unique political system they regard as their rightful due."[109] Furthermore, Hirst acknowledged even then that the Shi'a were the victims of the violence of Israel's anti-guerrilla operations in South Lebanon. Unfortunately, prior to 1975 no such attention was paid to the Shi`a in the American media and in the more popular *Times* (London).

REPORTING VIOLENCE AND CONFLATING RESISTANCE

At the beginning of 1975, the American and British press's coverage of the violence on the Lebanese–Israeli border often ignored the Shi`a and Musa al-Sadr. Additionally, reporters often conflated Lebanese Shi`a and Palestinian resistance fighters in their articles and dispatches. One such example unfolded on the night of December 31, 1974. That evening, members of the Israeli Defense Force (IDF) made preparations to cross into South Lebanon. The Israeli units were tasked with conducting an assault, purportedly against houses used by terrorists. The day before, Israeli forces killed three "Arab Guerrillas" in Northern Israel infiltrating from Lebanon.[110] As a result of a raid conducted by the Israeli forces on the morning of January 1, 1975, the *New York Times* reported, "Israeli military headquarters . . . said today an Israeli force searching for Arab guerrillas in South Lebanon blew up a house with guerrillas inside after an exchange of fire."[111] The same evening that the article appeared in the *New York Times*, American Broadcasting Corporation (ABC) nightly news anchor Howard K. Smith reported that the Israelis crossed the Lebanese border and raided two towns. No image of the damage wrought by the Israeli raid appeared in either the *New York Times* or in the report by Howard K. Smith.[112] Although the ABC report by Smith quoted Lebanese officials saying that "four Arab civilians were killed and two homes dynamited," key facts were not reported: the individuals killed were Shi`a, and the town raided by the Israelis was a predominantly Shi`i town.[113] This incident illustrates how the *New York Times* and the American media ignored and failed to report or place into context the Shi`a's exposure to violence and trauma in Lebanon.

Similar reports came from the *Times* (London). "Terror and counter-terror ushered in the new year for Israel as they had dominated the old" was the opening sentence of a January 2, 1975, *Times* article by reporter Eric Marsden.[114] Marsden, chronicling an attack by the IDF on two towns in South Lebanon for the British media at the beginning of 1975, chose to frame the attack as a battle between terror and counterterror. The next day the *Times* reported another attack by the IDF on the Lebanese village of Tabie. The report related the actions of the IDF as "fighting an hour-long gun battle with a number of guerrillas holding a house before they blew up the building with the Arabs inside."[115] Not once in either article did the authors mention that the towns' victims were Shi`a. An examination of the facts surrounding the attack on Tabie suggested something very unlike the characterization of the leading article of terror and counterterror. The Israeli attack resulted in the death of three civilians with no connection to the PLO or fighters opposing Israel.[116] The failure to capture the exposure of the Shi`a to the violence on the South Lebanese border, coupled with their conflation with the Palestinians and other Arab resistance movements, seriously affected the Shi`a representation in British press and media and mirrored their misrepresentation in the American press and media.

ANALYZING THE COVERAGE OF VIOLENCE AND REPRESENTATION OF MUSA AL-SADR

To provide an in-depth analysis of early coverage of violence against the Shi`a and the representation of Musa al-Sadr by the English-language media, it is instructive to examine the reporting in the first nine days of 1975. During that period four reports appeared in the *New York Times* relating to Israeli military actions into South Lebanon. These reports illustrated how the *New York Times* either ignored the violence perpetrated against the Lebanese Shi`a or conflated their community with other Arab independence movements in Lebanon. Two major sources for the reports were the Israeli military and reporter Juan de Onis. A detailed reading of all the reports revealed obvious inconsistencies between the Israeli press releases appearing in the *New York Times* and the information gathered by reporter Juan de Onis from eyewitness accounts. However, these inconsistencies were never highlighted, and as a result the *New York Times* never provided an accurate representation of the Lebanese Shi`a experience in the early part of 1975.

In a January 3, 1975, article covering the aftermath of an Israeli raid, de Onis quoted Israeli military sources as saying, "casualties in the town of Taibe were Arab guerrillas."[117] Five days later, he was in the village of Taibe and recorded a different account of what happened. The eyewitness account he gathered from the Shi`i family at Taibe put a different face on the people the Israelis referred to as "Arab guerrillas." De Onis recorded that an Israeli night patrol killed four men, including a father and two sons and blew up four houses. A fourteen-year-old boy, whose father and brother were killed, stated that the Israelis fired on their house and blew it up.[118] The young boy's account of the incident stated that his father went to the door of his home when he heard noises. When he opened the door, the Israelis shot him. They also shot his brother when he went to help. A third brother took a gun and fired out the window. He was killed also.[119] Later, it was revealed that the sixteen-year-old who fired the gun had been home on vacation from a vocational high school in Tyre established by Imam Musa al-Sadr. The curriculum of the school entailed imparting technical skills as well as military training that afforded Shi`i students the knowledge to use weapons to protect their villages.[120] This incident in Taibe was reported in the Lebanese press on

January 3, 1975, with an almost-identical corroboration of the eyewitness accounts gathered by Onis.[121] However, Onis made no mention of the contradicting report he had filed from the Israeli defense ministry just five days prior. The terms *terrorist* and *Arab guerrilla* were used frequently in *New York Times* reporting, but those words did not always accurately describe the victims of the fighting in South Lebanon.[122]

The term *Arab guerrilla* conflated all Arabs with fighting and resistance against Israel. Although Lebanon was predominantly Arab in ethnic makeup, its various confessional groups included Maronite Christians, Druze, Sunni, and Shi`a; not all were anti-Israel. Israel's adversaries in Lebanon were predominantly members of the PLO. The Shi`a composed the predominant population of South Lebanon. While some Shi`a willingly joined Fatah (the Palestinian resistance movement), others were forced into the resistance movement.[123] However, the majority of the Shi`a were more concerned about eking out a living from their meager fields than participating in the Palestinian resistance movement. Israeli attacks, like the one described above, hurt them the most.

Musa al-Sadr, the most prominent member of the Shi`i community, arrived on the scene soon after the incident in Taibe. As he had on numerous occasions when segments of the Shi`i community faced trauma, al-Sadr travelled to the town to console the victims of the Israeli attack and their families.[124] No mention was made of al-Sadr's visit to the town by the *New York Times* report covering the aftermath of the incident on January 1, 1975.

The *New York Times* reports on what transpired on the hills and in the towns in South Lebanon during that nine-day period in January are indicative of how the Shi`a were virtually ignored in the American prestige press and media. Their plight was subsumed into a different narrative of Palestinian and Arab nationalist movements. The contradictions in the stories of Israeli actions in January 1975 represent a lack of attention (intentional or otherwise) to the narrative of the Shi`a in the American press; their story was hidden and distorted. The *New York Times* failed to clearly outline that the attack and violence were perpetrated against a Lebanese Shi`a community and understand the resultant anger and angst caused within that community. This is but one instance in which the Shi`a were represented poorly by inadequate and imprecise *New York Times* reporting. A more conscientious effort by *New York Times* reporters would have captured an accurate narrative of the Lebanese Shi`a and crafted a reliable representation of their plight. Unfortunately, the *Times* (London) fared no better in its early representation of the Shi`a and Musa al-Sadr.

At the beginning of 1975 the reporting on Lebanon by the *Times* (London) focused on the cross-border violence between Israel and the Palestinian militias. However, the *Times* reports rarely mentioned Musa al-Sadr. Unnoticed by the *Times*, al-Sadr spent many religious and civil holidays in the southern border villages in Lebanon.[125] He presided over religious ceremonies and also engaged in symbolic acts of resistance against the Israelis and the Palestinians as a means of countering the violence occurring against the Shi`a population in the region. This resistance included calling on Shi`i villagers from the South not to abandon their homes in the wake of Israeli attacks but to stand and defend them against Israeli aggression.[126] But the *Times* characterized the fighting and the displacement of personnel in South Lebanon as Palestinians opposed to Israel. An example of that reporting took place in early in 1975.

On January 13, 1975, the *Times* (London) reported an Israeli attack on the small Southern Lebanese town of Kfar Shuba.[127] For two weeks, the *Times* reported fighting between the Israelis and what the paper said were "Palestinian guerrillas" in and around the town.[128] On January 21, 1975, the *New York Times* picked up the story involving fighting around Kfar Shuba. Their reports also chronicled the result of fighting between Israeli forces and Palestinian militias. However, there was a distinct difference in the reports from the *Times* (London) and the *New York Times*. The *New York Times* made definitive reference to the Lebanese Shi`a being a population affected by the fighting and also mentioned Musa al-Sadr, who, the paper said, "was the religious leader of the Shiite sect of Moslems in Lebanon and most of the small farmers and villages of the south are followers of the Imam."[129] Al-Sadr was the most important leader of the Lebanese Shi`a for over a decade, but according to the *New York Times Index* this was the first substantial mention of al-Sadr in the paper.[130] Although this *New York Times* article of January 21, 1975, was helpful in understanding the plight of the Shi`a, part of the article distorted the Shi`i narrative by conflating Musa al-Sadr's movement and the Lebanese Shi`a with a larger Arab resistance movement against Israel.

Onis reported that the town of Kfar Shuba was being used as a rallying point for all Lebanese political sectors to support the Palestinian guerrillas in a united "Arab front" against Israel. Listing the followers of the late Egyptian president Nasser (Nasserists), militants of the Arab nationalist Baath movement, the Palestinians, and the Shi`a, Onis suggested that there was the possibility of a coalition of these diverse entities.[131] In Onis's opinion, the most important factor in forming that united front was "Imam Moussa al-Sadr, the religious leader of the Shi`ite sect of Moslems in Lebanon."[132] The major evidence Onis put forward was that the imam believed the Palestinians had the right to attack Israel because international diplomacy had not enabled the refugees to return to their homes.[133] The article gave scant detail and background on the imam and did not put into context his stance on the Palestinians or the resistance to Israel. Although significant information on Musa al-Sadr existed in the Lebanese press in 1975, the *New York Times* report took al-Sadr's words out of context. As discussed previously, Musa al-

Sadr's support for the Palestinian resistance had weakened considerably due to their impressments of Shi`i men into their militias and encroachment on Lebanese Shi`a property and farms in the southern region.[134]

Another opportunity was missed by the English-language press and media in covering Musa al-Sadr and the story of the Lebanese Shi`a. The incident in Kfar Shuba brought to light once again the dispute between al-Sadr and the old power structure of the Lebanese Shi`a and his new conflict with the leftist community. The Beirut *Daily Star* covered al-Sadr's dispute with the *zaim* (old political bosses) and leftist leaders over the fighting and the displacement of Shi`a in Kfar Shuba. Kamel Assad (*zaim*) and Habib Sadek (socialist leader) criticized al-Sadr for failing to improve the plight of the Shi`a in the South, but both men were, in fact, jealous of the large following al-Sadr attracted among the Shi`i community.[135] The English-language press did not highlight the dispute or the changing dynamics of the Shi`a in Lebanon that Musa al-Sadr brought about, even though the information was available through Lebanese sources.

In February 1975, Musa al-Sadr traveled to the town of Kfar Shuba to pray at the town mosque. Reports in the Lebanese media chronicled al-Sadr's call upon villagers to return to the town and defend themselves from Israeli attacks.[136] However, there was no *New York Times* or *Times* (London) press coverage of Musa al-Sadr's efforts to rally the people of South Lebanon. As the fighting on the southern border of Lebanon continued, the story would soon be eclipsed by an even larger conflict upon which the English-language media would focus its coverage. Musa al-Sadr played a significant role in this conflict but, in this case, the *Times* of London did not represent his actions well.

THE LEBANESE CIVIL WAR, AL-SADR, AND THE MEDIA

On April 13, 1975, *New York Times* reporter Juan de Onis filed a report stating, "Gunmen of a right-wing party open fire on a bus filled with Palestinian militants, killing 22 Palestinians."[137] Palestinians and Christian militias had clashed previously, but this ambush by Christian militiamen was the catalyst for the Lebanese Civil War that lasted fifteen years. The beginning of the Lebanese Civil War prompted a change in the *New York Times* coverage of Lebanon and the Shi`a. While previous coverage had focused on cross-border clashes between "Arabs" and the Israelis, the level of violence in the civil war caused *New York Times* reporters to focus on Lebanon's internal divisions.

A week into the fighting, the *New York Times* reported 120 people killed and over 200 wounded.[138] In a country of less than 2.5 million, this was a significant casualty figure. By April 16, the Arab League and Egyptian president Anwar Sadat attempted a tentative cease-fire. A *New York Times* article on the same day mentioned Imam Musa al-Sadr, a leader of the "Shi`ite Moslems" in Lebanon, as an important influence on the cease-fire deal. The article identified al-Sadr as a political moderate trusted by both the Palestinian guerrilla leadership and the Lebanese Christians.[139] In describing al-Sadr as a political moderate, the *New York Times* failed to convey the personal stake that al-Sadr held for the Shi`a in the civil war. Al-Sadr was actually concerned that leftist militias involved in the civil war were recruiting Shi`a men into their organizations.[140] This recruitment weakened al-Sadr's "Movement of the Deprived" and exposed Shi`a men to a leftist philosophy that he did not support. Despite his disagreement with the Christian-dominated government, al-Sadr believed that the Shi`a had more to gain under the confessional system than beneath a leftist-dominated secular government. The *New York Times* also failed to capture that many of the victims of the civil war were Shi`a, again underreporting the violence to which the community was exposed.

Two days into the civil war, a correspondent for the *Times* (London) in Beirut, Paul Martin, reported that the death toll had reached more than one hundred.[141] Internal divisions within Lebanon had intensified to the extent that militia members were now battling in the streets. In his report, Martin acknowledged that calls for a cease-fire from Lebanese political leaders and from other Arab countries had been ignored.[142] Yet there was no mention of Musa al-Sadr, one of the key political leaders who called for the cessation of violence and who was involved as a mediator of the conflict from the beginning of the civil war.[143]

From the spring of 1975 to his disappearance in the summer of 1978, Musa al-Sadr played a small role in the *New York Times* coverage of the conflict in Lebanon. Although mentioned in articles about attempts to achieve a cease-fire and discussed in the revelation of a new Shi`i militia group, no *New York Times* article focused solely on Musa al-Sadr or the Shi`a during that period of time. As discussed previously, al-Sadr warned the Lebanese government of the potential for violence prior to the civil war.[144] Concerning the Shi`a in Lebanon, he said the plight of the community was a "time-bomb" for conflicts, yet the English-language press and media muted his voice.[145] This media approach was tantamount to covering the civil rights movement in America and not devoting considerable coverage to Martin Luther King Jr.[146] However, even when al-Sadr appeared in Western news reports, the Orientalist nature of the reporting was readily apparent.

New York Times press reports shrouded al-Sadr's persona in mystic allure. "Mysterious," one reporter called him; another described him as "powerfully built,"[147] yet few reports captured al-Sadr's importance to the Shi`i movement or the conflict in Lebanon.[148] In instances when the *New York Times* gave coverage to al-Sadr within the larger context of an article on

Lebanon, the paper either described him with a "mystic Orientalism" or distorted the role he played in Lebanon. For example, when covering al-Sadr's fast against the violence in the country in June 1975, the *New York Times* report ascribes an almost Gandhi-like quality to al-Sadr, yet five days after the end of his fast the *New York Times* reported the formation of al-Sadr's militia group.[149] Al-Sadr was no Gandhi, yet he was also no mystic snake charmer; he was a charismatic leader determined to guide his people out of the desperate situation in which they found themselves in Lebanon.

The *Times* (London) was silent on the topic of Musa al-Sadr and his efforts to restore peace in Lebanon. Promises by Lebanese political officials to work toward a cease-fire in the sectarian fighting were instrumental in al-Sadr ending his fast. Yet the *Times* never recorded this or chronicled the great political influence that Musa al-Sadr had within the country. However, another British media source did offer some insight into the role of Musa al-Sadr and the plight of the Shi`a in the Lebanese Civil War. The *Guardian* reporter David Hirst reported on June 28, 1975, with regard to the Shi`a and the fighting in Beirut: "Most Moslems in the Chiah district belong to the underprivileged but numerous Shi`ite sect and their spiritual leader Imam Moussa al-Sadr announced he was beginning a fast."[150] Hirst, who had covered the Shi`a and Musa al-Sadr since 1970, understood the importance of al-Sadr and the Shi`a. The *Times* did not demonstrate as much understanding or concern in its coverage of al-Sadr, despite the fact that his involvement was instrumental in helping the Lebanese politicians find a way to temporarily stop the fighting and begin the process of reconciliation.

On July 2, 1975, *Times* (London) reporter Paul Martin heralded the formation of a new cabinet. In his report, Martin stated, "The Cabinet has the blessing of the country's two main politico-religious factions the Christian Maronites and the Sunni Muslims."[151] Not once did Martin mention al-Sadr or the Shi`a. The paper would record a significant story involving al-Sadr and the Lebanese Shi`a several days after al-Sadr ended his fast: this was the announcement of the formation of his militia group Amal.

The coverage of Musa al-Sadr and the Shi`a increased briefly in the *New York Times* and the *Times* (London) after the revelation of the militia group Amal. On July 6, 1975, the *New York Times* reported an explosion at a training camp for "Moslem militiamen," exposing what it said was "military links between Palestinian guerrillas and Lebanese leftists."[152] In reality, the explosion occurred during a training session for Amal militiamen conducted by a member of Fatah, the Palestinian resistance movement. Fatah had the military expertise and the contacts within the Shi`i community to conduct the initial training of Amal.[153] Although the report identified most victims of the explosion as followers of Musa al-Sadr, the author of the *New York Times* article incorrectly linked the movement to leftist movements. Even the article's title, "Lebanese Blast, Fatal to 42, Discloses Leftist Links with Palestine Guerrillas," conflated al-Sadr and the Shi`a with the Left. The article stated that al-Sadr had appeared with large numbers of militiamen brandishing Soviet-designed Kalashnikov assault rifles and rocket grenade launchers.[154] In the bipolar world of 1975, placing Soviet manufactured weapons in the hands of al-Sadr's militia gave the reader the impression that al-Sadr's militia was aligned with the communist left. This was not the case.

The *New York Times* report on the explosion quoted Christian Phalangist sources, stating that the Palestinian guerrillas were supporting Lebanese leftists, most of whom were "Moslem."[155] *Leftist* was a code word for communist, and the Phalange traditionally used the word to garner the support of Western entities against their enemies.[156] However, al-Sadr and the Amal militia were vehemently anticommunist. Al-Sadr believed that communism was the negation of God.[157] However, nowhere in the *New York Times* reporting was this factor ever covered. The *New York Times* appeared fond of reporting the Lebanese violence in a binary fashion, recording the two sides fighting against one another as the Right and the Left. A more subtle and nuanced approach could have conveyed the complexity of the situation.

The *New York Times* did make minor attempts to clarify some of al-Sadr's issues. In the July 1975 article about the explosion in the training camp, the *New York Times* report did categorize Musa al-Sadr as a strong advocate of political and social change in Lebanon, desirous of giving "Moslems" a stronger voice in the government.[158] However, al-Sadr and his movement were often mentioned in conjunction with leftist groups in Lebanon.

The British reporting on Amal commenced on July 7, 1975, when the *Times* covered the accidental explosion at a Lebanese training camp that killed thirty militiamen. The report stated that the mishap occurred during mountain maneuvers for the followers of the imam Musa al-Sadr, the "Smia [this is how the intended word *Shi`a* appeared in the paper] Muslim leader near the town of Baalbeck."[159] The article further stated that "armed followers of Imam Musa form just one of the militias which were involved in the recent fighting."[160] There was no attempt by the paper to introduce any contextual statement by Musa al-Sadr or to discuss why the militia was formed and for what purpose it was intended. Al-Sadr, who stated in the local Lebanese press that Amal was formed to defend the country from repeated Israeli attacks, especially in the absence of any official reply, was never referenced or quoted in the *Times* article.[161]

After the revelation of Amal, the reporting on Musa al-Sadr slowed in the *Times* (London). In September 1975, Imam Musa al-Sadr was mentioned twice of in the *Times*. On September 15, reporter Paul Martin described how the newly appointed prime minister of Lebanon had avoided a nationwide strike. Prime Minister Rashid Karami announced in a special radio broadcast the successful conclusion of his day long negotiations with Socialist leaders and with Mr. Yassir Arafat Chairman of the Palestine Liberation Organization. Clearly, the manner in which Shaikh Hassan Khalid, the Sunni Mufti, and Imam Musa al-Sadr, the powerful Shi`i leader stood firmly against the leftist is a measure of their concern over the deteriorating situation in the country.[162]

This was the first reference in the *Times* to al-Sadr having played any significant role in the Lebanese peace efforts in the country. On September 24, Paul Martin mentioned Musa al-Sadr again—this time, as "the Shia leader, who recently formed themselves into a regular guerrilla force."[163] As in the article covering the explosion at the Amal training camp in July, no mention was made of al-Sadr's explanation of the militia's mission and purpose. As the Lebanese Civil War continued and the *Times* chronicled the tragedy, the paper failed to provide a true representation of Musa al-Sadr and his importance to the Shi`a in Lebanon. For the *Times*, he was just one of the many protagonists in the drama unfolding across Lebanon.

The *Times* (London) focused its attention on other actors in the Lebanese Civil War. A *Times* article of December 14, 1975, discussed at length the Muslim militia of Saeb Salam, a prominent Sunni Muslim leader and former prime minister.[164] Salam organized the Popular Resistance Militia, a group of conservative Muslims that purported to help maintain the traditional sources of Sunni political power in Lebanon. The group proved to be insignificant in comparison to Musa al-Sadr's Amal militia. Additional articles and editorials in the *Times* discussed the roles of sectarian leaders such as Kamal Jumblatt of the Druze and Bachir Gemayel of the Maronite Phalange militia.[165] The *Times* featured a report of a local Muslim leader in Tripoli, Lebanon, named Farouk Moqaddem but afforded no such feature to Musa al-Sadr.[166]

Again, the *Guardian* provided greater insight than the *Times* (London) into the role and the importance of Musa al-Sadr to the Lebanese Shi`i community. In an article in June 1976, David Hirst discussed the importance of Musa al-Sadr and the Shi`i community in accommodating the Syrian intervention in June.[167] Al-Sadr had negotiated many times with Syrian President Hafez al-Assad to have Syrian forces act as the honest broker in the fighting between the factions in Lebanon.[168] Unfortunately, this would later backfire for al-Sadr and the Shi`a, as Syrian forces pursued those entities allied with the Shi`a and al-Sadr. In September 1976, the *Guardian* published another article discussing al-Sadr's role in trying to facilitate peace in Lebanon by meeting with Syrian officials in Damascus.[169] Unfortunately, this coverage of al-Sadr was not forthcoming in the *Times* (London).

In a *New York Times* article in September 1976, Musa al-Sadr was mentioned with leftist leader Kamal Jumblatt as consulting with President Ford's special envoy to Lebanon, L. Dean Brown.[170] Kamal Jumblatt, the leader of the Druze sect in Lebanon and the head of the Progressive Socialist Party (PSP), was often at odds with al-Sadr and his vision of Lebanon. Despite that, the Shi`i movement of al-Sadr was often mentioned within the framework of Jumblatt's leftist political movement.

As an empowered and highly respected leader in Lebanon, al-Sadr earnestly attempted to broker a peace settlement early in the Lebanese Civil War. His efforts toward this end were outlined extensively in the Lebanese press.[171] However, when the *New York Times* covered these peace attempts, al-Sadr's role was mentioned only briefly. The reports in the *New York Times* also provided very little context for his role or that of the Shi`a.[172] During the Phalange siege of Nab`a in 1976, there was no mention of al-Sadr or the Shi`a, even though they suffered grievously from that battle. Al-Sadr's attempts to broker a deal or his reaction to the aftermath of the battle were never covered by the *New York Times*.

Finally, Musa al-Sadr's opposition to the shah of Iran was well known by sources within Lebanon.[173] However, the *New York Times* and the American media sources virtually ignored al-Sadr's statements or his beliefs on this issue. By 1974 Musa al-Sadr was openly criticizing the shah's policies in Iran and his support for Israel.[174] This linkage between Musa al-Sadr and the Shi`a of Lebanon with the opposition to the shah will be covered in depth in chapter 3; however, the American press and media missed an important opportunity to gain a better understanding of Musa al-Sadr and his connections with the transnational networks in the Shi`i community. This offers more support to the contention that by ignoring al-Sadr and not covering the transnational networks of the Shi`a, the English-language press failed to gain an accurate representation of the Shi`i narrative in Lebanon.

In August 1978, Musa al-Sadr disappeared during a trip to Libya. The American press did not immediately cover the event. Eventually, limited coverage of the imam's disappearance appeared in the *Los Angeles Times* and the *Washington Post*, but the *New York Times* would not feature the story in any of its columns.[175] Slowly, there was a trickle of information in reference to al-Sadr's disappearance in the *New York Times*. In January 1979, a brief notation in the World News section of the paper referenced "Shiite Moslem followers of the missing spiritual leader of Lebanon clashing with leftist forces."[176] On January 17, 1979, the *Washington Post* reported that a Middle East Airlines aircraft was hijacked by six Lebanese Shi`i Muslims seeking to publicize al-Sadr's disappearance, but the *New York Times* never carried an account of the hijacking or a detailed account of the missing imam.[177] Finally, two years after his disappearance and buried on page 7 of the *New York Times* was a report from Paris that a French radio station reported Imam Musa al-Sadr was being held captive in Libya.[178] Later, a series of reports on airline hijacking appeared in the paper in 1980. The *New York Times* began to attribute these hijacking attempts to "Shi`ites" wanting to draw attention to the case of the missing imam.[179] Yet the Lebanese Shi'a had focused the world's attention to their imam's plight on a number of occasions. A month after his disappearance, almost two hundred thousand Lebanese Shi'a traveled to an Arab summit in Damascus to protest the imam's disappearance.[180] However, the absence of protest coverage in the *New York Times* failed to convey the importance of Musa al-Sadr and the impact of his movement on Lebanese Shi'a.

In the British press, it was not until September 1978 that al-Sadr's disappearance received significant coverage in the *Times* (London). On September 13, 1978, *Times* reporter Robert Fisk wrote, "The political upheavals in Iran seem at last to have touched the Arab world with the mysterious disappearance of Imam 'Moussa' Sadr, the leader of the Shia Muslim community in Lebanon."[181] Fisk was one of the first Western reporters to comment on al-Sadr's disappearance. He speculated that SAVAK, the Iranian intelligence agency, might have kidnapped him for his opposition to the shah's regime.[182] In a follow-up article, Fisk reported on a strike by members of the Muslim community in Beirut to protest the disappearance of Musa al-Sadr. The protests shut down all of western Beirut, the predominantly Muslim area of the city.[183]

The *Guardian* covered the disappearance as well. Al-Sadr, the article said, was one of the most important religious figures in Lebanon. "He has been the first effective leader the Shi'a have had in a long time, while in Iran his disappearance is likely to fuel accusations that the Iranian authorities are trying to suppress all opposition to the Shah."[184] The *Guardian* also speculated that the shah's secret police, SAVAK, had something to do with al-Sadr's disappearance.

As a result of reports by the *Times* (London) and Manchester's *Guardian*, the impact of this most prominent of Shi'i leaders began to come to light. In his book *Pity the Nation: The Abduction of Lebanon* (1990), Robert Fisk states that in Lebanon "no militia or political leader is so powerful—his name so influential—as when he is dead, enshrined on wall posters and gatepost amid naively clusters of tulips and roses, the final artistic accolade of every armed martyr in Lebanon."[185] Fisk is correct. Al-Sadr was a prominent figure in Lebanese and Shi'i society, but after his disappearance and apparent death he took on mythical proportions. As covered previously, his picture appeared everywhere in the downtrodden Shi'i areas of West Beirut and in South Lebanon. Al-Sadr embodied the Lebanese Shi'i narrative, fighting against tremendous odds to do what is right, no matter the consequences.

In conclusion, there are times in history when a personality personifies a movement and a people. Martin Luther King personified the American civil rights movement and the African American plight. Nelson Mandela embodied the antiapartheid movement and black South Africans, as did Mahatma Gandhi for natives and the independence movement in India. Musa al-Sadr took on a similar personality for the Shi`a and their movement in Lebanon, yet the *New York Times* and the American media failed to capture his narrative and that of the Shi`a. Forty years after his disappearance, his picture still adorns neighborhoods in Lebanon. His legacy remains important to Lebanese Shi`a throughout the country.[186] The British media also failed to capture a true representation of Musa al-Sadr with the exception of some insightful reporting by the *Guardian*. Al-Sadr contributed considerable effort to transform the Lebanese Shi`a into a more activist community, one that demanded civil rights and demonstrated a willingness to defend the community by force. The dearth of coverage by the English-language press and media of the violence inflicted on the Lebanese Shi`a and the efforts of al-Sadr offered little context with which the consumers of this information could understand his importance to the Shi`i community or comprehend the Shi`a's narrative in Lebanon. The English-language media would also miss a critical opportunity to cover another event of significance to the Lebanese Shi`a, the battle of Nab`a. That story is covered in the next chapter.

NOTES

1. In Islam the title of *imam* is given to those who lead the community in prayer. Most imams have some form of advanced religious training. Within the Twelver Shi`a tradition, a distinction is made in regard to the first twelve imams in the religion, who they believe were endowed with certain gifts of religious discernment. In reference to these first twelve, the title *imam* has a completely different connotation than that of the normal prayer leader.

2. Augustus Richard Norton, *Amal and the Shi`a: Struggle for the Soul of Lebanon* (Austin: University of Texas Press, 1987), 39.

3. Majed Halawi, *A Lebanon Defied: Musa al-Sadr and the Shi`a Community* (Boulder, CO: Westview Press, 1992), 126.

4. Fouad Ajami, *The Vanished Imam: Musa al-Sadr and the Shia of Lebanon* (Ithaca, NY: Cornell University Press, 1986), 31.

5. See David Ignatius, "A Hero of Islam," *New York Times Book Review*, June 1986; Sarah Searight, "Third World Review (Books): Missing Martyr / Review of *The Vanished Imam: Musa al-Sadr and the Shia of Lebanon*," *Guardian*, October 17, 1986; Maurice Gent. "Review of *The Vanished Imam*," *International Affairs* 63, no. 1 (Winter 1986–1987), 150–51.

6. Ajami, *The Vanished Imam*, 24.

7. Ibid., 221.

8. Halawi, *A Lebanon Defied*, 20.

9. Ibid.

10. Ibid., 74–75.

11. Sandra Mackey, *Lebanon: A House Divided* (New York: W. W. Norton, 1989), 196.

12. Ajami, *The Vanished Imam*, 31.

13. Ibid., 85.

14. Roschanack Shaery-Eisenlohr, *Shi'ite Lebanon: Transnational Religion and the Making of National Identities* (New York: Columbia University Press, 2008), 26.

15. Ajami, *The Vanished Imam*, 123.

16. Fawwaz Traboulsi, *A History of Modern Lebanon* (London: Pluto Press, 2007), 179.

17. Ajami, *The Vanished Imam*, 48.

18. Ibid., 123.

19. Traboulsi, *A History of Modern Lebanon*, 178.

20. Ibid., 177.

21. Halawi, *A Lebanon Defied*, 136.
22. Norton, *Amal and the Shi`a*, 39.
23. H. E. Chehabi, ed., *Distant Relations: Iran and Lebanon in the Last 500 Years* (London: I. B. Tauris, 2006), 155.
24. Ajami, *The Vanished Imam*, 161.
25. Vali Nasr, *The Shia Revival: How Conflicts within Islam Will Shape the Future* (New York: W. W. Norton, 2006), 111.
26. Ajami, *The Vanished Imam*, 162.
27. Shaery-Eisenlohr, *Shi`ite Lebanon*, 99.
28. Chehabi, *Distant Relations*, 157.
29. Ibid., 168–69.
30. Martin Kramer, "How Syria's Ruling Sect Found Islamic Legitimacy," accessed June 2, 2012, http://www.geocities.com/martinkramerorg/Alawis.htm.
31. Halawi, *A Lebanon Defied*, 152.
32. Norton, *Amal and the Shi`a*, 46.
33. Ibid.
34. Shaery-Eisenlohr, *Shi`ite Lebanon*, 47.
35. V. Nasr, *The Shia Revival*, 86.
36. Ajami, *The Vanished Imam*, 168.
37. Norton, *Amal and the Shi`a*, 47.
38. "Israelis Kill Five in South: Victims Include Father, Two Sons," *Daily Star*, January 3, 1975.
39. "Lebanon Submits Complaint to U.N. over Israeli Raids," *Daily Star*, January 4, 1975.
40. Ajami, *The Vanished Imam*, 157.
41. "Sadr: Lebanon's Crisis Is Social Not Confessional," *Daily Star*, March 23, 1975.
42. Halawi, *A Lebanon Defied*, 191.
43. Ajami, *The Vanished Imam*, 161.
44. In *The Vanished Imam* (pp. 160–64), Fouad Ajami gives a compelling description of al-Sadr's predicament at beginning of the civil war. The Maronites, so supportive of him early in his career, felt themselves susceptible to the Pan-Islamism/Arabism of the Palestinians and were less supportive of al-Sadr's call for government reforms for the Shi`a. The Palestinians were always skeptical of al-Sadr's support for a Pan-Arab cause because of his Persian birth.
45. Ajami, *The Vanished Imam*, 134.
46. Norton, *Amal and the Shi`a*, 49.
47. "Khreish, al-Sadr Warn of Hidden Hands," *Daily Star*, April 18, 1975.
48. "Karami Sees Light at End of Tunnel," *Daily Star*, June 21, 1975.
49. Rodger Shanahan, *The Shi`a of Lebanon: Clans, Parties, and Clerics* (London: I. B. Tauris, 2005), 106.
50. Elizabeth Picard, *Lebanon: A Shattered Country* (New York: Holmes & Meier, 2002), 100.
51. Norton, *Amal and the Shi`a*, 38.
52. Ibid., 48.
53. Tabitha Petran, *The Struggle over Lebanon* (New York: Monthly Review Press, 1987), 264.
54. "Sadr Asserts Chiah Residents Won't Quit Devastated Areas," *Daily Star*, July 10, 1975.
55. Salim Nasr and Diane James, "Roots of the Shi`i Movement," *Middle East Research and Information Project*, no. 133 (June 1985), 15–16.
56. Ajami, *The Vanished Imam*, 165.
57. "Sadr's Condition Deteriorates," *Daily Star*, June 30, 1975.
58. Ajami, *The Vanished Imam*, 166–67.
59. Ibid., 168.
60. Ibid.
61. "Sadr Announces Formation of New Resistance Group," *Daily Star*, July 7, 1975.
62. Norton, *Amal and the Shi`a*, 48.
63. "Sadr Announces Formation of New Resistance Group," *Daily Star*, July 7, 1975.
64. Ajami, *The Vanished Imam*, 168.

65. Norton, *Amal and the Shi`a*, 65.
66. Ajami, *The Vanished Imam*, 171.
67. "Sadr Asserts Chiah Residents Won't Quit Devastated Areas," *Daily Star*, July 10, 1975.
68. Norton, *Amal and the Shi`a*, 48.
69. Ajami, *The Vanished Imam*, 132.
70. "Moslem Leaders Meet Issue Statement," trans. Foreign Broadcast Information Service (Lebanon), January 2, 1976.
71. "An-Nahar Report: May 16, 1976," trans. Foreign Broadcast Information Service (Lebanon), May 17, 1976.
72. Ibid.
73. Marius Deeb, *Syria's Terrorist War on Lebanon and the Peace Process* (New York: Palgrave Macmillan, 2003), 16–17.
74. Ibid., 17.
75. "Imam As-Sadr Appeals to Al-Asad for Cease-Fire—June 8, 1976," trans. Foreign Broadcast Information Service (Lebanon), June 9, 1976.
76. Ibid.
77. Memorandum of Conversation President Ford and Dr. Henry Kissinger, 30 March 1976, Oval Office National Security Adviser Memoranda of Conversation Collection, Gerald R. Ford Library.
78. Ajami, *The Vanished Imam*, 175.
79. "Imam's Headquarters Surrounded, Guards Disarmed," trans. Foreign Broadcast Information Service (Lebanon), June 18 1976.
80. Ibid.
81. "Radio Reports Shi`ite Council Premises Shelled," trans. Foreign Broadcast Information Service (Lebanon), June 29, 1976.
82. "Imam As-Sadr Makes Statement after Meeting Sarkis: April 9, 1977," trans. Foreign Broadcast Information Service (Lebanon), April 12, 1977.
83. "Talks on South Lebanon Urged," *New York Times*, July 1, 1977.
84. Zeina Maasri, *Off the Wall: Political Posters of the Lebanese Civil War* (London: I. B. Tauris, 2009), 42.
85. Marvine Howe, "Guerrillas Join Civilian Retreat from Attackers," *New York Times*, March 16, 1978.
86. Robert Fisk, *Pity the Nation: The Abduction of Lebanon* (New York: Thunder Mountain Press, 1990), 137.
87. "Shi'ite Leader on Lebanese–Palestinian Relations," *Amman Ad-Dustur,* trans. Foreign Broadcast Information Service (Lebanon), April 25, 1978.
88. Ajami, *The Vanished Imam*, 180.
89. "Shi'ite Council Issues Statement on Missing Leader," trans. Foreign Broadcast Information Service (Lebanon), September 12, 1978.
90. "Voice of Lebanon Reports Imam Detained in Libyan Prison: September 12, 1978," trans. Foreign Broadcast Information Service (Lebanon), September 13, 1978.
91. "Imam Rumored in Syria," trans. Foreign Broadcast Information Service (Lebanon), September 19, 1975.
92. "Shi`ite Council: Disregard Rumors," trans. Foreign Broadcast Information Service, (Lebanon), September 19, 1978.
93. "Mufti Meets with US Ambassador," trans. Foreign Broadcast Information Service, (Lebanon), September 19, 1978.
94. "Moslem Shi`ites Stage Religious Sit In," trans. Foreign Broadcast Information Service, (Lebanon), September 20, 1978.
95. "Shi`ites to Present Note on Imam to Rejectionist," *Voice of Lebanon (Clandestine)*, trans. Foreign Broadcast Information Service (Lebanon), September 22, 1978.
96. Ajami, *The Vanished Imam*, 185.
97. Maasri, *Off the Wall*, 65.
98. Shaery-Eisenlohr, *Shi`ite Lebanon*, 28.
99. Ibid., 89–90.
100. Robert J. Spitzer, *Media and Public Policy* (Westport, CT: Praeger, 1993), 190.

101. Edward Said, *Covering Islam: How the Media and the Experts Determine How We See the Rest of the World* (New York: Vintage Books, 1997), 54.
102. Raymond Stock, "Prestige Press at War: The *New York Times* and *Le Monde* in Lebanon, August 1–September 26, 1982," *Middle East Journal* 39, no. 3 (Summer 1985): 319.
103. Elizabeth Poole, *Reporting Islam: Media Representations of British Muslims* (London: I. B. Tauris, 2002), 55–56.
104. Ibid., 55.
105. Middle East Research and Information Project Reports, *Reading Guide*, no. 28 (May 1974), 22.
106. Ibid.
107. David Hirst, "Lebanese May Ask for Troops," *Guardian*, May 27, 1970.
108. David Hirst, "Arab Freedom That Hovers on the Brink of Violence," *Guardian*, April 18, 1974.
109. Ibid.
110. "Israeli Forces Raid 2 Lebanon Villages: 6 Houses Blown Up," *New York Times*, January 1, 1975.
111. "Israel Reports Attack on Guerrillas in House," *New York Times*, January 2, 1975.
112. The article "Israeli Forces Raid 2 Lebanon Villages; 6 Houses Blown Up" and the report by Howard K. Smith on the *ABC Nightly News* had no images associated with them.
113. *ABC Evening News*, January 2, 1975, Vanderbilt University news archive.
114. Eric Marsden, "Israeli Troops Raid Two Lebanese Villages," *Times* (London), January 2, 1975.
115. "Guerrillas Die in House Blown Up by Israelis," *Times* (London), January 3, 1975.
116. See the next section of this book, "Analyzing the Coverage of Violence and Representation of Musa al-Sadr" for analysis of the casualties from this Israeli attack.
117. "Lebanon Says 5 Are Killed in Border Raids by Israel," *New York Times*, January 3, 1975.
118. Juan de Onis, "Lebanese Live in Fear near the Israeli Border," *New York Times*, January 8, 1975.
119. The entire account is part of Juan de Onis's article, "Lebanese Live in Fear near the Israeli Border," *New York Times*, January 8, 1975.
120. Chehabi. *Distant Relations*, 194. The Vocational High School at Tyre was run by Mustafa Charman, one of Musa al-Sadr's closest confidants. As soon as students entered the school, they were taught fighting skills and how to handle weapons to defend themselves. The school had been subjected to attack by many entities wishing to disrupt the education of Shi`i children.
121. See earlier in this chapter, "Musa al-Sadr on the Eve of the Civil War 1975" and the *Lebanese Daily Star* report "Israelis Kill Five in South Victims Include Father, Two Sons."
122. In his article "Media Coverage of the Middle East: Perception and Foreign Policy" (*Annals of the American Academy of Political and Social Science* 482 [November 1985]), author Jack G. Shaheen quotes a report in the *Middle East International*: "Scores of Shiite Moslems have been killed during raids on villages in South Lebanon. Several times the Israeli Army has invaded a village and then later withdrawn claiming to have killed 20 or 30 terrorists. It is only when the bodies are inspected afterwards that so many 'terrorists' turn out to be young girls or old shepherds or families."
123. V. Nasr, *The Shia Revival*, 111.
124. "Lebanon Submits Complaint to U.N. over Israeli Raids," *Daily Star*, January 4, 1975.
125. S. Nasr and James, "Roots of the Shi`i Movement," 14.
126. Ibid.
127. "Two Israel Attacks on Lebanese Town," *Times* (London), January 13, 1975.
128. Paul Martin, "Syrians Greet King Faisal with Cry of Arab Unity," *Times* (London), January 15, 1975; Eric Marsden, "Israel Soldiers Wounded in Foray to Eliminate Terrorist Base in Lebanon Border Village," *Times* (London), January 16, 1975.
129. Juan de Onis, "1,500 Lebanese Abandon Israeli-Damaged Village," *New York Times*, January 22, 1975.

130. *The New York Times Index 1975* (New York: New York Times Company). The index is a book listing all stories and names of prominent individuals covered in *New York Times* articles during a specified year.

131. Juan de Onis, "1,500 Lebanese Abandon Israeli-Damaged Village," *New York Times*, January 22, 1975.

132. Ibid.

133. Ibid.

134. See earlier in this chapter, "The Rise of Musa al-Sadr in Lebanon."

135. "Politicians Bicker While South Suffers," *Daily Star*, February 3, 1975.

136. S. Nasr and James, "Roots of the Shi`i Movement," 14. Also see Ajami, *The Vanished Imam*, 186.

137. Juan de Onis, "22 Palestinians Killed in Beirut," *New York Times*, April 14, 1975.

138. Juan de Onis, "Guerrillas and the Lebanese Militia Reach a Cease-Fire Agreement," *New York Times*, April 17, 1975.

139. Ibid.

140. See earlier in this chapter, "The Rise of Musa al-Sadr in Lebanon."

141. Paul Martin, "Death Toll in Lebanon Fighting over 100," *Times* (London), April 15, 1975.

142. Ibid.

143. See earlier in this chapter, "Musa al-Sadr on the Eve of the Civil War."

144. Ibid.

145. Robin Wright, *Dreams and Shadows: The Future of the Middle East* (New York: Penguin Books, 2009), 163.

146. In a 2008 conference at the University of Michigan entitled "Shi`a Modernity and the Legacy of Musa al-Sadr," Lebanese Shi`a scholar Augustus Richard Norton likened Musa al-Sadr's leadership of the Shi`a in Lebanon to Martin Luther King's leadership of the civil rights movement in the United States. Last accessed June 14, 2011, http://www.arabamericanews.com/news/index.php?mod=article&catCommunity&article826.

147. Fouad Ajami, one the of the most prominent biographers of Musa al-Sadr, has numerous descriptions of al-Sadr in his book *The Vanished Imam*, yet none of them says that he was powerfully built. He was a tall man and well kept, but the term *powerfully built* is more characteristic of an Orientalist description of al-Sadr. Fouad Ajami also distinguishes al-Sadr from his Gandhi-like appeal during and immediately after his fast. On p. 168 of *The Vanished Imam*, Ajami states that al-Sadr was no Gandhi and that, for al-Sadr, violence was sometimes permissible to rectify injustice.

148. See Juan de Onis, "Lebanese Blast Fatal to 42, Discloses Leftist Links with Palestine Guerrillas," *New York Times*, July 7, 1975; and James Markham, "In Embattled Beirut, Nerves Are Taut and the Future Is Uncertain," *New York Times*, July 19, 1975.

149. Juan de Onis, "Lebanese Blast, Fatal to 42, Discloses Leftist Links with Palestine Guerrillas," *New York Times*, July 7, 1975.

150. David Hirst, "Beirut Fears of Civil War," *Guardian*, June 28, 1975.

151. Paul Martin, "New Lebanon Cabinet Brings Peace Hopes," *Times* (London), July 2, 1975.

152. Juan de Onis, "Lebanese Blast, Fatal to 42, Discloses Leftist Links with Palestine Guerrillas," *New York Times*, July 7, 1975.

153. Norton, *Amal and the Shi`a*, 48.

154. Juan de Onis, "Lebanese Blast, Fatal to 42, Discloses Leftist Links with Palestine Guerrillas," *New York Times*, July 7, 1975.

155. Ibid.

156. Itamar Rabinovich, *The War for Lebanon: 1970–1980* (Ithaca, NY: Cornell University Press, 1984), 91.

157. Norton, *Amal and the Shi`a*, 42.

158. Juan de Onis, "Lebanese Blast, Fatal to 42, Discloses Leftist Links with Palestine Guerrillas," *New York Times*, July 7, 1975.

159. Paul Martin, "PLO Embarrassed by Lebanese Disaster," *Times* (London), July 7, 1975.

160. Ibid.

161. "Sadr Announces Formation of New Resistance Group," *Daily Star*, July 7, 1975.
162. Paul Martin, "Nationwide Strike in Lebanon Averted," *Times* (London), September 15, 1975.
163. Paul Martin, "War Chaos Threatens Lebanon's Survival," *Times* (London), September 25, 1975.
164. Paul Martin, "Right-Wing Muslim Armies Challenge Leftist Tide in Lebanon," *Times* (London), December 14, 1975.
165. "Lebanon Falls Apart," *Times* (London), March 27, 1978; "Lebanon Leaders Meet As Syrians Press On," *Times* (London), June 2, 1976.
166. Robert Fisk, "Muslim Lord Holds Court in a Tripoli Castle," *Times* (London), November 22, 1976.
167. David Hirst, "Syria Prefers to Act by Stealth in Lebanese Struggle," *Guardian*, June 7, 1976.
168. See earlier in this chapter, "Musa al-Sadr on the Eve of the Civil War."
169. "Report of Israel Pact Ridiculous," *Guardian*, September 7, 1976.
170. Henry Tanner, "Lebanese Fight in Spite of Truce," *New York Times*, April 3, 1976.
171. See p. 52 of this book.
172. *New York Times* articles on May 17, 1976, September 3, 1976, September 16, 1976, and Mach 6, 1977, give brief mention of Musa al-Sadr as he attempted to facilitate peace and ceasefire efforts.
173. Chehabi, *Distant Relations*, 174.
174. See earlier in this chapter, "The Rise of Musa al-Sadr in Lebanon."
175. Thomas W. Lipman, "Moslem Dignitary Drops from Sight," *Washington Post*, September 18, 1978; "Demonstrating Moslems Seek Their Leader," *Los Angeles Times*, September 22, 1978.
176. "Clash Reported in Lebanon Involving Islamic Sect," *New York Times*, January 18, 1979.
177. "Lebanese Shiites Hijack Airliner," *Washington Post*, January 17, 1979.
178. "Missing Lebanese Cleric Called a Captive in Libya," *New York Times*, September 10, 1980.
179. Ibid.
180. Ajami, *The Vanished Imam*, 185.
181. Robert Fisk, "Mystery of Missing Shia Leader," *Times* (London), September 13, 1978.
182. Ibid.
183. Robert Fisk, "Muslim Area of Beirut Paralyzed by General Strike over Disappearance of Shia Leader," *Times* (London), September 16, 1978.
184. John Roberts, "Lebanon Begins Hunt for Shah Foe," *Guardian*, September 13, 1978.
185. Fisk, *Pity the Nation*, 93.
186. Lara Deeb, *An Enchanted Modern: Gender and Public Piety in Shi`i Lebanon* (Princeton, NJ: Princeton University Press, 2006), 55.

Chapter Two

The Shi`a Expulsion from Nab`a

Nab`a and the Shi`a Influence

Months after the start of the Lebanese Civil War, a skirmish began in an enclave east of Beirut that was to have far-reaching consequences for the Lebanese Shi`a. The battle of Nab`a made an indelible imprint on the minds of the Shi`a and helped to shape the community's notion of armed resistance to violence and injustice. This chapter will cover the origins of the battle of Nab`a and discuss the involvement of Sayyid[1] Muhammad Hussein Fadlallah, one of the key Shi`i advocates of the use of force in order to combat aggression and oppression.[2] Additionally, the chapter traces how the English-language press and media failed to convey an accurate representation of the horrors and the trauma that beset the Shi`i community during this battle. Failure of the English-language press and media to accurately cover this battle limited the opportunity for their consumers to comprehend the Shi`i narratives. It would be tantamount to ignoring, or misrepresenting, the Boston Massacre or the efforts of Thomas Jefferson in the narratives of the American Revolution. The battle of Nab`a was a critical event in the Lebanese Shi`i narrative.

No extensive archival sources or textual references to the battle of Nab`a exist. Occurring in the midst of the Lebanese Civil War, the battle was fought between militia groups who did not keep extensive documentation. In several published historical accounts of Lebanon, the battle is not given the prominence it deserves. Fawwaz Traboulsi and Helen Cobban, two prominent writers on modern Lebanon, make little mention of the tragedy in their books.[3] The fall of Nab`a merits a brief paragraph in each of their narratives on Lebanon. Augustus Richard Norton also mentions Nab`a and the tragedy that occurred there, but he devotes most of the space to discussing the controversial role of Musa al-Sadr in his attempt to end the fighting in the enclave. That controversy will be covered later in the chapter. An anecdotal reference to Nab`a appears in H. E. Chehabi's book *Distant Relations: Iran and Lebanon in the Last 500 Years* (2006); however, it focuses mainly on Musa al-Sadr and his role in attempting a peace settlement during the fighting. Jamal Sankari offers undoubtedly the most detailed coverage of the battle of Nab`a in his book *Fadlallah: The Making of a Radical Shi`ite Leader* (2005). This is certainly because Muhammad Hussein Fadlallah was such an important figure in the life of the enclave and his experience in the battle shaped a great deal of his politics and writing. In his book, Jamal Sankari makes a point of discussing the consequences of the enclave's fall and its impact on the Shi`a of Lebanon.[4] Even today, the expulsion of the Shi`a from this area east of Beirut resonates in their narrative of resistance to violence and oppression.

Before outlining Fadlallah's involvement in Nab`a or the origins of the battle, it is important to situate Nab`a geographically and politically within Lebanon. Nab`a constitutes part of a larger area in northeast Beirut named Bourj Hammoud. In 1975, Bourj Hammoud, Lebanon, was a mixed enclave of Orthodox Armenian Christians and Shi`a. Nab`a represented the southern quarter of this entity (see figure 2.1).

Nab`a was predominantly a poor district of young, semiskilled, and unskilled Shi`i workers. The Shi`a had come to the district in two waves: in the 1940s, in the wake of Palestinian–Israeli War, the Shi`a had moved up from South Lebanon to escape Palestinian refugees; and in the early 1970s a great many of the inhabitants of Nab`a came from South Lebanon, fleeing the ongoing violence between the Israelis and the Palestinians.[5] Many of the Shi`i residents of Nab`a worked at the docks of Beirut north of the area or did menial work around the city. Although there was a small emerging class of Shi`i entrepreneurs in the district, the majority of the population in the enclave remained poor and disaffected from the Lebanese government. The area of Bourj Hammoud, particularly the Nab`a district, constituted what was deemed the "belt of misery" which included the economically depressed areas that surrounded Beirut and extending from south of the city all the way through its northern suburbs. It was in this belt of misery, particularly in Nab`a, that the Shi`a began to develop communal and political consciousness as a group.[6] As they came into contact with the more affluent Lebanese in the Beirut area, a large, growing population of Shi`a yearned to have their problems of discrimination and poverty addressed. Leftist and communist groups attempted to exploit that dissatisfaction of young Shi`i men and recruit them into their militia groups. Despite that draw toward leftist groups, the relationship with the Christian Armenian population (adjacent to Nab`a in Bourj Hammoud) remained on relatively good terms.

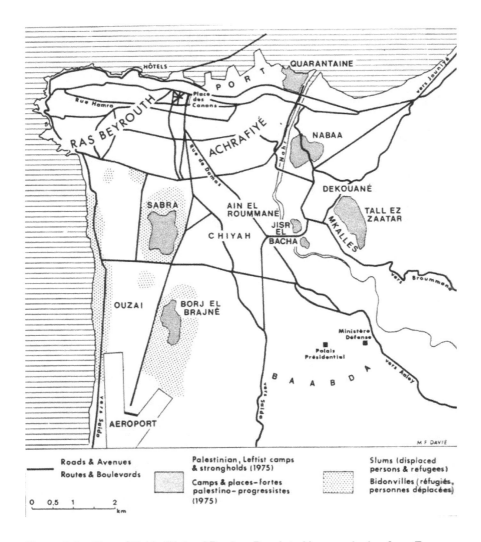

Figure 2.1. Map of Nab`a [Nabaa] Region. Reprinted by permission from Transaction Books, Joseph G. Chamai. *Days of Tragedy: Lebanon '75–'76* (London: Transaction Books, 1984), 398.

NAB`A AND SAYYID MUHAMMAD HUSSEIN FADLALLAH

Into this environment came one of the most important Shi`i scholars in a generation, Sayyid Muhammad Hussein Fadlallah (see figure 2.2).[7] Fadlallah was not an ordinary Shi`i cleric: He was one the most prominent and influential clerics teaching Islamic ideology in Lebanon and was revered by many in the Shi`i community for his scholarship and his piety.[8]

Like Musa al-Sadr, Fadlallah was born and reared outside of Lebanon. His upbringing in Najaf, Iraq, placed him in the heart of Shi`i scholarship. With only brief intellectual detours in poetry and journalism, Fadlallah followed the traditional path of the "ulama" through his religious studies in Najaf.[9] Although it is not in the scope of this book to examine his educational background extensively, Fadlallah's outstanding erudition and penchant for rhetorical studies put him at the heart of debates in the Shi`i community and marked him as an important Shi`i cleric. Fadlallah was renowned for his open-mindedness and his commitment to scrutiny and debate. He welcomed questions from any corner to clarify his positions on matters of religious beliefs and practices.[10]

In 1966, at the request of a Shi`i businessman from Nab`a, Fadlallah arrived in Lebanon to provide "services such as advanced religious education and juridical guidance on specific issues encountered by the local faithful."[11]

Figure 2.2. Sayyid Muhammad Hussein Fadlallah

Fadlallah's move from Iraq to Lebanon to perform religious duties reinforces again the transnational nature of the Shi`i networks throughout the Middle East. The Shi`i businessman from Lebanon who requested Fadlallah had traveled to Najaf to seek financial assistance in building a Shi`i religious center. Upon meeting Fadlallah, he was impressed enough to offer him a position to run the new Islamic center.[12]

During his time in Nab`a, Fadlallah obtained a sizable following. Although well acquainted with Musa al-Sadr, Fadlallah's strength lay in his theoretical and scholarly approach to the issues confronting the Shi`a of Lebanon. As founder of the Brotherhood Association in Nab`a, he built a grassroots network of schools and other social services to aid the Shi`i families in the town.[13] Fadlallah, a long-time resident of Nab`a, lived within the community when the fighting started. As one of the most influential Shi`a clerics in Lebanon, he used his position as collector of religious tithes and donations to help the most destitute during the siege of Nab`a.[14] He turned one of the Islamic centers he headed within Nab`a into a makeshift hospital and morgue to handle the growing casualties.[15] Despite his heroic efforts to care for those Shi`a who were suffering, Fadlallah is better known for his theory of Islamic resistance. Fadlallah produced his seminal work, *Islam and the Logic of Power* (1976), while enduring the horrendous siege in Nab`a. Although the book did not receive early acclaim, by the 1980s Hezbollah and similar groups viewed it as part of their foundational theory.[16]

THE ORIGINS OF THE TRAGEDY

The tragedy of Nab`a had its origins in a series of complex alliances forged by the Lebanese Shi`i community early in the civil war. Relationships in the Lebanese Civil War between antagonists were complicated, and simple labels proved inadequate to define the positions and equities held by the participants.[17] Calling people leftist or rightist, Muslim or Christian, revisionist or reactionary could never isolate the causes for which they fought. Even nation-states shifted their alliances in Lebanon to meet their own requirements. Such was the case for Syria, whose participation in the civil war had an adverse effect on the Shi`i community of Nab`a.

Early in 1976, Syria, a strong supporter of the PLO in its fight against Israel, faced a strategic problem that threatened its regime. The alliance of the Lebanese National Movement (LNM) and the PLO proved successful in battling Christian militias, and their success jeopardized the viability of the Lebanese government.[18] Syria was sure that Israel would not tolerate LNM/PLO de facto leadership of the Lebanese state.[19] For Syria, Israel's intervention into Lebanon would provide another avenue of approach to attack Damascus along the Beirut-Damascus Highway. Militarily, this would prove fatal to the Syrian regime in the event of another war between Syria and Israel. Additionally, the PLO was gaining supply and support from Iraq, Syria's not so friendly neighbor to the east. A PLO victory in Lebanon opened the possibility that hostile neighbors could surround Syria, which had attempted to subtly influence the outcome of the Lebanese Civil War by infiltrating small units of soldiers into Lebanon under the banner of the Syrian Palestinian Liberation Army (PLA). Although called "Palestinian," these forces were controlled by Syria.[20] However, as the coalition between the PLO and the Kamal Jumblatt's LNM began to dominate Christian militias, Syria saw an opportunity to use its military force to accomplish its strategic agenda of keeping Lebanon within its sphere of influence. The introduction of Syrian military forces in Lebanon in support of the Maronites would have dire consequences for the Shi`a living in Nab`a.

Regrettably, the people living in Nab`a had the misfortune of being situated between two very important areas to the Maronites: their traditional homeland of Mount Lebanon and their stronghold in East Beirut. The Maronites had inhabited the Mount Lebanon region of the country since the eleventh century.[21] The geographical position of Nab`a would also become problematic because of its proximity to the Palestinian stronghold of Tal al-Za`tar. Having dominated the Lebanese political and social structures since the birth of that nation, by 1975 the Maronites were in a deadly struggle with its Palestinian and Muslim rivals. Nab`a stood in the way of the Maronites' consolidation of their power center.

THE BATTLE FOR NAB`A

The initial battle for Nab`a actually commenced in December 1975, when Christian militiamen initiated their assault on the slum districts of Karantina and Maslakh, the districts adjacent to Nab`a.[22] This was part of a larger campaign by Christian militias to secure a contiguous area from which to defend itself from the PLO and the LNM. While the Palestinian stronghold of Tal al-Za`tar was the ultimate goal of the Phalangist campaign, non-Christian and Palestinian enclaves that surrounded the approaches to Tal al-Za`tar were fair game for their attacks. By the middle of January 1976, Christian forces had successfully eliminated most of the resistance from these towns. Nab`a, just north of the Palestinian stronghold of Tal al-Za`tar, was populated by over two hundred thousand Shi`a[23] and was viewed by Christian forces as the gateway for taking that more heavily fortified position.[24] However, Christian militias were also on the defensive in other parts of the Beirut area. In the city of Damur, a predominantly Christian city, Christian militias were soundly defeated and the town fell to a combined force of PLO and LNM militiamen. During this attack, the PLO and LMN forces committed a number of atrocities against townspeople.[25] These atrocities helped to fuel the ferocity of the attacks by Christian forces against Muslim and Palestinian targets in northeastern suburbs of Beirut. Yet it was the intervention of Syrian forces into Lebanon in the spring of 1976 that would dramatically change the situation and embolden Christian forces in their conquest of the area.

As discussed in chapter 1, Lebanese officials and Musa al-Sadr of the HISC were anxious for Syrian intervention as a means of quelling the fighting. They were taken aback by the level of violence and the new situation created by the intervening Syrian forces. Syrian troops attacked formations of the PLO and the LNM to preclude the destruction of Christian militias. The fighting between the PLO and the Syrian forces changed the dynamic within Lebanon. Christian militias, freed from their defensive posture of fighting major PLO and LNM units, initiated their own offensive action. At the end of July, the Christian militias began a vigorous attack on two towns in the northeast suburbs of Beirut, Tal al-Za`tar and Nab`a.[26]

When the siege of Nab`a intensified in July, the inhabitants demonstrated firm support for their Palestinian brethren (undergoing similar circumstances in the adjacent town of Tal al-Za`tar). From their association with Lebanese leftists, PLO fighters, and a small cadre of Islamists (who had coalesced around Sayyid Muhammad Hussein Fadlallah), the Shi`a in Nab`a had already been hardened in their resistance to Christian militia.[27] Musa al-Sadr sent one of his key deputies, Mostafa Chamran, to help organize the resistance in the enclave. Prior to his arrival, Amal maintained little presence within the town. As the siege continued and a sense of despair crept over the population, townspeople's support for the Palestinians and their cause waned. More Amal forces were rushed into the town, but, as al-Sadr's adviser Chamran recounted, they received no help from the Palestinians.[28]

According to historical accounts from Jamal Sankari and Elizabeth Picard, the fighting around Nab`a was brutal. Indiscriminate shelling of the enclave by Christian forces harmed civilians as well as fighters.[29] To make matters worse for the Shi`i residents, as fighting intensified in Nab`a, friction between Palestinian fighters and the Shi`a began to surface. The Palestinian leadership blamed Musa al-Sadr for involving the Syrians in the civil war. The Syrians had sided with the Christian militias and the town of Tal al-Za`tar was also taking a fierce pummeling from Christian guns. The Palestinians had fortified the town with bunkers and fighting positions, and Arafat was prepared to have the town's residents fight to the bitter end.[30] There were conflicting reports that, in an effort to relieve the pressure on Tal al-Za`tar, Palestinian fighters fired on the Christian militia from the neighboring town of Nab`a to cause the Christians to concentrate their major efforts in that area.[31] However, both the Palestinians and the Shi`a were in the crosshairs of the Christian militia. By the middle of July, both Tal al-Za`tar and Nab`a were taking a relentless pounding from the Christian militias.

On July 23, Shaykh Muhammad Mahdi Shams ad-Din, the deputy of the HISC of Lebanon, issued an appeal to the Lebanese people to avert a massacre in Nab`a. The shaykh skillfully contrasted the plight of Nab`a to that of Tal al-Za`tar. "Nab`a," he said, "had never been a camp but a residential area inhabited by thousands of Shi`a alongside their brother Christian Armenians."[32] It was not difficult to read between the lines of his statement. Shams wanted to make sure that the Christians understood Tal al-Za`tar was a Palestinian refugee camp and should be considered different from the religiously mixed Lebanese town of Nab`a. Despite the appeal of the shaykh, the Christian militias' siege of the two towns continued.

By the beginning of August 1976 it was apparent that the Shi`i and Palestinian fighters could not hold out against the Christian militias' siege of Nab`a and Tal al-Za`tar. Although Yasir Arafat was committed to holding out to the last man, al-Sadr contacted Bachir Gemayel, head of the Phalange, in an attempt to work out a clandestine agreement that would allow the Shi`i residents to peacefully evacuate Nab`a.[33] Part of this agreement would include the forceful eviction of the Palestinian minority. However, a delay in alerting the Shi`i fighters of the pending cease-fire prompted Gemayel to renege on his agreement. The forces of Gemayel battered the town with heavy artillery fire and eventually overran the defenses. In the end, tens of thousands of Shi`a were violently expelled from their neighborhood, and the district was subjected to two days of wanton looting and destruction.[34]

Considerable historical disagreement exists on the role of al-Sadr and his attempted negotiation with the Christian militia. Richard August Norton supports the notion that al-Sadr's dealings with the Christian militia facilitated the fall of Nab`a.[35] However, H. E. Chehabi discounts that report by sourcing the accounts of Mostafa Chamran, al-Sadr's key adviser in Nab`a. Chamran blamed the fall of Nab`a on the duplicitous dealing of the PLO.[36] The entire truth about this incident may never be known, but certainly Musa al-Sadr's prestige suffered as a result of his perceived collusion with the enemy.

The adverse impact that the fighting and exodus from Nab`a had on the Shi`a would be difficult to overstate. The massacre and tragedy of the Palestinians in Tal al-Za`tar should not be minimized, yet many Shi`i men were also massacred, and refugees from Nab`a were forced to inhabit squalid conditions in the teeming slums of West Beirut.[37] One of the most prominent Shi`i clerics of the next four decades, Sayyid Fadlallah, would never return to Nab`a. Even after the civil war, when he received a personal offer from the Maronite president Gemayel to return to the community, he declined.[38] He would not forget what had happened during the siege. Eventually, Fadlallah resettled in the southern suburb of Beirut and continued to write, focusing his studies on Shi`i jurisprudence and the principles of *ijtihād* (the process of arriving at an independent interpretation of Islamic law). His writings continued to shape a generation of Shi`i theology until his death in 2010.[39] Jamal

Sankari, author of *Fadlallah: The Making of a Radical Shi`ite Leader* (2005), insisted that Fadlallah, "as Islamist theoretician and activist," was a pragmatic radical who took up a more informal association with radical Shi`i organizations.[40] Although his expulsion from Nab`a helped to shape his intellectual development, Fadlallah was much more concerned with the political advancement of Islam within the Lebanese state. Years later, after an attempted assassination of Fadlallah by intelligence operatives sponsored by the American Central Intelligence Agency (CIA), Fadlallah distanced himself again from any formal relationship with the radical group Hezbullah.[41] However, his belief in Islam's legal authority to resist aggression was continually influenced by his experience in Nab`a and other attacks against Muslims in Lebanon.

As mentioned previously, Musa al-Sadr suffered the hardest fate of the Shi`i leadership after the fall of Nab`a. His attempt to negotiate with the Christians to secure the peaceful evacuation of the town was seen as naive and duplicitous.[42] Though he lost prestige and much of his standing within the Shi`i community, he continued attempts to resuscitate his leadership until his disappearance in 1978. Reports surfaced that, after the Nab`a incident, Musa al-Sadr devoted most of his time to organizing opposition to the shah of Iran within Lebanon.[43] While these reports could never be verified, Lebanon's role as an incubator for opposition to the shah cannot be denied and will be covered in the next chapter. Within the Shi`i rank and file, more radical voices were being heard.

After the trauma of Nab`a, different voices emerged from the Shi`i community. Beirut radio broadcast messages from a group calling itself the Shi`ite Revolutionary Organization. The group demanded that the Shi`i view be acknowledged and that all members of the Arab League and the entire Arab world know their position.[44] Additionally, the group stated that it was compelled to take up arms in opposition to the Palestinians, communists, and others who deviated from the core principles of the Palestinian revolution and those who would not support the integrity of Lebanese sovereignty.[45] In another statement broadcast on Beirut radio, the group proclaimed, "The armed Shi`ite Revolutionary Organization will only lay down arms after Lebanon regains its sovereignty and independence and its land is purged of every foreign saboteur."[46] This new group of Shi`a expressed a more activist notion of what they sought and how they should be represented. The voices of moderation and accommodation in the Lebanese Shi`i community became less prominent, and their narrative began to be shaped by the larger Shi`i discourse taking place in and around Iran.

In the end, the battle of Nab`a helped to solidify several things in the minds of the Lebanese Shi`a. First, within the Lebanese polity, the Shi`a had to be self-reliant. States such as Syria and the Palestinian people, who traditionally supported their community, would turn their backs on them when it was advantageous to do so. Second, the Shi`i clerical establishment, in the forms of Sayyid Fadlallah and Musa al-Sadr, offered the community the best source of succor. For most Shi`a it was clear that the *zuama* (old-time political clan leaders), could do nothing to stop their suffering. It was only the actions of the Shi`i "ulama" that provided any support. Finally, the Shi`a understood that they must be prepared to fight to stop their expulsion from their homes. Sayyid Fadlallah had given them the legal justification in his writing of *Islam and the Logic of Power*, and al-Sadr had provided a small cadre of militia fighters (Amal) to help stem the tide in the fighting around Nab`a. These themes of Shi`a self-dependency and resistance would continue to grow within the Lebanese Shi`i community.

NAB`A IN THE ENGLISH-LANGUAGE PRESS AND MEDIA

Another tragic occurrence as a result of the battle of Nab`a was the lack of coverage the Shi`a received in the English-language press and media. This was particularly true in the American prestige press and media. Although the siege of Tal al-Za`tar and the plight of the Palestinians received considerable coverage in the *New York Times,* the fall of Nab`a received relatively little attention from the paper. Missed in the *New York Times* coverage of Nab`a were the narrative and the personal stories of the Shi`a in that enclave.

The limited coverage of Nab`a in the *New York Times* began on January 20, 1976. In an article chronicling the fighting in Lebanon, the *New York Times* referred to Nab`a as "a shantytown and the origin of Moslem attacks on Christian positions."[47] In fact, Nab`a was one of the largest Shi`i neighborhoods in the Beirut area. The next day, the *New York Times* reported that Phalangists were "mopping up" the last pockets of resistance in the shantytown of Maslakh and that the Muslims feared they would push toward Nab`a.[48] Within that *New York Times* report there were indications that "mopping up" meant something horrific for the inhabitants of the towns. The testimony of a thirty-five-year-old woman in a *New York Times* news report stated that three of her brothers and four of her nephews were forced to curse the Prophet Mohammad and then were shot to death by Phalangist militiamen.[49] Yet the *New York Times* never focused on the fact that the Christian militiamen were religiously cleansing the area of Sunni and Shi`i Muslims. In that same report appeared a denial from a Phalangist spokesman that anything nefarious had happened in the towns they had taken over.[50] However, in the aftermath of the attack by the Christian forces, a number of civilians were massacred or expelled to West Beirut. The takeover of those districts, and the indiscriminate killing of civilians, helped to further radicalize the district of Nab`a to support the forces fighting against the Phalange.[51]

The phrase "ethnic cleansing" is extremely controversial. Although there is no precise definition of the term under international law, an independent United Nations Commission looked into violations of international humanitarian law and defined the phrase as, "the purposeful policy designed by one ethnic or religious group to remove by violent and terror-inspiring means the civilian population of another ethnic or religious group from certain geographic territory."[52] There is very little doubt that the forced displacement of Shi`a in the areas around Eastern Beirut fits the United Nations' definition of ethnic cleansing. In a 2016 dissertation, Nils Hagerdal chronicled ethnic cleansing in Lebanon during its civil war. Hagerdal specifically looked at the actions around Karantina and Nab`a and characterized the attack by Christian forces on those enclaves as ethnic cleansing.[53] Additionally, after returning from Lebanon, Jonathan Randal, Beirut news reporter for the *Washington Post*, documented his experiences and eyewitness account of the battles in Eastern Beirut. "Karantina was the first Lebanese massacre I witnessed," Randal said. "Christian militiamen with outsized wooden crosses around their necks, high on hashish or cocaine, and some wearing Nazi surplus helmets, killed to their hearts' content."[54] Randal later documented the battle of Maslakh, the town adjacent to Karantina with over thirty thousand residences of mostly poor Shi`a and a sprinkling of Kurds and Armenians. According to Randal, the town was purged of its inhabitants by the same forces that attacked and devastated Karantina. Later that year he recorded the even bigger catastrophe at Tal al-Za`tar.

For the British press, coverage of the fighting in and around Nab`a began in early January. On January 7, 1976, the *Times* (London) reported fighting between neighboring Christian and Muslim areas adjacent to the encircled 'Tel Zaatar' camp.[55] On January 9, 1975, the *Times* reported Christian forces advancing from two different directions and were at that point overlooking Muslim Nab`a.[56] The paper reported that the core of the latest crisis in the Lebanon Civil War was the Christian blockade of Tal al-Za`tar and Jisr al-Basha.[57] Any witness to the efforts of Christian militias to displace other Muslim populations during the civil war would be surprised that the article gave no hint of a looming disaster in the expulsion of thousands of Shi`a from their homes in Nab`a.[58] A *Times* article on January 20, 1976, described Phalangist forces "bulldozing the blazing ruins of the Karantina shantytown . . . in one of the most pitiless battles of the Lebanese civil war"; however, the article gave no indication that the Shi`i population of Nab`a was at risk.[59] The Karantina area was a mixture of Syrian Kurds, Palestinians, and Shi`a, but as Christian forces tightened the noose around their prize, Tal al-Za`tar, they made no effort to differentiate the Lebanese Shi`a in Nab`a from the Palestinians or any other Muslims. In April, the *Times* analysis of the situation in Lebanon mirrored what many Maronite Christians put forward as the Lebanese narrative: that "the Muslim Left wished to destroy the

Christian Right in Lebanon once and for all."[60] Of course, this was much too simplistic an analysis of the situation, and conflating all Muslims with the so-called Left did not take into account the different positions many of the Shi`a held. As the British press and media missed the important differences between the Shi`i and the rest of the Islamic community, the American press continued to cover Nab`a in a monolithic fashion.

On April 23, 1976, the *New York Times* reported the shelling of Nab`a by Christian forces. Again, the *New York Times* description of Nab`a as a "Moslem enclave" never indicated that the area was predominantly Shi`a.[61] Three days later, a *New York Times* report stated that over one hundred people had been killed in the shelling.[62] However, the article conveyed none of the hardship and the deprivation that the community experienced within the enclave. Shelling and fighting continued around the town from April until June 1976, when a total blockade was imposed on Nab`a by Christian forces.[63] Two months passed before Nab`a was mentioned again in the *New York Times*. The later report referenced the heavy shelling by Christian militia into the enclave, but once again there was no mention of it being a Shi`i community.[64]

In the middle of June 1976 the *New York Times* portrayed the chaos and violence surrounding Nab`a as anecdotal to the larger narrative of the Palestinian and Maronite Christian fight. *New York Times* reporter James Markham reported on protests surrounding Christian attacks on Nab`a and linked Palestinian and Lebanese leftists to the enclave.[65] Never once did he mention the area's predominantly Shi`i population. In another part of his article, Markham reports almost euphemistically about what was taking place.

> The Nabaa Moslem section and the Tell Zaatar camp are impoverished quarters that have long been regarded by Christians as a tormenting problem. It is widely believed that the Christians would like to remove the pockets to smooth out the boundaries of what has become in effect a portioned city and nation.[66]

Terms such as *ethnic cleansing* or *religious cleansing* were never used by Markham to describe what was happening to the Shi`a of Nab`a, although that is exactly what took place. Nab`a was ethnically cleansed by Christian militias because they believed the town offered support for the PLO and its allies.[67] Additionally, the Christian militias viewed the political organization within Nab`a as a threat because it fell outside of the local Christian-dominated political parties.

On June 29, Bernard Gwertzman, writing for the *New York Times*, penned "Officials in Washington Fear Wave of Killing If 2 Camps Are Taken." His reference was to Tal al-Za`tar and Jisr al-Basha and the Palestinians; he never mentioned the plight of the Shi`a in the area. In a July 3, 1976, report, the *New York Times* stated the "Lebanese Rightists Closing In on Palestinian

Camp."[68] The report continually referenced Tal al-Za'tar and the Palestinians. No mention was made of Nab'a and the Shi'a. An editorial on July 4, 1976, by James Markham entitled "Lebanon, a Country Destroying Itself" again makes no mention of the Shi'a or any of its leaders. Nowhere in the American prestige press did this monumental event receive the coverage it deserved.

By August 1976, the *New York Times* recorded some of the most intensive artillery bombing of the war inflicted against Nab'a by the Christian militia. Reporter Henry Tanner gives a brief mention of the Palestinian garrison in Nab'a but failed to acknowledge the Shi'a. On August 7, in a special to the *New York Times*, Nab'a is mentioned again but this time as a "Moslem slum area surrounded by Christian quarters in the eastern suburbs of Beirut."[69] Shi'i representation is missing from the entire series of articles.

Embedded in one article on the fighting was an Associated Press picture, the caption under which stated, "Moslem refugees flee from Christian sector of Beirut" (see figure 2.3). Nowhere does it indicate that the people fleeing their homes were being expelled by Christian forces. Many of the Shi'i families had lived in Nab'a for a generation. The Christian militia was making Nab'a a Christian enclave where none existed before. This was truly religious cleansing.

The *New York Times* and the prestige American press never fully captured the horror of this incident and the trauma inflicted on the Shi'a of Lebanon.

The situation was much the same for American televised news coverage of the siege of Tal al-Za'tar and Nab'a. From the end of June until the fall of these towns in August 1976, the CBS, NBC, and ABC nightly news broadcasts provided extensive coverage of the siege of Tal al-Za'tar.[70] However, Nab'a was mentioned only twice, while no mention was made of the Shi'a population within the town.[71] The brief reference to Nab'a made by reporter Jerry King was as a slum quarter that had given up their fight. However, in keeping with the tendency for American media to conflate the Shi'i narrative with those of other groups and movements in Lebanon, King linked the "Muslims" in Nab'a with the Palestinians in the Tal al-Za'tar region.[72]

If ever an opportunity existed for American media sources to highlight the trauma of the Lebanese Shi'a in Nab'a, it was in the television coverage of this event. The coverage of the siege's aftermath was disturbing. There were video accounts of men from the besieged towns surrendering and being treated harshly by their Christian militia captors. The NBC news broadcast of August 13, 1976, even mentioned possible massacres by Christian forces who had taken over the town, but nothing was said about the plight of the Shi'a.[73] Nowhere did the *New York Times* or the American television coverage mention the role of Musa al-Sadr or Sayyid Muhammad Hussein Fadlallah.

Lebanese Truce Hopes Dashed Again

By HENRY TANNER
Special to The New York Times

BEIRUT, Lebanon, Aug. 5—Hopes for an immediate cease-fire in Lebanon, which had sprung up overnight, were dashed today when Interior Minister Camille Chamoun, one of the main right-wing Christian leaders, accused Iraq of having sent troops into Beirut to fight on the side of the Palestinians.

A meeting of the Lebanese-Syrian-Palestinian cease-fire commission, which had been set for this afternoon, was abruptly canceled after Mr. Chamoun made his accusations. No new date was set.

Mr. Chamoun charged that two soldiers of the Iraqi People's Army were taken prisoner last night during fighting on the front of Ain Rummaneh, a Christian suburb southeast of Beirut. He said they had confessed that they were part of an Iraqi force sent to Egypt and from there to southern Lebanon by ship a few days ago.

Iraq and Egypt are involved in a bitter feud with Syria, which is playing the predominant role here.

The Iraqi People's Army is the militia of the ruling Iraqi Baath Party. The Syrian-Iraqi feud had its roots in the split of the Baath Party into Syrian and Iraqi wings. Mr. Chamoun's charges thus seemed calculated to disturb the political leadership in Damascus.

Moslem and Palestinian officials were quick to say that Mr. Chamoun had made his charges to gain time for Christian militias to press their attack on the beleaguered Palestinian camp of Tell Zaatar and to try to force the surrender of the Palestinian garrison in Nabaa, an isolated Moslem slum area in eastern Beirut.

All through the night, Tell Zaatar and Nabaa were subjected to one of the most intensive artillery bombardments of the war. Palestinian and leftist-Moslem forces in turn fired on Christian positions and some residential areas with mortars, field artillery and rockets.

On some of the other fronts, notably in the port area of Beirut and in the mountains east of the city, the fighting subsided this morning.

A cease-fire was signed yesterday at the military level by the commanders of the principal Christian militias in a meeting with Gen. Abdel Hassan Ghoneim, the commander of the Arab League peace keeping force here. Palestinian and Lebanese Moslem commanders also gave their agreement to the cease-fire.

The military agreement took on political dimensions late last night when Dr. Hassan Sabry el-Kholy, the special envoy of the Arab League, announced after talks with Syrian Government leaders in Damascus that he would convene the first meeting of the mixed cease-fire commission this afternoon in the mountain village of Sofar, on the Beirut-Damascus highway.

This is the meeting that has now been postponed.

The mixed commission was to consist of officers of the opposing Lebanese factions, Syria and the Palestine Liberation Organization. Its chairman is Dr. Kholy. It was set up under the agreement reached a week ago in Damascus by Syrian and Palestinian delegations.

Moslem refugees flee from a Christian sector of Beirut

Associated Press

Figure 2.3. Shi`a fleeing their homes in Nab`a. Reproduced by permission from the *New York Times*, August 6, 1976.

In the British press and media the culmination of the battle of Nab'a received even less coverage than it did in the American media. The *Times* (London) articles continued to focus on the siege of Tal al-Za'tar and Jisr al-Basha. On June 30, 1976, the paper reported that over three thousand shells had fallen on those enclaves during a three-hour period.[74] By the beginning of July, the *Times* reported that Jisr al-Basha had fallen to the Christian militias, and the paper predicted that the leftists and Palestinians would open a new front to relieve the pressure on Tal al-Za'tar and Nab'a.[75] Reports from the Palestinian news agency WAFA recounted atrocities committed by Christian forces in the aftermath of the conquest of Jisr al-Basha, but the *Times* stated that no neutral account existed of the battle or its aftermath to verify these reports.[76] Instead of trying to confirm or deny these reports, *Times* correspondents conjectured "that the allegations of atrocities could result in reprisals against Christians and Christian communities."[77] With Jisr al-Basha subdued, the Christian militia was free to focus most of its energy on Nab'a.

The battle of Nab'a culminated in August 1976. In its aftermath, other reports on Nab'a appeared in the British media. The noted British magazine weekly the *Economist* incorrectly stated that Musa al-Sadr handed over the district of Nab'a to the Maronites after token resistance.[78] As discussed earlier in this chapter, al-Sadr's role in the battle of Nab'a was controversial. Yet, the *Economist* article failed to mention that al-Sadr attempted to negotiate a peaceful evacuation of Shi'a from the enclave with Bachir Gemayel.[79] The Maronite militia overran the defenses of the enclave, and, as described earlier in this book, there were numerous accounts of massacres of unarmed people and looting in the area.[80] The *Guardian* reported, "Nab'a has been destroyed. After the shelling and the mortars came the looters in lorries and cars, stripping homes and shops until nothing remained."[81] The *Guardian* report also highlighted how plentiful the signs of the battles that raged around Nab'a were. Bullet holes and smoke-soiled buildings pervaded the area. Yet there was no mention in the *Guardian* article that Nab'a was predominantly Shi'a. The majority of the Shi'a who fled Nab'a relocated to shantytowns in Southwest Beirut. Already teeming with displaced Palestinian civilians and the Shi'a who had fled the fighting in South Lebanon, southwest Beirut became a hotbed of Shi'a resistance to the Lebanese government and to other foreign entities.

In conclusion, the fall of Nab'a embodies one of the great tragedies of a horrific civil war in Lebanon. It is widely believed that up to two hundred thousand Shi'i residents were expelled from Nab'a at the conclusion of the battles.[82] The displacement and killing of thousands would affect the mindset of the Shi'i for many years. In a 1985 interview with the French media, Nabih Berri, leader of Amal, referenced Nab'a when he told a reporter why his militia forces were battling Lebanese government troops in the predominantly Shi'i area of West Beirut: "I tried to warn the government against establishing such a presence. It was necessary to prevent a repetition of the tragedy that took place at Nabaa another poor Shiite neighborhood where the inhabitants were chased out by the Phalangist in 1976."[83] Additionally, in a February 1985 open letter from Hezbullah to the "Downtrodden in Lebanon and the World," Nab'a was mentioned again as part of the Shi'i narrative in Lebanon: "Nearly one half million Muslims have been displaced and their quarters of al-Nab'a, Burj Hammud, al-Dikwana, Tall al Za'tar . . . have been almost totally destroyed."[84] Nab'a resonates in the mind and the history of the Lebanese Shi'a.

The tragedy of Nab'a was then and still is today an enduring part of the Shi'i legacy. The *New York Times* and the American media failed to understand and interpret the importance of this critical event in the Shi'i narrative in Lebanon. By ignoring the Shi'i accounts of this tragedy and conflating their story with the Palestinian liberation movement, the American media missed an important opportunity to properly represent the Shi'a of Lebanon. The tenacity with which Lebanese Shi'a resisted and fought over future attempts to displace them from areas in Lebanon was a direct consequence of the battle of Nab'a. The British press and media missed some of the same opportunities to understand the foundational arguments of Shi'a resistance theory by not closely covering this event or examining the experiences of Sayyid Fadlallah during the siege of Nab'a. As discussed previously, Sayyid Fadlallah completed his seminal work in Shi'i theology entitled *Islam and the Logic of Power* (1976) during the siege. It was Fadlallah's experience under siege that honed his intellectual approach to Islam and the use of power and force. Repeatedly, Western news reports would present derogatory information about the radical Shi'i cleric Fadlallah. Years after the siege on Nab'a, the *New York Times* linked him to Hezbollah and the bombing of the Marine Corps barracks in Beirut in 1983, an accusation that Fadlallah consistently denied.[85] Never in its reporting on Fadlallah did the *New York Times* reference his time in Nab'a and his efforts to help the residents.

The Lebanese Shi'a developed a keen sense of the importance of armed resistance to violence and injustice. This notion of resistance and self-empowerment would be further strengthened based on the Lebanese experience with the Iranian Revolution. Those connections and the importance of the transnational networks in Shi'i Islam will be examined in chapter 3.

NOTES

1. In Shi'i Islam, this is the designation of descendants of the Prophet Muhammad. See Moojan Momen, *An Introduction to Shi'i Islam: The History and Doctrines of Twelver Shi'ism* (New Haven, CT: Yale University Press, 1985), xxii.

2. Jamal Sankari, *Fadlallah: The Making of a Radical Shi'ite Leader* (London: SAQI, 2005), 157.

3. See Helena Cobban, *The Making of Modern Lebanon* (Boulder, CO: Westview Press, 1985), 141; and Fawwaz Traboulsi, *A History of Modern Lebanon* (London: Pluto Press, 2007), 201.

4. Sankari, *Fadlallah*, 158–62.

5. Sankari, *Fadlallah*, 129.

6. Amal Saad-Ghorayeb, *Hizbu`llah: Politics and Religion* (New York: Pluto Press, 2002), 7.

7. Sankari, *Fadlallah*, 10.

8. Ibid., 132.

9. Ibid., 47–49.

10. Ibid., 136.

11. Ibid., 131.

12. Ibid.

13. Naim Qassem, *Hizbullah: The Story from Within* (London: SAQI, 2005), 16.

14. Sankari, *Fadlallah*, 156.

15. Ibid.

16. Ibid., 200–201.

17. Itamar Rabinovich, *The War for Lebanon: 1970–1985* (Ithaca, NY: Cornell University Press, 1984), 44.

18. Marius Deeb, *Syria's Terrorist War on Lebanon and the Peace Process* (New York: Macmillan, 2003), 16.

19. Rabinovich, *The War for Lebanon*, 48.

20. Elizabeth Picard, *Lebanon: Shattered Country* (New York: Homes & Meir, 2002), 108.

21. Kamal Salibi, *A House of Many Mansions: The History of Lebanon Reconsidered* (Berkeley: University of California Press, 1988), 13.

22. Sankari, *Fadlallah*, 154.

23. Traboulsi, *A History of Modern Lebanon*, 201. The number of two hundred thousand is controversial among historians. Sankari's book *Fadlallah: The Making of a Radical Shi`ite Leader* places the number of Shi`i in Nab`a between sixty thousand and one hundred thousand. Amal Saad-Ghorayeb, in his book *Hizbu`llah Politics and Religion*, estimates that over one hundred thousand Shi`i were eventually expelled from Nab`a. Due to the lack of official statistics on the Shi`i population and the density of population in the urban area of Nab`a, Traboulsi's estimation is as accurate as one can expect.

24. Sankari, *Fadlallah*, 155.

25. Traboulsi, *A History of Modern Lebanon*, 193.

26. Ibid., 199.

27. Sankari, *Fadlallah*, 155.

28. For a detailed discussion of Mostafa Chamran's estimation of the role of the Palestinians in the defense of Nab`a, see H. E. Chehabi, *Distant Relations: Iran and Lebanon in the Last 500 Years* (London: I. B. Tauris, 2006), 194, and Sankari, *Fadlallah*, 156.

29. Picard, *Lebanon*, 110; Sankari, *Fadlallah*, 156.

30. Robert Fisk, *Pity the Nation: The Abduction of Lebanon* (New York: Thunder Mountain Press, 1987), 86.

31. Chehabi, *Distant Relations*, 194.

32. "Shi`ite Leader Urges Halting Conflict in An-Nab`ah," trans. Foreign Broadcast Information Service (Lebanon), July 29, 1976.

33. Chehabi, *Distant Relations*, 195.

34. Sankari, *Fadlallah*, 159.

35. Augustus Richard Norton, *Amal and the Shi`a: Struggle for the Soul of Lebanon* (Austin: University of Texas Press, 1987), 197.

36. Chehabi, *Distant Relations*, 194–95.

37. Chehabi, *Distant Relations*, 194.

38. Sankari, *Fadlallah*, 159.

39. Ibid., 15.

40. Ibid., 190.

41. Rodger Shanahan, *The Shi`a of Lebanon: Clans, Parties, and Cleries* (New York: I. B. Tauris, 2005), 155; "C.I.A. Linked to Beirut Bomb," *New York Times*, May 12, 1985.
42. Shanahan, *The Shi`a of Lebanon*, 160.
43. Norton, *Amal and the Shi`a*, 48.
44. "Shi`ite Revolutionary Organization Issues Statement," trans. Foreign Broadcast Information Service (Lebanon), August 2, 1976.
45. Ibid.
46. Ibid.
47. James M. Markham, "Beirut Ex-Premier Balks at Return without Truce," *New York Times*, January 20, 1976.
48. "Strife in Lebanon Worsens as Town Falls to Moslems," *New York Times*, January 21, 1975.
49. Ibid.
50. Ibid.
51. Sankari, *Fadlallah*, 154.
52. "Ethnic Cleansing" definition, www.un.org/en/genocideprevention/ethnic-cleansing.html, accessed May 22, 2018.
53. Nils Hagerdal, "Ethnic Cleansing as Military Strategy: Lessons from Lebanon, 1975–1990" (Doctoral dissertation, Harvard University, Graduate School of Arts & Sciences), 2, 91, http://nrs.harvard.edu/urn-3:HUL.InstRepos:33493501, accessed August 4, 2017.
54. Jonathan Randal, *Going all the Way: Christian Warlords, Israeli Adventurers, and the War in Lebanon* (New York: Vintage Books, 1984), 12.
55. "Lebanon Truce Crumbling," *Times* (London), January 7, 1976.
56. "Israel Warns Syria to Keep Out of Lebanon," *Times* (London), January 9, 1976.
57. Paul Martin, "Fears of Army Coup in Lebanon as Christians and Muslims Blockade Each Other's Communities," *Times* (London), January 14, 1976.
58. Traboulsi, *A History of Modern Lebanon*, 192–93.
59. "Lebanon Alleges Invasion of 15,000 Syrians," *Times* (London), January 20, 1976.
60. "Massacre That Sparked Off War in the Lebanon," *Times* (London), April 13, 1976.
61. "Franjieh's Foes Threaten to Set Up Rival Regimes," *New York Times*, April 23, 1976.
62. James M. Markham, "Drive to Replace Franjieh Is Stepped Up," *New York Times*, April 26, 1975.
63. Sankari, *Fadlallah*, 155.
64. "US Bids Citizens Leave Lebanon; Convoy Departs," *New York Times*, June 19, 1976.
65. James M. Markham, "Gun Duels Resume in Beirut as Syria Begins a Pullback," *New York Times*, June 23, 1976.
66. Ibid.
67. Hagerdal, "Ethnic Cleansing as Military Strategy: Lessons from Lebanon, 1975–1990," 95–96.
68. "Lebanon Rightists Closing In on Palestinian Camp," *New York Times*, July 3, 1976.
69. "Sniping at Wounded Halts Evacuation at Beirut Camp," special to the *New York Times*, August 7, 1976.
70. Starting on June 29, 1976, there were televised reports of the fighting and the siege around Tal al-Za`tar on the CBS, NBC, and ABC nightly news reports. Vanderbilt University Television News Archive.
71. A review of the Television News Archive at Vanderbilt University revealed only two mentions of Nab`a during the period.
72. *ABC Evening News*, July 26, 1976, correspondent Jerry King, Vanderbilt University Television News Archive.
73. *NBC Nightly News*, August 13, 1976, John Chancellor Vanderbilt University Television News Archive.
74. "Threat of Total War in Lebanon If Palestinian Refugee Camp Falls," *Times* (London), June 30, 1976.
75. "Refugees and Gunmen Flee As Christians Seize Lebanon Camp," *Times* (London), July 1, 1976.

76. "Arab League Truce Mission Leaves for Lebanon Where Fighting Rages beyond Cease-fire Deadline," *Times* (London), July 2, 1976.
77. Ibid.
78. "The Unpopular Ones," *Economist*, August 21, 1976.
79. Sankari, *Fadlallah*, 159.
80. See earlier in this chapter, "The Batttle for Nab`a."
81. Peter Nesewand, "The Dumping of the Dead—a Beirut Peepshow," *Guardian*, August 10, 1976.
82. Traboulsi, *A History of Modern Lebanon*, 201.
83. "Memo for Gemayel," *Guardian*, February 21, 1984.
84. Norton, *Amal and the Shi`a*, 171.
85. "Beirut Bombing Trigger Threats against U.S.," *New York Times*, March 10, 1985; Sankari, *Fadlallah*, 208.

Chapter Three

The Effects of the Iranian Revolution on the Lebanese Shi`a

No event outside of their country more keenly affected the Lebanese Shi`a than the Iranian Revolution of 1978 and 1979.¹ During that period, the shah of Iran, touted by many Westerners as the most progressive and enlightened leader in the Middle East, lost control of his government to an enigmatic Shi`i leader, Ayatollah Khomeini.² The Shi`a-inspired revolution in Iran sent shock waves around the world and had a profound influence on the narratives of the Shi`a of Lebanon. It motivated the Lebanese Shi`a to continue their civil rights drive and reinforced their commitment to armed resistance against violence and injustice. The Iranian Revolution also exposed the transnational nature of Shi`i networks in education, finance, and support between Lebanon, Iran, and other centers of Shi`i power. The coverage of the revolution in the English-language press and media failed to capture or convey the importance of these transnational networks. Concurrently, the negative press coverage of the Shi`a-inspired revolution in Iran had a harmful effect on the representation of Lebanese Shi`a.

In outlining the importance of the Iranian Revolution to the Shi`i narratives in Lebanon, this chapter will also expose the inadequacy and the Orientalist nature of the English-language media coverage of the Iranian Revolution. The *New York Times*, the *Times* (London), and to a lesser extent the *Guardian* missed important opportunities to adequately represent the revolution and connect its impact to the story of the Shi`a in Lebanon. As historians cull from the volumes of material available to journalists from this era, it is clear that adequate material existed to make the connections between the Iranian Revolution and its influence on Lebanese Shi`a.

The two most important scholarly works for understanding the linkage between the Lebanese Shi`a and the Iranian Revolution are *Distant Rela-*

tions: Iran and Lebanon in the Last 500 Years (2006), by H. E. Chehabi, and *The Iranian Revolution: Its Global Impact* (1990), edited by John Esposito. As covered in the introduction of this book, the relationship between the Lebanese and the Iranian Shi`a span several hundred years, but, as Chehabi states in his book,

> Events of the last two decades seem to have compelled the media to reduce the Iranian-Lebanese connection to the support afforded by some centers of power within the Islamic Republic of Iran to the Lebanese militant group Hizballah, notably in its confrontation with Israel.[3]

Although Chehabi expends considerable effort tracing the early connections between the Lebanese Shi`a and Iran, his chapter "Iran and Lebanon in the Revolutionary Decade" provides a comprehensive account of the linkage between the two Shi`i communities during the revolution.[4] Upon reviewing this chapter, it is easy to discern important connections between Lebanon and Iran that were missed by the media during the critical periods surrounding the Iranian Revolution.

In *The Iranian Revolution: Its Global Impact* (1990), John Esposito exposes the impact of a larger discourse on the nature of Islamic Revolution throughout the globe caused specifically by the Iranian Revolution. The Lebanese Shi`a were a part of that discourse, but according to Esposito the discourse was often contentious: "On the one hand, the downfall of the Shah proved that an illegitimate government did not have to be lithely suffered . . . on the other hand, it was widely recognized that Iranian solutions would not necessarily solve Lebanese problems."[5] Throughout, this chapter will outline the continuities and the discontinuities between the Lebanese Shi`i movement and the Iranian Revolution. Although the extent of influence between Iranian Shi`a and the Lebanese may never be resolved historically, what is not in doubt are the enduring connections between the Lebanese and Iranian Shi`i communities.

MODERN IRAN AND THE EARLY CONNECTIONS TO LEBANON

The political connection between the modern state of Iran and Lebanon began in the 1950s, when Iran formally established diplomatic relations. Iran, the most populous Shi`i state in the world, coveted its relationship with Lebanon. The ruler of Iran, Shah Reza Pahlavi, had a great affinity for the Maronite political establishment in Lebanon. He considered the Lebanese regime a bulwark against Arab nationalism and a window into the Western world.[6] This meshed with the shah's own beliefs, which would entail moving Iran away from its historical and cultural ties to the Middle East and adopting a new, more Western approach to its society.[7] From the 1950s through the start of the Lebanese Civil War, the shah of Iran maintained a relatively good relationship with the Lebanese government and supported the Shi`i community within Lebanon.[8] However, within Iran, the shah established policies much less supportive of the Shi`i religious community.

The shah's initial political problems in Iran stemmed from his attempt to extend government control of the religious domain of the Shi`i clergy ("ulama").[9] New Iranian government reforms limited the revenues of Shi`i institutions and lessened the status of the "ulama" throughout the country. As the shah initiated his policy of economic reforms in Iran, he also alienated the merchant class, fomenting more opposition to his regime.[10]

Early in the 1960s, Ayatollah Ruhollah Khomeini (a revered Islamic scholar in Qom, Iran) emerged as a key antigovernment activist in opposition to the shah's Western-style reforms. Khomeini considered the White Revolution, as the shah's reforms were labeled, a direct assault on the "ulama." He denounced the shah's policies and the Iranian government's support for the United States and Israel.[11] The shah reacted harshly to Khomeini, arresting him and ultimately deporting him to Turkey. Khomeini eventually made his way to Najaf, Iraq, one of the traditional centers for Shi`i learning and scholarship established hundreds of years before.

Najaf was, and continues to be, an incubator for Shi`i thought. It is the burial site of the first, and most prominent, of the Shi`i imams.[12] Many of the religion's most talented jurists received training in Najaf. Between 1954 and 1957, Musa al-Sadr spent time there under the tutelage of an Islamic scholar.[13] He honed his skill in Islamic law and *ijtihād*.[14] Muhammad Mahdi Shams al-Din, the vice president of the HISC in Lebanon, also trained there along with Sayyid Muhammad Hussein Fadlallah, who later braved the siege of Nab`a.[15]

Qom, Iran, another important center of Shi`i learning and the city from which Ayatollah Khomeini was deported, also had a strong connection to the Lebanese "ulama." Having established themselves in Lebanon, two of the most prominent Shi`i clerics in the country had enduring ties to the city of Qom. Sayyid Hussein Fadlallah had sent a number of his most prominent scholars from his religious school in Lebanon to study at the religious centers in Qom.[16] These students would return to Lebanon and teach in Fadlallah's school, reinforcing the religious and educational bonds between the two communities. Musa al-Sadr was born in Qom and maintained ties to the religious institutions within the city. These factors again reinforced the transnational nature of the Shi`a educational networks and the enduring kinship and support mechanisms within the community. Yet it was the teachings of Khomeini that would have the most impact on the Shi`i community during this time.

Throughout his time in Najaf, Ayatollah Khomeini exerted a powerful influence on a number of Shi`i clergy and scholars. While many of the

Islamic scholars sought alternatives to Western-style governance, Khomeini formulated his doctrine on Islamic government, calling it *vilāyat-i faqīh* ("government of the jurist"). His theory postulated that Islamic clerics should oversee the running of government to ensure that the state practiced Islamic principles. This theory placed great power in the hands of Islamic jurists.[17] This philosophy would have a profound effect on the antishah movement and later on the formation of Hezbollah in Lebanon. Political upheaval in Iraq facilitated the dissemination of these theories.

In 1968, a coup in Iraq installed the secular Baathist party as head of the government. This regime, dominated by Sunni Muslims, exhibited extreme hostility to the majority Shi`i population of Iraq.[18] During his exile to Iraq, Khomeini encouraged Shi`i dissidents of the Iraqi regime and induced Shi`a men and women to shun their affiliation with communist revolutionary movements. His close affiliation with prominent Iraqi cleric Ayatollah Muhammad Baqr al-Sadr helped frame the intellectual foundation of the al-Da`wa party, a religious, anticommunist, and anti-Western Shi`i movement.[19] The Iraqi government initiated a concerted crackdown on Shi`i activists, especially members of the al-Da`wa party. These actions of the Iraqi government caused many Shi`i clerics to flee to Lebanon, where they continued to support Khomeini's ideology and work in opposition to the shah.[20] Eventually (probably at the behest of the Iranian government) Iraqi authorities deported Khomeini. He fled to Paris, where he continued to work against the government of the shah of Iran.[21] Despite government efforts to isolate and minimize the influence of Ayatollah Khomeini, his writings and his doctrine gained ground within the Shi`i communities, and his opposition to the shah continued to grow.

LEBANON AND THE IRANIAN RESISTANCE

Although beset by opposition on many fronts, by 1975 a great deal of the resistance to the shah of Iran's regime came from Lebanon, as it developed into a key location for recruiting and training Iranian antishah dissidents and insurgents.[22] Additionally, many of the prominent intelligentsia working against the shah's government found fertile ground in the Shi`i areas in Lebanon. According to the shah's intelligence service, the Liberation Movement of Iran (LMI) and the People's Mujahedeen of Iran were two of the most active resistance groups in Lebanon, where they received key military training.[23] In fact, Roschanack Shaery-Eisenlohr called the relationship between the LMI and Musa al-Sadr's Amal movement the most important transnational network between Iranian and Lebanese Shi`a in the 1970s.[24] This alliance was certainly problematic for the shah's regime. Nevertheless, he continued to find ways to combat his opposition.

From the early 1970s until the Islamic Revolution unfolded in the streets of Iran in 1978–1979, a low-level guerrilla war waged between the shah and his opponents. The shah used his secret police (*Sazeman-i Ettela' at Va Amniyat Kishvar* or SAVAK) to fight a counterinsurgency against his opposition groups.[25] The level of violence remained relatively low, yet the scope of the battle became global as SAVAK agents attempted to assassinate or marginalize members of these groups. The early stages of this war resulted in the deaths of 341 guerrillas; 42 died by torture at the hands of SAVAK.[26] The murder of Ayatollah Khomeini's son, Mustafa, in Iraq in October 1977 is widely assumed to have been the work of SAVAK.[27] Within Lebanon, SAVAK took a more nuanced approach. Its agents attempted to manipulate the Lebanese government toward Iranian policies and maintained a high degree of surveillance on Iranian dissidents throughout Lebanon.[28] Despite that surveillance, opposition to the shah's regime flourished in Lebanon.

The most prominent of the intelligentsia working in opposition to the shah in Lebanon was Mostafa Chamran.[29] An Iranian-born, American-educated intellectual, Chamran had been exiled from Iran for his opposition to the shah. Having spent time in America, and later Egypt, instigating and training resistance cadres against the shah, early in the 1970s Chamran found himself in Lebanon.[30] His activism on behalf of Shi`a endeared him to Musa al-Sadr, and he quickly rose to become a key leader in the Lebanese Shi`i movement. In 1974, as the head of Burj al-Shimali Technical School (founded by al-Sadr in Tyre), Chamran trained hundreds of Iranian resistance fighters opposed to the shah's regime and developed himself as a skilled military leader and tactician.[31] This was the same Mostafa Chamran that Musa al-Sadr commissioned to travel to Nab`a to organize the enclave's defense. Mostafa Chamran's work with Iranian dissidents drew the notice of Iranian diplomats in Lebanon who petitioned the Lebanese government to curtail his activities.[32] However, the Lebanese government proved too weak to take any action. Despite SAVAK's attention on the activities of Chamran, they were never able to eliminate him, and eventually he would play a key role in the revolutionary government of Iran. SAVAK and the Iranian diplomats' corps in Lebanon were unable to cope with other problems from the Shi`i leadership in Lebanon. Among these problems was Musa al-Sadr, the Iranian immigrant to Lebanon who now considered the Lebanese Shi`a his most important concern.

Musa al-Sadr had an ambiguous relationship with the shah of Iran. As the most important Shi`i leader in Lebanon he often appealed to the shah for financial support for his "Movement of the Deprived." The shah, as ruler of the most populous Shi`i nation, often acceded to the financial support requested by al-Sadr.[33] However, as time passed and opposition to the shah grew in Lebanon, al-Sadr was pressed hard by the shah to give something back in return for his financial support. In 1972, the Iranian ambassador to

Lebanon approached al-Sadr and requested that he provide information on Iranian dissidents in Lebanon.[34] Al-Sadr refused the request, not wanting to be associated with the shah's repressive policies or his notorious intelligence agency SAVAK. By 1974, al-Sadr was openly criticizing the shah's policies in Iran and his support for Israel. Eventually, the Iranian government's anger and disapproval of al-Sadr's actions caused them to withdraw his Iranian passport and strip him of his Iranian citizenship.[35] Although al-Sadr's major focus remained the plight of Shi`a in Lebanon, he continued to side with the Iranian resistance fighters and the most prominent antishah cleric at the time, Ayatollah Khomeini. Prior to his disappearance in 1978, it was reported that al-Sadr spent most of his time working with groups opposing the shah.[36]

Throughout the 1970s Lebanon continued to be a key outpost for funneling information and material to the Shi`i opposition in Iran. Ayatollah Khomeini's famous book *Islamic Government,* in which he articulated the concept of the guardianship of the jurist, or *vilāyat-i faqīh*, was first printed in Beirut, Lebanon, by his supporters.[37] This book and other tapes and messages from Khomeini were later smuggled into Iran and helped inspire and incite the Islamic opposition to the shah. The mujahidin (Islamic fighters) opposed to the shah also used Lebanon as a place to buy weapons and transship them to Iran.[38] All of this occurred in Lebanon in a less than clandestine atmosphere. There was no doubt that the cross-fertilization between Lebanese and Iranian revolutionaries was a significant factor in the successful return of Ayatollah Khomeini to Iran in February 1979.

In *Vanguard of the Imam: Religion, Politics and Iran's Revolutionary Guards*, Naval Postgraduate School professor Afshon Ostovar chronicles the long relationship between Iranian activists and the Lebanese Shi'a. Notably Ostovar discusses the prominent Iranian cleric, Ali Akbar Motashami, who had traveled several times to Lebanon beginning in the 1970s to establish strong relations with Lebanese clerics in the Bekaa valley.[39] These ties, established by Mostashami, facilitated networks that enabled antishah activists to travel to Lebanon and receive guerrilla warfare training in Palestinian camps.

The triumph of the Iranian Revolution and the Ayatollah Khomeini's subsequent return to Tehran provided the Shi`a of Lebanon another example of the power of activism. In a March 1980 sermon, Khomeini praised the Iranian people for freeing themselves from the oppressive power of the "world-devouring America."[40] During that same speech, he gave voice to his support for "beloved Palestine and beloved Lebanon," linking his message of liberation from domination for all downtrodden people to both the East (Soviet Union) and the West (the United States).[41] Khomeini articulated a form of governance new to the West—an Islamic model in which the Iranian Shi`i clergy would act as the guardians and protectors of the country.

The Shi`i revolution in Iran inspired and empowered the Shi`a in Lebanon and throughout the rest of the Middle East. In Lebanon, posters appeared in Shi`i neighborhoods with Khomeini's picture and that of the missing imam, Musa al-Sadr (see figure 3.1). The poster cited contained the flag of the Islamic Republic of Iran flying next to the flag of Amal, the group founded by al-Sadr. In the middle of the poster is the Azadi tower monument in Tehran, which symbolizes freedom.

Considerable intellectual discourse continues to debate how much the Iranian Revolution guided or subsumed the Shi`i movement in Lebanon. Roschanack Shaery-Eisenlohr minimizes the direction the revolution gave to the Lebanese Shi`a. In Shaery-Eisenlohr's view, the discourse and the interaction between the more strident views of Khomeini's supporters and those Shi`a in Lebanon following the line of Musa al-Sadr helped to sharpen Lebanese Shi`a identity.[42] Despite the calls by newly formed Shi`i revolutionary organizations to support a Khomeini style of government, a majority of Shi`i activists in Lebanon did not initially accept his model of Islamic governance. Nabih Berri, a lawyer by trade and a Shi`i activist, had assumed the mantle of Amal leadership after Musa al-Sadr's disappearance. He articulated the predominant attitude of the Shi`a, saying, "We support the Islamic revolution in

Figure 3.1. Poster with pictures of the Ayatollah Khomeini and Musa al-Sadr. Reproduced by permission of American University of Beirut Libraries, Archives and Special Collections.

Iran but . . . we do not want an Islamic revolution in Lebanon."[43] He embraced Musa al-Sadr's call toward activism, but within the construct of the Lebanese constitution and the national pact. Even Muhammad Hussein Fadlallah, the leading Shi`i Cleric in Lebanon and a staunch supporter of Khomeini's revolution in Iran, understood the difficulty of transporting that revolution in total to Lebanon. Fadlallah said, "Lebanon cannot be transformed into an Islamic republic, but the Islamists should give free reign to their ideas in Lebanon. . . . Lebanon could be a pulpit from which to spread the word of God, just as it has always been a theatre for political action."[44]

Other scholars place more emphasis on the fact that Lebanon was the only nation where the Islamic Revolution gained considerable influence. Among this scholarship, Vali Nasr's book *The Shia Revival: How Conflicts within Islam Will Shape the Future* outlines the enormous influence that the Iranian Revolutionary Guard, and Khomeini's concept of *vilāyat-i faqīh*, had on Hezbullah, the Lebanese resistance group and political organization.[45] Although there is a great deal of evidence that supports the transnational effects on the Iranian Revolution, it would be a mistake not to grant that the Lebanese Shi`a had their own agency in determining what was right for their population. Most Lebanese Shi`a supported the movement of Ayatollah Khomeini in Iran, but the political movement in Iran was not the same as the Shi`a political movement in Lebanon.

To conclude this section, the historical ties between the Shi`a in Lebanon and the Shi`a in Iran fostered a natural affinity between the two groups. Despite the shah of Iran's efforts to develop a good relationship between the secular government of Lebanon and the Shi`a religious community, opposition to his rule grew significantly in Lebanon as he disenfranchised the Shi`i religious establishment in Iran. The traditional transnational networks of education, financing, and kinship allowed the flow of ideas, arms, and money between the Shi`i communities in Lebanon and Iran. The growth of Shi`i activism in Lebanon helped to buttress the Shi`i revolution in Iran that eventually overthrew the shah. The success of the Iranian Revolution and the installation of a Shi`i government in Iran reinforced the ideals in the Shi`i master narrative in Lebanon. It was now possible to achieve civil rights through the use of armed struggle under the leadership of Shi`i clergy. However, there were still unique differences between the Shi`i movement in Lebanon and the one in Iran. The next section will cover how the English-language press and media dealt with the Iranian Revolution and its representation of the connections and involvement of the Lebanese Shi`a.

THE ENGLISH-LANGUAGE MEDIA AND THE IRANIAN REVOLUTION

The major issues with the English-language media's coverage of the Iranian Revolution center on its marginalization of the Shi`i revolutionary movement and its lack of understanding about the nature of the revolution. The media's descriptions and representation of the Shi`a of Iran were often at odds with reality. This, in turn, directly affected the news narrative constructed about the Lebanese Shi`a. The violence and excesses occurring during the Iranian Revolution were attributed to the Shi`i religion as a whole and not to aberrant actors within the revolution. The English-language media made only modest attempts to deconstruct the complex factors involved in the Shi`i revolt in Iran. Additionally, many aspects of the revolution in Iran were conflated with the Shi`i movement in Lebanon, particularly in the American media. As addressed by Shaery-Eisenlohr, the role of religion and the secular state was a topic of debate among the Lebanese Shi`a as they struggled for civil rights and fought to defend themselves from numerous rivals.[46] However, the media made little attempt to outline the subtle differences between the movement in Lebanon and what was happening in Iran.

Among the numerous critiques of Western press coverage of the Iranian Revolution, three standout accounts provided important information for this book. First, Martin Walker's *Powers of the Press: Twelve of the World's Influential Newspapers* examines the prestige press across the globe. Through a focus on the *New York Times* and *Times* (London), Walker highlights how each paper covered the fall of the shah. In his conclusion, Walker states,

> The US government was confused, America surprised, and the journalists were confounded by the toppling of the Shah—in large part because of the way the *New York Times* had defined the story throughout the 1970s. As the leading American paper the *New York Times* had set the tone for American perception, and it had not done it well.[47]

Walker levels a similar critique against the *Times* (London). Using the paper's own words, he quotes from an editorial: "All that has emerged so far is that the Shah is far more unpopular with his own people that most Western observers had realized."[48] In *The U.S. Press and Iran: Foreign Policy and the Journalism of Deference* (1987), William A. Dorman and Mansour Farhang outline that US press coverage of Iran was inadequate because reporters ignored the internal politics of Iran and ascribed very little importance to the subaltern within Iranian society.[49] Finally, in *Covering Islam: How the Media and the Experts Determine How We See the Rest of the World*, Edward Said wrote in regard to the Iranian Revolution, the American consumer of news was given a sustained diet of information about a people, a culture, a religion—really no more than a poorly defined and badly misunderstood abstraction always, in the case of Iran, represented as militant, dangerous and anti-American.[50]

In these three works, the authors clearly outline and demonstrate the dysfunctional nature of Western media coverage of the Iranian Revolution. Said confronted the Orientalism in the American reporting on the Iranian Revolution. However, all three works fail to link the importance of the Iranian Revolution to the larger Shi`i community, especially in Lebanon. Extrapolating the coverage of the Iranian Revolution to the misrepresentation of the Lebanese Shi`a in the English-language press would have enhanced the argument of the authors. During the Iranian Revolution, the English-language media clearly lacked contextual coverage of the transnational link between Iran and the Lebanese Shi`a. Despite the previously mentioned scholars' inability to expand the analysis of the Iranian revolution coverage to a wider Shi`i community, they still exposed important aspects of Western news reporting that misrepresented the news narrative of the Lebanese Shi`a. Among these aspects were Orientalism, cultural misunderstanding, and a lack of knowledge of the Shi`i religion.

As outlined previously in this book, prior to 1975 the English-language media provided limited coverage of the Lebanese Shi`a; however, even the most populous Shi`i nation in the world, Iran, received little attention about its religious aspects.[51] The shah and the huge economic interest that Western nations held in his country dominated the American and European press and media in regard to Iran. This did not occur by happenstance. The shah valued the positive images of himself and Iran created in the American media and press. He hired polling firms to ascertain the type of impression and representation he received in the American press.[52] Islam and Shi`ism were not the dominant themes that the shah wished to convey about his nation. Instead, he linked Iran to its ancient past with an ostentatious celebration of twenty-five thousand years of Persian monocracy at the ancient city of Persepolis. In America, NBC News beamed this one event in October 1971 by satellite (new technology at that time) to ten million viewers.[53] With few exceptions, leading American newspapers, particularly the *New York Times,* offered favorable coverage of the shah and his regime up until the height of the revolution.[54] In fact, in 1975, at the height of the shah's well-documented human-rights abuses, the *New York Times* had referenced only peripherally three instances of human rights violations in Iran.[55] Yet, in the British press, early cracks appeared in the favorable reports produced on Iran.

THE BRITISH PRESS AND MEDIA AND SHI`I REVOLUTION IN IRAN

Although early revolutionary activities against the shah were not systematically covered in the *Times* (London), the paper did outline the extensive police apparatus in place in Iran and the draconian measures used to control the population. On January 19, 1975, the *Sunday Times* printed a major feature entitled "Torture in Iran." The reporter, Philip Jacobson, documented the Iranian secret police's (SAVAK) abuses of political prisoners. The *Sunday Times* stated that the prisoners who were alleged to have been tortured fell into three broad categories: left-wing activists who either supported or took part in guerrilla operations, "Moslem" dissidents opposed to what they regarded as the religious and political repression by the shah, and those predominantly middle-class intellectuals who were unwise enough to have criticized the regime.[56] Unfortunately, never once in the article did the author mention that Iran was a predominantly Shi`i country or that the religious opposition originated from the Shi`i clerical establishment. Instead, prominence was given to the communist and leftist parties as the key resistance leaders to the shah and his policies. Although the article uncovered abuses by the shah's security apparatus, it constructed the story that the shah's regime fought predominantly communist insurgents. The paper failed to uncover that by 1975 there was a key Shi'i religious opposition to the shah located in Lebanon. Years after the article on torture, a *Times* reporter would have direct evidence of the linkage between Lebanon and the Shi`i opposition to the shah but would fail to connect the dots for the British readers.

In *Pity the Nation: The Abduction of Lebanon*, *Times* (London) journalist and author Robert Fisk recalled a run-in with an antishah Iranian. During a 1977 visit to a Shi`i area in South Lebanon, Fisk and his friend Edward Cody came across an armed man listening to a Palestinian officer giving weapons instruction. The man asked in English if the two journalists could interpret what the officer was saying. Unaware of the man's nationality, they inquired why the man needed interpretation. "Because I am not an Arab. I am from Iran. I am from the opposition in Iran. I have come to learn here how to fight. We understand a common cause with our Palestinian brothers. With their help we can learn to destroy the Shah."[57] Both Fisk and Cody remember scoffing at the man's claim, yet, less than two years from that date, the dissident they were exposed to and others like him would be instrumental in the overthrow of the shah of Iran. Robert Fisk, an astute chronicler of Middle Eastern affairs, never reported that story in the British press and thus missed a critical opportunity to uncover the transnational linkage between Lebanon and the Iranian Shi`a.

There were other instances in the British press where reporters failed to correctly characterize the nature of the Shi`i movement in Iran and the Iranian Revolution. The protest taking place in Iran had a decidedly religious tenor, but the British press was unable to characterize the importance of Shi`ism to the uprising. By January 1978, the pace of protest against the shah increased. The *Times* (London) reported on January 11 that more than twenty protestors were killed when Iranian police opened fire on demonstrators. The killings took place in the city of Qom, Iran, one of the holiest sites in Shi'i Islam, which had been one of the focal points of Shi`i protest and opposition to the shah's reform movement. Not once in the article did the *Times* acknowledge that the protest movement involved Shi`a[58] when, in fact, the protest began as a reaction to a slanderous article printed in the Iranian press instigated by the shah's information minister.[59] The article conflated Marxist and Shi`i opposition as a red–black coalition united with the single purpose of colonizing the Iranian people. The article also directly offended and disparaged Ayatollah Khomeini. The resulting violence by the shah's security establishment against the protest helped to solidify Shi`i opposition to the regime. By ignoring the central role of the Shi`a in this protest and not uncovering the esteem in which the community held Ayatollah Khomeini, the paper failed to convey an accurate representation of the Shi`i community.

In February 1978, the *Times* (London) reported more violence on the streets of Iran. On this occasion crowds fought in Tabriz, Iran's second largest city. According to an Iranian government spokesman, as reported by the *Times*, these rioters were led by "Marxist-Muslims." The *Times* made no effort to deconstruct that term: *Marxist-Muslims* would be looked at skeptically in today's context, but this early linkage of Shi`i theology with Marxism was common in Western media circles.[60] In the Iranian context, there was some validity to this linkage based upon the writings of Ali Shariati, a lay Iranian intellectual who died in 1977 just prior to the revolution.[61] He attempted to couple Shi`i activism with Marxist revolutionary doctrine; however, among the Shi`i religious establishment he was widely criticized.[62] Those knowledgeable about Ayatollah Khomeini and his Shi`i movement understood that he was anti-Marxist. Khomeini steadfastly believed that citizens had the right to own private property.[63] During his exile to Iraq, Khomeini had encouraged Shi`i dissidents of the Iraqi regime to shun their affiliation with communist revolutionary movements. His close affiliation with prominent Iraqi cleric Ayatollah Muhammad Baqr al-Sadr helped frame the intellectual foundation of the al-Da`wa party—a religious, anticommunist, and anti-Western Shi`i movement.[64] Yet the conflation of Marxism and Islam would continue to distort a true representation of the Shi`i religion in the British and the American press and would affect the representation of the Lebanese Shi`a. Despite the distortion between Islam and Marxism, coverage of the turmoil in Iran did afford some reporters the opportunity to understand the linkage between the Shi`a in Iran and what was happening in Lebanon.

In September 1978, almost nine months after the confrontation in Qom, *Times* (London) reporter Robert Fisk linked the political upheavals in Iran to events in Lebanon. Fisk believed that the political unrest in Iran had finally touched the Arab world as a result of the disappearance of a prominent Shi`i cleric. Reporting on the "Lebanese cleric" who had been missing for almost three weeks after his trip to Libya, Fisk commented, "Musa al-Sadr, who was born in the holy city of Qom . . . made no secret of his sympathy for Ayatollah Khomeini, the Shah's principal Shia opponent."[65] Fisk reported that a Beirut paper speculated that al-Sadr had been kidnapped by SAVAK, the Iranian secret police. What went unreported by Fisk was that Musa al-Sadr had made it possible for Iranian dissident groups to be present and active in the south of Lebanon for a number of years. There were a number of cases in which some of these dissidents were picked up by the Lebanese police and taken to the Beirut airport to be deported. Musa al-Sadr's intervention facilitated their release and often saved them from the hands of the shah's secret police.[66] This connection between the Shi`i revolutionaries, who had trained and were supported in Lebanon, and the events happening in Iran was never clearly expressed in *Times*. Rather, the stories most prominent in the *Times* coverage of Iran concerned the financial issues that faced Great Britain about Iran.

Summarizing the early British media representation of the Iranian Revolution and the Shi`a, it is clear the British press excavated the abuses of the shah against the revolutionaries but failed to outline the importance of the Shi`a in that revolutionary movement. By not highlighting the Shi`i opposition when the pace of protest quickened, the British paper left the impression upon its readers that a Marxist–Islamic alliance represented a major factor in the shah's troubles. Only brief reports from journalist Robert Fisk offered any insight into the link between the Lebanese Shi`a and Iran. Yet this early reporting in Great Britain on Iran and the Shi`a gave a more open perspective about the Shi`a than the American press and media.

IRAN AND THE AMERICAN PRESS AND MEDIA

Coverage in the American media of Iran and the shah was very favorable prior to the revolution of 1978–1979.[67] Much of the coverage on Iran was driven by the large financial stakes American businessmen had in the country. This contrasted with the American media's coverage of Lebanon, where the financial and geopolitical outcomes for the United States were more acute. The US government had invested millions of dollars in the shah's regime in support of his military and internal security apparatus.[68] American corporations made excellent profits from arms sales and infrastructure improvements in Iran, while the shah's military ensured the free flow of oil through the Persian Gulf to the United States.[69] In the late 1970s, thousands of Americans lived and worked in Iran. Most lived in their own Western-style cantons, oblivious to the realities of Iranian society. When the revolution unfolded, reporters and correspondents were unprepared for the dramatic paradigm shift away from the model of Iran that they had created.

From the beginning of the Iranian Revolution, the *New York Times* mischaracterized the events in Iran and the role of the Shi`i religious community. On April 2, 1978, Paul Hofmann wrote an article discussing opposition groups who were beginning to align against the shah of Iran. He said, "The regime of Shah Mohammed Riza Pahlevi has for years asserted that 'Islamic-Marxists'—an underground coalition between ultraconservative Moslems and leftist extremists—are behind the illegal dissent and intermittent terrorism in Iran."[70] Hoffman called this a "Black–Red alliance," black being the color of the turbans and cloaks worn by the leaders of "Shiah Islam," and red the color assigned to communism.[71] As mentioned above, the term *red–black alliance* came directly from an article planted in the Iranian paper by the information ministry of the shah. In January 1978, the article so enflamed the Shi`i community in Qom that its members rioted against the government for several days to protest the regime's slander of Ayatollah Khomeini.[72] In an attempt to balance the coverage in his article, Hoffman questioned whether the shah was really identifying the true cause of the opposition and not looking at his own oppressive and paternalistic rule as the major factor in the unrest. Nevertheless, Hoffman missed a critical opportunity to explain, or deconstruct, the notion of a red–black alliance. He identified Tabriz, Iran, as the center of Shi`i conservatism, where religious militants opposed greater freedom for women and land-reform programs, but he discounted the religious aspect of the opposition, suggesting "that large number of Iranians who were not primarily motivated by religion joined in to vent their hostility to the Shah."[73] Terms like *Shi`ite conservatism* and *religious militants* were used in his article with no amplifying explanation or discussion of the deeper reasons for Shi`i opposition to the shah. More confusion would result from the *New York Times* as it conflated Shi`i aspirations with those of the Sunni sect in Saudi Arabia.

In a *New York Times* article entitled "The Moslem World Rekindles Its Militancy," Christopher Wren linked the flogging of two Britons in Saudi Arabia for making beer to conservative Muslims of the Shi`i sect spearheading riots in Iran.[74] Again, no effort was made to deconstruct these events or to discuss the different environments in which these actions took place. The author placed both events together as a means of describing Islamic conservatism. The Kingdom of Saudi Arabia and the Islamic law (shari`a) practiced there had no connection with the struggle of the Shi`a against the dictatorship of the shah. The Saudi rulers, Sunni Wahhabis, considered some of the Shi`a in Iran apostates.⁷⁵ Yet these comparisons and conflations persisted in the American media's representations of the Shi`a in Iran.

The same article discussed antishah activists in Iran as having joined with Shi`i religious conservatives as a pretext for opposition to the shah's regime.⁷⁶ There was no need for a pretext for secular opposition to the shah's regime: it was not only the Shi`i activists who found reasons to oppose the shah's regime, as the shah's actions in Iran had alienated him from a number of groups. Opponents of the shah spanned the spectrum from secular democratic to hardcore communist. Throughout this article, Wren tied together the concepts of Islamic militancy, Shi`ism, and radicalism. Nowhere in the article did he make an effort to unpack the phenomenon of Islam or Shi`ism.⁷⁷ Wren even suggested that the effort of Palestinian entities in Lebanon to play on Muslim sympathies during the civil war was directly connected to the Islamic Revolution in Iran. He never mentioned that Lebanese Shi`a frequently clashed with Sunni Palestinians over territorial and property disputes. This was part of the distorted picture of the Shi`a painted by *New York Times* reporters taken from their exposure to the protests in Iran.

Toward the end of 1978, the shah of Iran's political situation became critical. The *New York Times* and the rest of America's media now devoted more resources and attention to reporting the crisis within Iran. As a result, more content reported on Shi`i Islam. The analysis, however, woefully lacked context. The inability to accurately portray the relationship between the Shi`a in Lebanon and Iran limited the American public's ability to understand the dynamics accurately. As discussed earlier in this chapter, many of the groups in opposition to the shah were located in Lebanon and provided military training to the shah's opponents. However, the American media focused on the awakening of the Shi`a in Iran—despite the fact that this awakening had already gained a firm foothold in Lebanon.

One can find any number of intellectual critiques of American media's coverage of the shah and Iran prior to the revolution and the inability to "get it right."⁷⁸ However, none of these critiques focus specifically on the coverage of the Shi`a or explain how the distorted representation of the group affected the news narrative of Lebanese Shi`a. There was a distinct tendency to misrepresent the Shi`a as a group throughout the media's coverage of the Iranian Revolution, with only few exceptions. Even those attempts to accurately cover and represent the Shi`a fell short of the mark. More often, the English-language press employed Orientalist jargon and conflated the Shi`a with communism in the representation offered to their readers. Both the American and British press exhibited these trends during this critical timeframe.

ORIENTALISM, COMMUNISM, AND SHI`ISM

The deterioration of the political situation in Iran accelerated at the end of November 1978. The English-language press struggled to make sense of a new reality in Iran. During that month, a number of *New York Times* articles reported that the violence in Iran included the death of many opponents of the shah's regime.[79] Even to the casual reader this large loss of life signaled that all was not well in Iran. What was missing from the *New York Times* previous coverage was the context in which this widescale violence took place. During this period, articles in the *New York Times* attempted to provide insight into the Shi`i movement in Iran. In his report "Islam's Most Devout Are the Most Devoutly Opposed," *New York Times* correspondent Eric Pace started out with this description of Ayatollah Khomeini: "The fire-breathing utterances of Ayatollah Mohammed Khomeini, exiled leader of Iran's Moslem fundamentalists have helped shape the popular conception of Iran's trouble as a conflict between medieval mullahs and a modernizing Shah."[80] Despite the initial Orientalist description of Khomeini as a fire breather, the article is one of the few that attempts to give context to the Shi`a and to Khomeini's opposition to the shah. Pace stated that his initial description of Khomeini truly oversimplified the deep Islamic opposition that threatened the shah's throne.[81] He outlined how the suppression of many of the Shi`i religious institutions by the shah's government fomented much of the religious community's resentment to his regime.[82] However, as if this were the only hallmark of the religion, most of the other coverage of the Shi`a was typified by statements linking Shi`i opposition to the shah with their readiness to die and become martyrs.[83] This fascination with martyrdom would continue to be a theme in the *New York Times* coverage of the upheaval in Iran.

At the end of November 1978 the British press also began to focus attention on the Shi`a. The *Times* (London) devoted an entire article to the Shi`a entitled "Iran's Brand of Islam a Religion of Opposition."[84] Again, despite the Orientalist title of the article (one which categorized the Shi`i religion as oppositional), *Times* reporter Edward Mortimer wrote a detailed and comprehensive description of the religion. In the article, he explained the religion's major tenets and covered the belief systems of other sects within the religion. Although the article was focused on the Shi`a in Iran, Mortimer mentioned that substantial populations of Shi`a existed in Lebanon. Still, there was no mention of the historic connection between the Shi`a in Lebanon and those in Iran. There was no discussion on the origins of Islam in Iran via the introduction of Shi`i scholars to the Safavid dynasty in Persia in the sixteenth century. Mortimer's article, however, presented a much more enlightened representation of the Shi`a than did the *New York Times* focus on the idea of Shi`i martyrdom.

As fighting intensified in Iran, the *New York Times* continued to focus on the negative aspects of the Shi`i revolution taking place within the country. The journalists missed the importance of Shi'ism as a cultural force and focused more on fanaticism.[85] This focus on fanaticism encompassed more than just the religious aspect of the Shi`i revolution. Suggestions of a link between Khomeini and the communists came in an article published on December 8, 1978. In that article, the *New York Times* questioned whether the Ayatollah Khomeini was subject to Communist manipulation. Citing a European intelligence source, the report states, "some of his circle seem to have more in common with Libya and the Italian Communist Party than with Shi`ite Moslem tradition."[86] Surprisingly, an American intelligence report nine months prior came to the opposite conclusion. The American intelligence summary stated, "The Shia Islamic movement dominated by Ayatollah Khomeini is far better organized, enlightened and able to resist communism than its detractors would lead us to believe."[87] The intelligence assessment goes on to say that the movement was rooted more in the Iranian people than in Western ideologies to include communism.[88] It would not be unusual to expect equal or better assessment about foreign crisis coming from the *New York Times* then from American intelligence. By 1978, the *New York Times* had become such a media powerhouse that its data-gathering capabilities rivaled that of American intelligence agencies; however, the paper failed to analyze the data properly.[89] In fact, key government officials, who had access to the most highly classified documents, said that they would rather get their information from the *New York Times* than from the documents produced by American intelligence agencies.[90] Yet in this case the *New York Times* was off the mark in its assessment of communism and its influence on the Shi`i movement in Iran.

Why this disconnect between the *New York Times* reporting on the Shi`a and the conclusions of some American intelligence organizations? One factor to consider is that the authors of such articles did not believe these movements could act independently from a movement with Western origins. This reporting mind-set ensured that many of the *New York Times* forecasts of events in Iran were inaccurate. A December 1978 article supports this point. When discussing the opposition to the shah, the report stated, "Khomeini is unlikely to prevail in his revolution unless the more flexible opposition leaders are driven into his camp by clumsiness on the part of the Shah and his American friends."[91] *Clumsy* would not be an appropriate adjective to describe the shah's actions between December 14, 1978, and January 16, 1979, when he fled Iran. Yet no amount of deft maneuvering by the shah could have saved him from his inevitable ouster. On February 1, 1979, Khomeini returned to Iran, and on March 31 a referendum passed that abolished the monarchy and established the Islamic Republic of Iran. The support of other opposition leaders was not critical to Khomeini's ascension to power. The

New York Times prognostication was inaccurate because it failed to understand and interpret the motivation and skill of the Shi`i movement in Iran.

Not all the analysis and reporting on the Shi`i movement in Iran was flawed. On January 1, 1979, *New York Times* reporter Anthony Lewis wrote a scathing article in which he said that the American relationship with the shah was "self-feeding":[92] "We created him, put him in power, helped shape his economic and political policies and then acted as if the Shah truly represented the desires of the Iranian people."[93] Not only did Lewis lambaste American diplomats for their failure to predict the shah's fall—he also criticized American journalists for failing to perceive the political reality in Iran:

> Until very recently, most of the press kept telling Americans that, as Time put it last June 5, the Shah "has a broad base of popular support." His trouble, the stories said, came only from the far right and the far left both angered by the Shah's successful land reform and other liberal economic measures that were bringing the country up from feudalism.[94]

As Lewis stated in his article, the events made it clear that it was not only religious fanatics and political radicals who wanted the shah out of power; the majority of Iranians opposed the shah.[95] However, Lewis's report was the exception, not the rule, for the *New York Times* and most of the English-language prestige press.

When the shah of Iran flew into exile on January 16, 1979, so did thirty-three years of US foreign policy in the region. As the *New York Times* had reported, Iran was pivotal to American security interests in the region. However, in the aftermath of the shah's departure, a great many of the Iranian people held tremendous resentment for America's support of the shah's regime. This resentment was certainly not unfounded. American intelligence agencies had trained and worked with SAVAK, which the shah used to repress his religious and political opponents.[96] America also supported and equipped the Iranian military, which the shah employed (especially toward the end of his reign) as an instrument of internal repression. However, some in the American government still harbored hope, as echoed in the American media, that the shah's departure would not lead to the installation of Shi`i Islamic government.[97] The British press reports appeared more realistic in their assessment by providing a better understanding of the depth of Khomeini's support in Iran and outlining his virulent opposition to the remnants of the shah's regime.

The shah appointed a new government to succeed him prior to his departure, but, as reported in the *Sunday Times* (London), Ayatollah Khomeini denounced the new government and urged his followers to fight for its downfall, "lest the blood spilled until now for Islam and liberty be lost forever."[98] Later, the British press noted that a million Iranians marched through the streets of Tehran in support of the return of the Ayatollah from exile in France.⁹⁹ This was indicative of the wide range of support within Iran for Khomeini and his Shi`i revolution. Without editorializing, the British press indicated that Khomeini's support was more widespread than that of the transitional government appointed by the shah. Meanwhile, the *New York Times* featured a story on one of the shah's military units. The "Immortals," as the unit was designated, put on a "show of force" for foreign correspondents demonstrating their loyalty to the shah and the interim government. The unit's leaders opposed Khomeini, yet the demonstration proved merely farcical as the Shi`i revolution continued unabated.¹⁰⁰ Again, the *New York Times* seemed incredulous of the notion that a Shi`i revolution could overpower a Western-oriented government, a very Orientalist notion. By the end of 1978, a domestic labor issue would affect the *Times* (London), which had provided some balance to the Orientalist notions offered in the American press. A strike forced the paper to shut down production temporarily in November 1978. From this point, the most comprehensive news in the British press about the Iranian Revolution and its relation to the Shi`a in Lebanon would come from the *Guardian*.

The *Guardian* provided some accurate and detailed coverage of the Shi`a in Iran and reported their linkage to the Shi`a in Lebanon. The *Guardian* covered two important connections between the Iranian Revolution and the Lebanese Shi`a. First, it outlined Khomeini's support for finding the missing Lebanese cleric Musa al-Sadr and, second, it highlighted the importance the Lebanese Shi`a held for the revolution's success.

When Khomeini arrived in Iran in February 1979, Musa al-Sadr had been missing for six months. Even while exiled in France, Khomeini had expressed concern over al-Sadr's whereabouts. Soon after the arrival of Khomeini in Iran, a Shi`i delegation from Lebanon (including Nabih Berri, Muhammad Shams-al Din, and al-Sadr's close acquaintance Mustafa Chamran) traveled to Iran and asked Khomeini to inquire of the Libyans about the status of Musa al-Sadr. They also made a point to pledge their support for the Shi`i revolution in Iran.¹⁰¹ As Khomeini consolidated his power base in Iran and acted as head of state, he took the opportunity to accede to the wishes of the Lebanese delegation. In May 1979, the *Guardian* reported on Khomeini's reception of a delegation from Libya, which had never truly accounted for the missing Lebanese Shi`i leader. The *Guardian* reported that Khomeini gave the Libyan delegation a cool reception during their visit. The Ayatollah told the Libyans that the problems between Iran and Libya could only be solved if the Tripoli government provided a successful accounting for Musa al-Sadr's disappearance.¹⁰² Although Khomeini's pressure never resulted in a full accounting of Musa al-Sadr's whereabouts, Khomeini's actions established the linkage of the Iranian revolutionary state as a champion of Shi`i causes. Yet it was not a one-way relationship. The fledgling Iranian government needed help, particularly military and security expertise, that the Lebanese Shi`a and Amal had acquired during the Lebanese Civil War.

Mustafa Chamran, the Iranian-born, American-educated confidant of Musa al-Sadr, had been fighting for the overthrow of the shah for many years, particularly during his time in Lebanon, where he helped organize and support the Shi`i causes.[103] Chamran acquired a great deal of military expertise in Lebanon during the civil war, particularly in his defense of the Shi`a enclave of Nab`a. During his visit to Iran in February 1979 to seek assistance in finding al-Sadr, Chamran decided to stay in that country and help the fledgling government of Ayatollah Khomeini. Chamran became a leading figure in forming the Iranian Revolutionary Guard, the highly motivated, religiously indoctrinated military group charged with the role of protecting the revolution. He was later named Iran's minister of defense in September 1979.[104] The *Guardian* also uncovered that this and other links existed between the Lebanese Shi`i and the fledgling Iranian government.

During reporting of the assassination of Ayatollah Moretez Motahari, an aide to Khomeini on May 3, 1979, the *Guardian* uncovered contacts between the Lebanese militia Amal and the new Iranian government. The paper stated that an ultra-right-wing group calling itself Forqan carried out the assassination. According to the *Guardian* article, a representative of Amal had called a Western media source in Iran saying "they were seeking [Iranian] government approval to hunt *Forqan* . . . and that *Forqan* was made up of American and Israeli intelligence agents."[105] Although the *Guardian* failed to follow up on the claim, the mere fact that the paper recorded a linkage between the Shi`i Amal militia and the Iranian government marked a significant step in capturing a portion of the Lebanese Shi`i narrative. Many of the Shi`a in Lebanon were invested in the success of the Iranian Revolution and, according to the *Guardian* article, willing to use armed force to preserve the regime.

When the *Times* (London) resumed operations and coverage of the Iranian Revolution in November 1979, the paper did not uncover the linkage or connection between the Iranian and the Lebanese Shi`a that the *Guardian* offered. For example, the *Times* missed the opportunity to cover that connection while reporting on the fighting between the Kurdish insurgents and the newly formed Iranian government. During that fighting in November 1979, the *Times* mentioned that Mustafa Chamran was the defense minister leading the Iranian effort. However, the paper never mentioned his connection with the Lebanese Shi`a.[106] Instead, the animosity between Khomeini and the West (particularly America) continued to shape the English-language news coverage of Iran.

The majority of the news about Shi`a and the Iranian Revolution continued to bend toward negative in the American press. Their representation in the *New York Times* characterized the Shi`a as antimodernization, anti-Western, and inclined toward authoritarianism. Western news reports and coverage from Lebanon would continue to link the Shi`a with these presumably negative positions. American and Western officials viewed a visit to Tehran by a delegation of the Lebanese Shi`i militia group Amal as an ominous sign. They speculated that the group was providing security expertise to the new Iranian government in opposition to American policies.[107] However, American policies were already dedicated to work against the new Iranian government. American policymakers strongly supported the so-called "moderate leaders" installed by shah before he left Iran.[108] This again placed American government policy in direct opposition to the majority of the Iranian people.

It was no secret that America opposed the government of Ayatollah Khomeini. In a January 1979 *New York Times* article, Iranians had expressed enmity toward President Jimmy Carter for his support of Prime Minister Shahpur Baktiar, the leader who had been appointed by the shah just before he fled the country. The news report quoted an Iranian demonstrator as saying, "Tell President Carter Khomeini is our leader. Tell Carter to shut his mouth."[109] As Khomeini continued his consolidation of power in Iran, his rhetoric against the United States became more strident.

On November 4 that rhetoric morphed into something Khomeini did not anticipate. President Carter's decision to allow the shah to come to the United States for medical treatment infuriated many Iranians. On the streets of Tehran, students from the Islamic movement were overcome with anger. As a protest against America's involvement in Iran, a cadre of students called the Muslim Students Following the Imam's Line plotted to seize the American embassy.[110] That morning, the students climbed the walls of the American embassy and took Americans hostage. Ayatollah Khomeini had no prior knowledge of the student plot to overtake the embassy.[111] When initially informed of the takeover by the Iranian foreign minister, Khomeini reportedly told the minister to "kick them out."[112] Later that evening, during his trip back from speaking with Khomeini, the Iranian foreign minister heard that the Ayatollah had publicly made a statement endorsing the goals of the student takeover. Khomeini's failure to act against the taking of American hostages dramatically changed the words and images employed by the American press and media. These news outlets placed their focus on the militancy and anti-Americanism of Khomeini and the Shi`a.[113]

The news outlets turned Khomeini, the leader and the symbol of the Shi`i revolution in Iran, into the ultimate "other" along with the millions of Shi`i Muslims he represented. In the English-language prestige press and Western media, a sinister, more threatening image of the Shi`a was presented. Chosen as *Time* magazine's 1979 man of the year, Ayatollah Khomeini's cover image portrayed him with a dark, menacing expression (see figure 3.2).

The British press and media took a more measured approach in their reporting. In an article on November 18, 1979, the *Sunday Times* offered that

Figure 3.2. The Ayatollah Khomeini. Reprinted by permission of *Time* magazine's 1979 man-of-the-year cover image.

different voices were emerging from America. Many Americans voiced anger and frustration that the shah of Iran had been admitted to a New York City hospital for cancer treatment, the incident that precipitated the hostage takeover at the embassy.[114] Later, in a *Times* (London) article, reporters explained why the Iranian government had expelled reporters from the American-based *Time* magazine. The article quoted an Iranian spokesperson saying, "Since the problem of hostages has come up *Time* has done nothing but arouse the hatred of the American people."[115] The article also went on to report how disparaging the American broadcast media had been toward the

Shi'i students who had seized the embassy. The Iranian government spokesman was critical of ABC and CBS news reports, which compared the students to the German terrorist group the Baader-Meinhof Gang—another instance of the American press and media's tendency to present the Shi'a with a broad brush of negative imagery and representation.[116]

Without the emotional baggage of their countrymen being held hostage, the British press and media were able to discern different viewpoints of the event including the source of the Iranian Shi'i populations' anger against the West. In an editorial in the *Guardian,* reporter James Dickie stated, "The frustrations of the disposed majority have now boiled over in Iran, to the amazement of the stunned and incredulous West whose inhabitants find themselves blamed for the connivance and support their governments lent to the tyranny under which the Iranians groaned for 26 years."[117]

In some regard, the hostage crisis changed and improved the overall *Times* (London) coverage of the Iranian Revolution. Reporters took a more expansive view of the impact of the Shi'i revolution in Iran, particularly its effect on the Shi'i population in Lebanon. Robert Fisk of the *Times* followed the link between the Iranian Revolution and the Shi'a in Lebanon. In a May 29, 1980, article Fisk reported on fighting between the Shi'i militiamen and Iraqi supporters of the Palestinian movement in Lebanon. He correctly ascertained that the militia in Lebanon had looked to the Iranian Revolution and Ayatollah Khomeini for spiritual guidance in its struggle against the secular Baathist supporters of the Palestinians.[118] He went on to recognize that the Iranian Revolution had given Lebanese Shi'a cohesion, creating another force within the country's broken political structure.

No reporting of the link between Lebanese Shi'a and the Iranian Revolution was forthcoming in the *New York Times* during this period. Instead of recognizing revolution in Iran as a source of global Shi'i pride and cohesiveness, the *New York Times* produced articles attributing the negative actions of the Iranian students as characteristic of all Shi'i Muslims. According to one article, attributes of Shi'a Islam included dissimulation (the right not to reveal the truth in times of crisis), support of authoritarian rule, and the concept of martyrdom.[119] Basically, the *New York Times* represented the Shi'a as people who lie, support dictators, and long for death. Further, the *New York Times* articles suggested that Khomeini exerted little influence among the Shi'a outside of Iran, yet his picture began to appear everywhere in the downtrodden Shi'i communities, particularly in Lebanon.[120] Edward Said was the most critical of the *New York Times* coverage. In his book, *Covering Islam*, Said contends that reporters subjected Islam to a dizzying array of misinterpretation and Orientalism during the Iranian crisis.[121] In his estimation, the *New York Times* represented Shi'a as those who longed for martyrdom and were unwilling to compromise.[122]

The American television media also contributed to the unfavorable representation of the Shi`a based upon the Iranian hostage crisis. For a number of months after the embassy takeover, ABC scheduled a late-night news broadcast entitled *America Held Hostage*. Every evening, the number of days since the seizure of the hostages was flashed on the television screen, reminding the American public of their government's impotence in the face of this new Shi`i regime in Iran. Distortions and inaccuracies about the Shi`a also went unchallenged in television news reporting. In a CBS Evening News segment, a reporter characterized Muharram as a period when Shi`i Muslims celebrate Mohammed's challenge to world leaders.[123] In fact, *Muharram* is the name of a month in the Islamic calendar; during the first ten days, Shi`a honor and commemorate the martyrdom of Husayn, the grandson of the prophet Muhammad. Such misrepresentation of Shi`i history may not have mattered to the average American, but it was certainly indicative of Western media outlets' careless treatment of Shi`i Islam.

Part of the media misrepresentation of the Iranian Revolution and the Shi`a included the tendency by papers such as the *New York Times* to frame the new revolutionary government in Iran as incapable of managing modern political activities.[124] The *New York Times* editorialists framed the battle between Khomeini and his opponents as a conflict between old and new ways. The *New York Times* also conflated the fighting between Christians and Muslims in Lebanon as representing a struggle between the old ways of Islam and the new and modern ways of the West.[125] However, it was not modernity that the Shi`a rejected in Iran and Lebanon—it was the imposition of different cultural and religious norms that they eschewed.[126]

A great deal of evidence was available to Western reports to allow them to discount the notion of rejection of modernity by Shi`a. Michel Foucault, the prominent French historian and philosopher, traveled to Iran during the revolution and provided insight into this topic. Foucault did not frame the conflict in Iran as a fight between the old and the new, as did most *New York Times* journalists and Western media outlets. He noted that a new kind of modernity could arrive out of the Iranian Revolution, one based on an Eastern model that rejoined spirituality and politics.[127] Many politico-religious thinkers in Iran supported modernization and rejected aspects of the traditional past.[128] However, there was no such suggestion of that in the coverage by the *New York Times*.

The American media relentlessly characterized Ayatollah Khomeini and the Iranian Revolution as backward and evil. One such example, captured in a *Time* magazine article, stated, "As the leader of Iran's revolution he [Khomeini] gave the 20th century world a frightening lesson in the shattering power of irrationality, of the ease with which terrorism can be adopted as government policy."[129] Irrationality and terrorism now became part of the parlance that the prestige press and media used to describe Khomeini and the

Shi`a. The use of the word *irrationality* is curious in the context of Khomeini and the Shi`a because Khomeini was trained in Aristotelian logic, and many Shi`i clerics pride themselves on *ijtihād*, a form of logical steps and debate to arrive at an issue's proper solution.[130] Concerning government policies, Khomeini sought to articulate and practice a new form of governance, one that had its own unique decision-making style quite different from Western models.

LINKING THE LEBANESE SHI`A TO IRAN

While American media riveted its attention to the events in Iran and the overwhelmingly negative imagery and representation of the Shi`a, coverage of the Shi`a in Lebanon went underreported. Israel continued its raids against targets in Lebanon and, once again, much of the collateral damage was falling on the Shi`a. One of the few stories in the American media regarding the Lebanese Shi`a came not from the *New York Times* but from the *Washington Post*.

In November 1979, *Washington Post* reporter Edward Cody wrote an article entitled "Arab Shiites, Inspired by Iran, Show New Force in Lebanon, the Strength of Numbers."[131] This is one of the few times that a Western press outlet provided a clear analysis of what was happening to the Shi`a in Lebanon in the aftermath of the Iranian Revolution. He stated in his article:

> The growth in Shiite self-awareness and political organization here flows in part from inspiration generated throughout the Moslem world by Ayatollah Ruhollah Khomeini and his Shiite led revolution in Iran. It also reflects a particular outrage at the suffering of Shiite villagers in South Lebanon's battlegrounds and a new realization of strength of numbers in Lebanon's sectarian power sharing.[132]

A seasoned Associated Press reporter, Cody had spent a great deal of time in Lebanon during the early civil war years. He understood quite well the events on the ground and how the continued fighting in South Lebanon and the Iranian Revolution were affecting the Shi`a throughout Lebanon.

In his article, Cody devoted attention to the Shi`i militia group Amal. He reported that Amal had gained in strength and stature since the Iranian Revolution and that most Shi`a in Lebanon looked to Ayatollah Khomeini for leadership.[133] However, while Ayatollah Khomeini inspired many of the Shi`a in Lebanon, not all of them looked to him for leadership. Nabih Berri, leader of Amal, reiterated that fact in a 1980 interview in the *Washington Post*[134]: "We were founded six years ago, before the Iranian revolution surfaced. . . . However we have learned a number of things from the Iranian revolution, among them is that reason is stronger than arms, and the word is stronger than the bomb, and religion has its own revolutionary impact."[135]

It was not until the beginning of 1980 that the *New York Times* focused any effort on the Lebanese Shi`a and their involvement in the wider Shi'i revival throughout the Middle East. The majority of the initial coverage focused on hijackings and violent clashes between Shi`i militia groups and other groups in Lebanon. An April 1980 *New York Times* article discussed a clash in Lebanon between "Moslem Shi`ite militants" and pro-Iraqi guerrillas.[136] The paper freely used such words as *militants* to describe Shi`i militia groups. The article traced the origin of the conflict between Shi`i militiamen and pro-Iraqi guerillas to the death of Imam Muhammad Baqr al-Sadr in Iraq. The paper said that Baqr al-Sadr was a key figure in a secret organization known as al-Da`wa that allegedly had direct links with Ayatollah Khomeini of Iran.[137] The article gave no context of the importance of this Shi`i scholar and leader from Najaf, Iraq. Additionally, the article never discussed that a number of the Shi`i religious community's members (followers of Baqr al-Sadr) had been expelled or fled Iraq based upon a crackdown by the Iraqi government. The article never clarified the connection between the Lebanese Shi`a and Muhammad Baqr al-Sadr and Khomeini, nor did it expose a link between a wider Shi`a revival throughout the Middle East.

However, in the early 1980s the *New York Times* provided glimpses into what was happening to the Lebanese Shi`a. In one article, reporter Nicholas Gage chronicled what he stated was the "growing assertiveness of Lebanon's Shiite Moslems."[138] In that article, Gage discussed the origins of the conflict between the Palestinians and the Shi`i and outlined Iran's growing financial support for Amal.[139] Growing financial support, however, did not translate into Iranian leadership of the Amal movement. That influence and leadership would change dramatically with the Israeli invasion of Lebanon and the introduction of the Iranian revolutionary guard as a vanguard of the Shi`i resistance movement against the Israelis.

In conclusion, the Iranian Revolution had a profound impact on the Shi`a of Lebanon, as it did on the Shi`i movement throughout the world. Much of the support and initial resistance to the shah's regime was situated in Lebanon, which exposed the importance of the transnational connections of the Shi`i religious movement. The ultimate success of the revolutionary movement in Iran inspired the Lebanese Shi`a and helped to reinforce their own narrative of civil rights and armed resistance to violence and injustice. The English-language press and media were slow to capture the effects of the revolution on the Shi`a population in Lebanon. Instead, popular characterization and the news narrative constructed of the Shi`a was predominantly negative. This was particularly true of the American press. Edward Said provided the most incisive critique of the coverage by the *New York Times* and the American media on the Shi`a and the revolution in Iran. In *Covering Islam:*

How the Media and the Experts Determine How We See the Rest of the World, Said remarked,

> Whether they did so consciously or not, the news media were in fact using their powers of representation to accomplish a purpose, similar to that intended by the United States government in the past: namely, the extension of an American presence, or what to Iranians amounted to the same thing as negation of the Iranian Revolution.[140]

In this Orientalist tradition, the revolution was seen as something negative because it did not fit into a Western construct. Despite Said's historical critique of the American press and media coverage, his account, and those of other authors outlined in this chapter, did not directly link the Orientalist representation of the Iranian Revolution to the Shi'a movement in Lebanon. As indicated thus far, the American media missed the importance of that connection. The British media and press, although not perfect, were able to discern some of the links between the Iranian Revolution and the Shi'a in Lebanon. Although they also editorialized and demonized aspects of the Shi'i movement, they provided a clearer understanding of this part of the Shi'i narrative. For the English-language press and media, the impact of the Iranian revolution on the Lebanese Shi'a would be increasingly important as the Israeli invasion of Lebanon unfolded in 1982. This aspect of the media representation of the Lebanese Shi'a and their narrative will be covered in the next chapter.

NOTES

1. Augustus Richard Norton, *Amal and the Shi'a: Struggle for the Soul of Lebanon* (Austin: University of Texas Press, 1987), 56.
2. James A. Bill, *The Eagle and the Lion: The Tragedy of American–Iranian Relations* (New Haven, CT: Yale University Press, 1988), 192–93.
3. H. E. Chehabi, *Distant Relations: Iran and Lebanon in the Last 500 Years* (London: I. B. Tauris, 2006), 1.
4. Ibid. See pp. 201–30.
5. John Esposito, *The Iranian Revolution: Its Global Impact* (Miami: Florida International University Press, 1990), 122.
6. Chehabi, *Distant Relations*, 24.
7. Esposito, *The Iranian Revolution*, 20.
8. Chehabi, *Distant Relations*, 25.
9. Esposito, *The Iranian Revolution*, 21.
10. Nikki R. Keddie, *Modern Iran: Roots and Results of Revolution* (New Haven, CT: Yale University Press, 2003), 168.
11. Esposito, *The Iranian Revolution*, 21.
12. The Shi'i religion is named for its first imam, Ali, the son-in-law and cousin of the Prophet. Those who follow Ali were said to be part of the party or (Shi'i) of Ali.
13. Chehabi, *Distant Relations*, 143.
14. Ibid.
15. Esposito, *The Iranian Revolution*, 125.

16. Jamal Sankari, *Fadlallah: The Making of a Radical Shi`ite Leader* (London: SAQI, 2005), 132.
17. Keddie, *Modern Iran*, 226–27.
18. Chehabi, *Distant Relations*, 155.
19. Esposito, *The Iranian Revolution*, 104.
20. Chehabi, *Distant Relations*, 155.
21. Keddie, *Modern Iran*, 148.
22. Vali Nasr, *The Shia Revival: How Conflicts within Islam Will Shape the Future* (New York: W. W. Norton, 2006), 164.
23. Chehabi, *Distant Relations*, 162.
24. Roschanack Shaery-Eisenlohr, *Shi`ite Lebanon: Transnational Religion and the Making of National Identities* (New York: Columbia University Press, 2008), 94.
25. Keddie, *Modern Iran*, 217.
26. Ervand Abrahamian, "The Guerrilla Movement in Iran, 1963–1977," *Middle East Research and Information Project Reports*, no. 86 (March–April 1980), 3.
27. Keddie, *Modern Iran*, 225.
28. Abbas W. Sammii, "The Shah's Lebanon Policy: The Role of SAVAK," *Middle Eastern Journal* 33, no. 1 (January 1997), 73.
29. Chehabi, *Distant Relations*, 183–84.
30. Shaery-Eisenlohr, *Shi`ite Lebanon*, 94–95.
31. Chehabi, *Distant Relations*, 183–84.
32. Ibid., 184.
33. Norton, *Amal and the Shi`a*, 41.
34. Ibid., 176.
35. Chehabi, *Distant Relations*, 177.
36. Norton, *Amal and the Shi`a*, 48.
37. Ruhollah Khomeini, *Islamic Government*, USA: *Studies in Islam and the Middle East*, http://majalla.org, accessed December 27, 2011.
38. Chehabi, *Distant Relations*, 187.
39. Afshon Ostovar, *Vanguard of the Imam: Religion, Politics, and Iran's Revolutionary Guards* (New York: Oxford University Press, 2016), 113.
40. Ruhollah Khomeini, "We Shall Confront the World with Our Ideology," *Middle East Research and Information Project Reports*, no. 88 (June 1980), 22.
41. Ibid.
42. Shaery-Eisenlohr, *Shi`ite Lebanon*, 34.
43. David C. Martin and John Walcott, *Best Laid Plans: The Inside Story of America's War against Terrorism* (New York: Harper & Row, 1988), 87.
44. Shanahan, *The Shi`a of Lebanon*, 154.
45. V. Nasr, *The Shia Revival*, 142.
46. Shaery-Eisenlohr, *The Shi`a of Lebanon*, 108.
47. Martin Walker, *Powers of the Press: Twelve of the World's Influential Newspapers* (New York: Pilgrim Press, 1983), 376.
48. Ibid., 350.
49. William A. Dorman and Mansour Farhang, *The U.S. Press and Iran: Foreign Policy and the Journalism of Deference* (Berkeley: University of California Press, 1987), 13.
50. Edward Said, *Covering Islam: How the Media and the Experts Determine How We See the Rest of the World* (New York: Vintage Books, 1997), 83.
51. See "The Influence of English-Language Press and Media" in chapter 1.
52. Bill, *The Eagle and the Lion*, 367.
53. Ibid., 184.
54. Ibid., 369.
55. Yahya R. Kamalipour, ed., *The U.S. Media and the Middle East: Image and Perception* (Westport, CT: Praeger, 1995), 93.
56. Philip Jacobson, "Torture in Iran," *Sunday Times*, January 19, 1975.
57. Fisk, *Pity the Nation*, 115.
58. "20 Killed as Police Open Fire in Iran," *Times* (London), January 11, 1978.

59. Keddie, *Modern Iran*, 225.
60. In the binary world of the Cold War, it was much easier for journalists and intellectuals to view everything through the lens of communism versus capitalism. The Islamic movements that grew to prominence in late twentieth century were not being considered outside that binary construct.
61. V. Nasr, *The Shia Revival*, 127.
62. Ibid., 129.
63. Ervand Abrahamian, *Khomeinism: Essays on the Islamic Republic* (Berkeley: University of California Press, 1993), 39.
64. Esposito, *The Iranian Revolution*, 104.
65. Robert Fisk, "Mystery of Missing Shia leader," *Times* (London), September 13, 1978.
66. Chehabi, *Distant Relations*, 198.
67. Bill, *The Eagle and the Lion*, 369.
68. Khosrow Fatemi, "The Iranian Revolution: Its Impact on Economic Relations with the United States," *International Journal of Middle East Studies* 12, no. 3 (November 1980): 303.
69. Ibid.
70. Paul Hoffmann, "However Slight, an Opposition Does Exist in Iran," *New York Times*, April 2, 1978.
71. Ibid.
72. Keddie, *Modern Iran*, 225.
73. Paul Hoffmann, "However Slight, an Opposition Does Exist in Iran," *New York Times*, April 2, 1978.
74. Christopher S. Wren, "The Moslem World Rekindles Its Militancy," *New York Times*, June 18, 1978.
75. The origins of the Wahhabi Movement of Islam lie in an eighteenth-century Saudi Arabian religious upheaval. Its teachings are based upon the purification of the Islamic faith. The Wahhabis reject the Sufi and the Shi`a Islamic sects because they hold too much veneration for human beings, such as the twelve imams who succeeded Muhammad. The Wahhabis believe that a greater emphasis should be placed on Allah and the teachings of the Quran. See V. Nasr, *The Shia Revival*, 96.
76. Christopher S. Wren, "The Moslem World Rekindles Its Militancy," *New York Times*, June 18, 1978.
77. Ibid.
78. See Bill, *The Eagle and the Lion*, 368–74. See also note on page 501. Dorman and Mansour, *The U.S. Press and Iran*, and Walker, *Powers of the Press*, 342–93, offer great critiques on press coverage of the shah and the Iranian Revolution.
79. Between November 6 and 19, 1978, there were numerous articles in the *New York Times* on Iran and the precarious position of the shah. They included reports from Hendrick Smith, Nicholas Gage, and Jonathan Randal—all reporting on the trouble and violence in Iran.
80. Eric Pace, "Islam's Most Devout Are the Most Devoutly Opposed," *New York Times*, November 12, 1978.
81. Ibid.
82. Ibid.
83. Youssef M. Ibrahim, "Teheran Is Decked with Symbols of Death," *New York Times*, December 3, 1978.
84. Edward Mortimer, "Iran's Brand of Islam a Religion of Opposition," *Times* (London), November 23, 1978.
85. Dorman and Farhang, *The U.S. Press and Iran*, 174.
86. R. W. Apple, "Iranian Unrest: Whose Influence at Work?," *New York Times*, December 8, 1978.
87. "Iran: Understanding the Shi'ite Islamic Movement," message from American embassy in Tehran to US State Department, February 3, 1978, Digital National Security Archive.
88. Ibid.
89. Said, *Covering Islam*, 89.
90. Discussion with Leslie Gelb, senior State Department and defense official, on October 12, 2010. About the value of the *New York Times* and intelligence sources, see also Fawaz A.

Gerges, "Islam and Muslims in the Mind of America: Influences on the Making of U.S. Policy," *Journal of Palestine Studies* 26, no. 2 (Winter 1997): 74.

91. "On the Ropes in Iran," *New York Times*, December 14, 1978.
92. Anthony Lewis, "Who Lost Iran?" *New York Times*, January 1, 1979.
93. Ibid.
94. Ibid.
95. Ibid.
96. Esposito, *The Iranian Revolution*, 20.
97. Edward Cody, "Khomeini Declares Indignant Rejection of Carter's Appeal," *Washington Post*, January 19, 1979. The article includes the following quote: "Whatever the composition of the provisional government, American officials clearly seem more at home with the Western-oriented parliamentary system Bakhtiar is trying to organize in Tehran. A French-educated intellectual, Bakhtiar almost certainly would be easier to deal with that the elderly holy man whose call for a return to traditional Moslem values has driven the shah abroad and transformed Iran from a dependable U.S. ally to a potentially unfriendly unknown."
98. James Allan, "Tired Shah Hints He Will Leave Iran," *Sunday Times*, January 7, 1979.
99. James Allan, "Bakhtiar flies to Khomeini," *The Telegraph*, January 1979.
100. R. W. Apple, "Immortal March to Fealty to Shah," *New York Times*, January 24, 1979.
101. Chehabi, *Distant Relations*, 204.
102. Liz Thurgood, "Khomeini Gives Libyans Cool Reception in Iran," *Guardian*, April 26, 1979.
103. Chehabi, *Distant Relations*, 156.
104. Ibid., 204.
105. Liz Thurgood, "Hit List Warning as Iran Leader Murdered," *Guardian,* May 3, 1979.
106. Robert Fisk, "Glint of New Steel in Iran Army," *Times* (London), November 27, 1979.
107. "Request for Moshem Slim to Collect Information on Lebanon and Syria from His Lebanese Contacts," secret CIA cable, September 26, 1979, Digital National Security Archive.
108. Bill, *The Eagle and the Lion*, 278.
109. R. W. Apple, "New Anti-American Wave Spreads in Iran," *New York Times*, January 22, 1979.
110. Mark Bowden, *Guest of the Ayatollah: The First Battle in America's War with Militant Islam* (New York: Grove Press, 2006), 93.
111. Ibid., 14.
112. Ibid., 90.
113. Said, *Covering Islam*, 83.
114. David MacGregor and Petger Pringle, "Free Blacks and Woman Hostages Says Khomeini," *Sunday Times*, November 18, 1979.
115. "Foreign Press Lectured on Why Iran Must Expel 'Time' Men," *Times* (London), December 18, 1979.
116. See "Iran and the American Press and Media" earlier in this chapter.
117. James Dickie, "Between the Devil and the Deep Red Sea," *Guardian*, November 26, 1979.
118. Robert Fisk, "Shia Militiamen in Beirut Clash with Palestinians," *Times* (London), May 29, 1980.
119. George Vecsey, "Iran's Moslem Sect Assessed by Experts," *New York Times*, November 18, 1979.
120. Ibid. See also Martin and Walcott, *Best Laid Plans*, 86
121. Said, *Covering Islam*, 103.
122. Edward Said, "Whose Islam," *New York Times*, January 29, 1979.
123. Said, *Covering Islam*, 104.
124. Dorman and Farhang, *The U.S. Press and Iran*, 180.
125. James Reston, "Counterrevolutions," *New York Times*, November 19, 1978.
126. Esposito, *The Iranian Revolution*, 31–32.
127. Janet Afary and Levin B. Anderson, *Foucault and the Iranian Revolution: Gender and the Seductions of Islamism* (Chicago: University of Chicago Press, 2005), 99.
128. Dorman and Farhang, *The U.S. Press and Iran*, 172.

129. "The Mystic Who Lit the Fire of Hatred," *Time*, January 7, 1980.
130. V. Nasr, *The Shia Revival*, 119.
131. Edward Cody, "Arab Shiites, Inspired by Iran, Show New Force in Lebanon, the Strength of Numbers," *Washington Post,* November 13, 1979.
132. Ibid.
133. "14 Die in Lebanon in Fighting Linked to a Murder," *New York Times*, July 28, 1980.
134. Loren Jenkins, "Lebanon's Shiites: A Major New Force," *Washington Post*, August 5, 1980.
135. Ibid.
136. "5 Killed in Shiite Clash in Lebanon," *New York Times*, April 16, 1980.
137. Ibid.
138. Nicholas Gage, "Lebanon's Shiites Growing Assertive against Palestinians," *New York Times*, June 11, 1980.
139. Ibid.
140. Said, *Covering Islam*, 101.

Chapter Four

The Israeli Invasion of Lebanon 1982

The 1982 Israeli invasion of Lebanon profoundly affected the dominant narrative of the Lebanese Shi`a. The results of the invasion helped to cement within the Shi`i community the desire for civil rights and the need for armed resistance against its adversaries. It also reinforced the importance of the transnational networks to support the community, as help for resistance to the Israeli occupation would come from Iran. The Shi`i community's representation in the English-language press and media initially marginalized the group's importance and then grudgingly attempted to explain the nature of the Shi`i resistance. Unfortunately, to describe the Lebanese Shi`a, the media employed terms like *terrorist* and *violent extremist* without adequate explanation or accurate description of the situation within Lebanon. This chapter explores the importance of the invasion to the Lebanese Shi`a and the news narrative constructed by the English-language press and media. The aftermath of the invasion resulted in a unified, more virulent Shi`i resistance to Israel and strong opposition to US policies in Lebanon.

At the beginning of 1980, the Lebanese Shi`i community was in a precarious position. Caught in a cauldron of armed militia groups and foreign forces, each with its own agenda, the Shi`a desire for change in Lebanon's society was palpable. More than ever, the community wanted security and equality. Divided internally about the best way to advance their interest in Lebanon, the Shi`a struggled between two different models.[1] One model suggested that the Shi`a could coexist within the Lebanese confessional system as long as they received equal consideration. Wrested from the "quietist" approach of Musa al-Sadr and other Shi`i clergy, supporters of this model were willing to work within the Lebanese governmental structure. The second model proffered lessons from the Iranian Revolution, which reinforced within the Lebanese Shi`i community the importance of transnational networks for overcoming obstacles in support of their civil rights drive. Based upon the Khomeini model, this group took a more strident approach to advancing Shi`i interests.[2] They saw the possibility of an Islamic government taking hold in Lebanon. The Israeli invasion of Lebanon in 1982 would have an overwhelming effect on this internal Shi`i debate and the community's approach to achieving security and equality.

There is no lack of scholarship on the 1982 Israeli invasion of Lebanon. Numerous articles and books cover many aspects of the invasion. One of the most heralded accounts is Ze'ev Schiff and Ehud Ya'ri's *Israel's Lebanon War*, which provides in-depth commentary on the motivation for and the results of the Israeli invasion.[3] Additionally, *Pity the Nation: The Abduction of Lebanon* by Robert Fisk provides a graphic portrayal of the events prior to and during the Israel invasion.[4] Fisk's book is particularly poignant. As a reporter for the *Times* (London), Fisk had unrivaled experience in reporting from Lebanon. In many instances, he was a primary source of information, witnessing firsthand the fighting and violence during the Israeli invasion. Although these books are useful, they, along with other journalist accounts from Thomas Friedman (*New York Times* correspondent) and Larry Pintak (CBS News correspondent), did not focus exclusively on the Lebanese Shi`a and the effects of the invasion on that community.[5] Yet Robert Fisk recorded in his book what he and other reporters had missed in covering the conflict in Lebanon. On the kidnapping of American University president David Dodge in Beirut after the Israeli invasion, Fisk said:

> None of us knew then how important Dodge's kidnap really was. We had still not heard of *Al-Jihad Al-Islami* —Islamic Jihad, or Holy War—and we had no idea that the Iranian revolution had penetrated so deeply into the aspirations of the Shia population in west Beirut. We had not connected the extraordinarily brave resistance of the Shia militiamen at Khalde with anything other than hatred of the invading Israelis.[6]

Prior to the Israeli invasion of 1982, a number of signs indicated that the Shi`i community in Lebanon had transformed itself to a much more activist entity. These events, not cloaked in mystery, indicated the growing tenacity and efficiency of Shi`i militia groups and political organizations, but the English-language press was unable to discern the importance of these occurrences before, during, and after the Israeli invasion.

PRELUDE TO THE ISRAELI INVASION OF 1982

By 1980, the civil war in Lebanon had exacerbated an already difficult situation for the Shi`i community. Amal, the Shi`i militia group in Lebanon, continued to assert itself against the Palestinians and other leftist militias that threatened their communities. In April 1980, the Amal militia clashed with leftist, pro-Iraqi militia forces in Lebanon after the Iraqi execution of Shi`i cleric Muhammad Baqr-al-Sadr. As covered previously, Baqr-al-Sadr was the prominent Shi`i cleric that opposed the Sunni Baathist regime in Iraq. Those Shi`i clerics and activists who fled Iraq when the Baathists assumed power now focused their enmity against Iraqi-supported militias in Lebanon. These actions further demonstrated that the Shi`i community in Lebanon would not remain passive when it perceived that the wider community was being harmed.[7]

In South Lebanon, Amal was continuously engaged, protecting Shi`i villagers from Palestinian and Christian militias. After the invasion of 1978, the Israelis installed a rogue Lebanese military officer, Major Saad Haddad, to protect their interests in the southern region of Lebanon. He received money, supplies, and training from the Israelis as he built a force used to suppress any Palestinian or "leftist Moslem" activities along the Israeli–Lebanese border.[8] Though loath to do so, when Palestinian fighters threatened Shi`i villages in South Lebanon, Amal joined forces with Major Saad Haddad's militia to attack PLO positions.[9] This was not a natural tendency for the Shi`a or Amal, but it signaled their growing tendency toward self-interest and self-empowerment. For years, Shi`a had served as members of leftist groups and Palestinian organizations. However, in the early 1980s the growing power of the Amal militia in the South Lebanon better served Shi`i basic needs.[10]

The cooperation between the Shi`a and Major Saad Haddad's militia was not an enduring alliance but one of convenience. Haddad would often express his support for the Shi`a but disparage their principle organization, Amal. In one of his weekly speeches on his radio station "Voice of Hope," he enjoined the Shi`a to support him: "We and the Shiites are in the same boat, facing the same danger."[11] He condemned the Amal movement and its leader Nabih Berri and encouraged the Shi`a to take up arms against the Syrians and the Palestinians. He even invoked the name of Musa al-Sadr, saying that Libya and its leader Muammar al-Qaddafi had al-Sadr killed and controlled Syria.[12] Haddad's request for Shi`i support belied his tactics of raiding Shi`i villages in concert with Israel and causing considerable damage to their towns.[13] The Shi`a were only useful to Major Haddad and other Christian leaders, such as the Bachir Gemayel, when they could use them against the Palestinians and Syrians. By the end of 1980, the environment in Lebanon was set for one of the most important events to shape the Shi`a in Lebanon— the Israeli invasion of 1982. The fighting and conflict between Palestinians and Christians strengthened Amal and fortified the Shi`i notion of resistance to outside forces.[14] However, it was the July 1982 Israeli invasion that galvanized the Shi`i community against any attempt to place them back into the realm of second-class citizens within the Lebanese state.

AMERICA, THE SHI`A, AND THE ISRAELI INVASION OF 1982

It is important to understand the connection between Israel's invasion of Lebanon and the Shi`i perception of America's intentions toward their community. The Shi`a of Lebanon were not the primary concern of American policymakers in the early 1980s.[15] However, American actions in Lebanon helped to shape the Shi`i narrative and caused many of the Lebanese Shi`a to believe that America was acting in concert with Israel against their interest. Prior to the 1982 Israeli invasion of Lebanon, the US government viewed the conflict through the prism of the Cold War.[16] The Soviet Union supported the PLO and Syria, and the United States was a strong ally of Israel. When fighting between various factions in Lebanon threatened to ignite an international conflict involving the United States and the Soviet Union, the US president engaged American envoy Phillip Habib to negotiate a cease-fire in the region.[17] The cease-fire that Habib arranged between the PLO and the Israelis along the southern border of Lebanon worked well from July 1981 to June 1982. However, a new Israeli administration desired to change the PLO's proximity to Israeli territory.

The new Israeli defense minister, Ariel Sharon, and the Israeli prime minister, Menachem Begin, wanted to rid Israel of threat from the PLO.[18] Although they had agreed upon a cease-fire with the PLO, Sharon and Begin looked for an excuse to attack the PLO infrastructure within Lebanon.[19] In June 1982, they had their excuse. Sharon and Begin viewed an attempted assassination of the Israeli ambassador to London on June 3 as an abrogation of the cease-fire agreement. In retrospect, the assassination attempt in London had nothing to do with the PLO. The Abu Nidal Organization (ANO) carried it out.

Abu Nidal, the mastermind of the assassination, was a founding member of Fatah but had split from the group years before the attack. He formed his own organization, ANO, which targeted members of the PLO he considered too moderate for the Palestinian cause. Arafat placed a death sentence on him for his actions against PLO members and Fatah. Nidal and his organization also freelanced, working not only against the PLO but also against other political entities as long as his group was funded and supported. The ANO was most likely fulfilling a contract from the Iraqi government to attack Israeli interests as a response to Israel's assault on an Iraqi nuclear facility.[20] Though Israeli intelligence was aware of the "disconnect" between the attack and the PLO, Prime Minister Begin was in no mood to make distinctions.[21] Israel launched a full-scale invasion of Lebanon as a response to the attack. Initially, Defense Minister Sharon told Prime Minister Begin and the Israeli cabinet that the attack into South Lebanon was to clear out PLO infrastructure in the southern region similar to the invasion that had taken place in 1978. Several days into the attacks, the Israelis had destroyed Syrian missile batteries in Lebanon, had directly confronted Syrian troops in combat, and were on the outskirts of Beirut. Although this had long been anticipated, perhaps no one but Sharon and his chief of defense staff knew the ultimate objective of the attack.[22]

For the Shi`a in Lebanon, the Israeli attack presented a dilemma. Unfortunately, the result of a military attack in South Lebanon was that much collateral damage was inflicted on Shi`i civilians, the majority of the population in the area. Yet there was always a hope that the Israeli action would free the Shi`a from Palestinian control of the region and lessen the impact of the Christian militia in the area.

As the leader of Amal, Nabih Berri put out the word to his militia not to oppose the invasion, but not all members heeded his command. The closer Israeli forces advanced toward Beirut, the stronger the resistance offered by some factions grew.[23] When a column of Israeli armored vehicles reached the town of Khalde in the southern Beirut, a combined group of Amal militiamen and PLO guerrillas halted them.[24] Another Shi`i force stopped an Israeli military advance coming from a beachfront suburb of Ouzai. The difference in the Shi`i reaction in the Beirut area can be attributed to their solidarity with the Palestinians, forged by the intense and often indiscriminate Israeli bombing of mixed Shi`a and Palestinian areas in and around the city.[25] Despite their resistance, Israel's conventional force proved much too powerful, and Shi`i forces could not halt their advance indefinitely.

Ariel Sharon's design on Lebanon was simple. He wanted to crush the PLO and make the organization ineffective.[26] In its place, he would install the Maronite Phalange as the head of the Lebanese government. The Phalange, grateful for Israeli help in ridding it of the Palestinians, would sign a peace treaty with Israel that allowed it to secure its northern borders from the PLO.[27] Nowhere in Sharon's planning had he considered the Shi`a.[28] Despite the fact that the Israelis had been raiding Shi`i villages in South Lebanon for over ten years, Israeli policymakers knew very little about what was happening in these communities.[29] The initial support for Israeli invaders by Shi`a in the south was ephemeral. A meeting of Shi`i clergy in Iran during the time of the invasion would have much greater consequences for the Israelis than did the initial support from local Shi`a.

Prior to the Israeli attack in June 1982, Lebanese Shi`i religious leaders travelled to Iran for a conference on the "dispossessed." The conference, sponsored by Medhi Hashemi (head of the Iranian Pasdaran Unit for Liberation Movements), was attended by Sayyid Fadlallah, Shaykh Shams-al Din, Raghib Harb, and Subhi al Tufaylia, the intellectual force of the Shi`i clergy in Lebanon.[30] These leaders appealed directly to the Iranian government for help in defending Lebanon from the Israeli invasion.[31] One of the reasons the Iranians agreed to help lay in the long-standing relationship between the Lebanese and Mostafa Chamran, one of Musa al-Sadr's closest confidants.

As covered previously Chamran left Lebanon in 1979 to take part in the Iranian Revolution and eventually became the country's Defense Minister. He was killed in 1981 during the Iran–Iraq War, but the Iranians never forgot their historic connection with the Lebanese.

With the Syrian government's agreement to facilitate the movement of Iranian troops and logistics into Lebanon, the Iranian support for the resistance began. Eventually, groups of Iranian Revolutionary Guard made their way into the Bekaa Valley and Baalbek and began training Shi`i fighters to resist the Israeli occupation. This initial cadre of trained Shi`i fighters, coupled with their support from the most prominent Shi`i clerics in Lebanon, began the formation of Hezbullah. Eventually, Hezbullah would offer the fiercest resistance to Israeli and American interests within Lebanon.[32]

The Israeli invasion into Lebanon convinced many of the Shi`a in the country that the United States and Israel colluded to invade their country.[33] After all, American manufactured aircraft and equipment operated by the Israelis were involved in the violence, and American ambassador Phillip Habib, tasked to work out a cease-fire between the Palestinians and the Israelis, proved ineffective at stopping the Israeli onslaught. For the Shi`a it was a matter of fairness. The United States condemned resistance attacks on the Israelis while failing to call on the Israelis to adhere to United Nations Resolution 425, which called for their complete withdrawal from Lebanon.[34]

Ambassador Habib worked tirelessly with the governments of Israel, Syria, and Lebanon to broker a deal for a cease-fire and the evacuation of the PLO. He was also determined to ensure the construction of a strong, meaningful government in Beirut capable of controlling the entire country. Toward that end, Habib met with the leader of the Phalange, Bachir Gemayel, because he believed that he was the strongest and best hope for building a strong central government in Lebanon.[35] In his efforts to establish a new and more effective government, Habib conducted deliberations with the sitting President Sarkis. Habib convinced the president to set up the National Salvation Committee, whose goals were to stop the fighting between Israel and the PLO and to start the negotiation process for a peace settlement.[36] Seeking participation of the major sects within Lebanon, Lebanese President Sarkis reached out to the Amal leader, Nabih Berri, to join in the conference. Berri accepted his offer, but this infuriated other members of Amal.[37]

Berri's decision to participate in the conference exacerbated a long-simmering division within the ranks of Amal. A number of the more religiously oriented members of Amal sought to "Islamicize" the movement.[38] Among these key leaders were Hussein Musawi and Hassan Nasrallah. These two clerics would later become associated with the founding of Hezbullah ("the party of God"). In June 1982 this group of disillusioned Amal members left the party and moved to Baalbek, where members of the Iranian Revolutionary Guard trained Shi`i resistance fighters. The new group, calling itself

Islamic Amal,[39] eschewed the notion of Shi`i secularism. They fully endorsed the teachings of Ayatollah Khomeini and his ideal of an Islamic state under his principal of *vilāyat-i faqīh* (or guardianship by the clerics).[40]

A number of other contentious issues existed between Amal and the newly founded group in Baalbek. Islamic Amal rejected any accommodation with Israel due to its invasion of Lebanon. The group also vehemently opposed Bachir Gemayel. Its members viewed him as an Israeli collaborator and never forgot his involvement in the expulsions of thousands of Shi`a from Nab`a in 1978.[41] This group also viewed America as an adversary. America's failure to stop the Israeli invasion and the continued destruction wrought by the Israelis in Beirut supported the view that America was complicit in Israel's desire to dominate Lebanon.[42]

The fracture between Amal and this new group of Shi`i activists would have important consequences for the Lebanese Shi`i community. In the late 1980s, Amal and its scion, Islamic Amal (Hezbullah), battled in the suburbs of Beirut to establish which group would dominate in Lebanon. However, in the summer and fall of 1982 it was Islamic Amal, with the help of the Iranian Revolutionary Guard, that provided Lebanese Shi`a its most potent means of resisting the Israeli occupation. The military and religious indoctrination that the Shi`a received in Baalbek proved instrumental in fortifying their resistance to the Israeli occupation.[43]

As the Israeli occupation of Lebanon continued, Amal's tolerance for Israeli actions diminished as well. Israel confiscated weapons from members of Amal and formed their own home-guard militia made up of poor, disaffected Shi`i men, whom most of the townspeople held in disregard.[44] Amal also despised Israel's economic policy in South Lebanon. After the invasion, Israel introduced inexpensive goods and produce to the area, devastating the region's economy.[45] The Amal leader, Nabih Berri, warned the Israelis that "the Shi`ites will be the new Palestinians and will become Israel's worst enemies if the Israeli army remains in South Lebanon."[46] Unfortunately, the Israelis did not heed Berri's warning.

On September 23, 1982, Bachir Gemayel, the president-elect of Lebanon whom the Israelis had courted for several years and had counted on for securing a peace treaty, was assassinated by a bomb blast.[47] This event further complicated the situation in Lebanon for the Israelis and began a chain reaction that directly affected the Shi`i community in Lebanon. After Gemayel's assassination, Israeli forces reacted quickly to enter the predominantly Palestinian and Shi`i area of West Beirut. Prior to his death, the Israelis had agreed with the United States not to enter the predominantly Muslim areas of West Beirut.[48] It was known that family members of the Palestinian fighters who had been evacuated by the multinational force were still living in West Beirut. Phillip Habib, the American negotiator for the evacuation of the PLO, had guaranteed the safety of these civilians once the

Palestinian fighters left.[49] Unbeknownst to the United States, the Israelis had concluded an agreement with Bachir for his Phalangists to clean out what they thought were pockets of Palestinian guerrillas in the area.[50] With his death, the Israelis took it on their own to abrogate their assurances to the United States and attack what they believed was the remaining PLO structure in Lebanon.[51] Although American officials and diplomats could never ascertain the source of the Israeli belief that thousands of Palestinian fighters remained in the camps of West Beirut, Defense Minister Sharon seemed convinced that many PLO fighters had stayed behind.[52] Unfortunately, Shi`i families had lived in West Beirut beside Palestinian refugees for more than a decade, and many of them inhabited the refugee camps Sabra and Chatila. When the Israelis entered West Beirut, they surrounded Sabra and Chatila, the consequences of which would be devastating for Shi`i camp members.

Israel allowed Christian militias into the camps. Many of these militia members, convinced that the PLO had been behind Bachir's assassination, sought revenge for his death. Still others were seeking revenge for PLO atrocities committed against Christians earlier in the civil war. The outcome was predictable. The number killed in camps has never been accurately verified. The report by Israel's Kahan Commission,[53] tasked with an inquiry into the massacre, placed the total between 700 and 800.[54] Palestinian and Lebanese civil defense forces place the number at 1,239 dead and missing.[55] Those killed were mostly unarmed old men, women, and children—not the fighters that Sharon had told the Americans were there. Among the dead were a number of Shi`i families.[56]

Members of the Shi`i community were horrified by the loss of so many innocents. America, which had guaranteed the safety of Palestinian civilians when Yasir Arafat left, now felt obligated to do something to save face. On September 29, 1982, by the order of the president of the United States, American Marines reentered Beirut as part of a multinational force. This force was supposed to allow the Lebanese government the time and space to reconstitute itself and to "assist the efforts of the Lebanese government to assure the safety of persons in the area and bring an end to violence."[57] However, the Shi`a were determined not to allow themselves to be subjugated by the Maronite minority or to continue to live under the thumb of an Israeli occupation. Their recent history in Lebanon had informed their community that only their own institutions could protect them.

When the Lebanese government tried to reconstitute itself under the leadership of the newly elected president Amin Gemayel, Shi`i opposition to his rule persisted. In January 1983, Nabih Berri, leader of Amal, demanded that Gemayel's government disband the Phalange militia.[58] He did not trust the government of Amin Gemayel to form an integrated Lebanese army with Muslims and Christians. He believed that Gemayel intended to keep the Phalange as the dominant force in Lebanon. He also did not trust the negotiation between Gemayel's government and the Israelis to work out an equitable peace settlement.⁵⁹ Any possibility of accommodation among Israel, the newly formed Lebanese government, and Amal was gone by the beginning of 1983.

Initially, the Shi`i resistance to the Israeli occupation of South Lebanon was minimal. Individuals and small groups engaged in minor protests and acts of defiance, boycotted Israeli products, and sometimes attacked the homes of Israeli collaborators.⁶⁰ As cadres of Islamic Amal and other Shi`i groups increased their activities, the casualty count increased. By early 1983, Israel was experiencing an average of one casualty per day.⁶¹

By the start of 1983, the Israeli invasion of Lebanon had gone terribly awry. The Israeli effort to destroy the PLO and install the Maronite Phalange had failed. Bachir Gemayel, the leader Israel had hoped to install as the president of Lebanon, was dead from an assassin's bomb. Any of the goodwill the Israelis had garnered in their initial invasion evaporated in their siege of Beirut and the massacre of civilians at two Palestinian refugee camps on the outskirts of Beirut. The Kahan Commission's report on the aftermath of a massacre of Palestinian and Shi`i civilians at the refugee camps of Sabra and Chatila implicated Ariel Sharon for his complicity in the tragedy, and he was forced to give up his position as minister of defense.⁶² The peace treaty with Lebanon, which Israel envisioned after its invasion, had also fallen through. Israel gradually retreated from areas around Beirut and the Shouf Mountains to what it considered positions that were more defensible, south of the Latani River. However, in South Lebanon resistance by various Shi`i factions continued to increase.

Prominent Shi`i clergy such as Imam Ragheb Harb in South Lebanon were targeted by the Israelis in an attempt to break the resistance.⁶³ This same Imam attended the "conference on the dispossessed" in Iran prior to the Israeli invasion. He condemned the Israeli invasion, and now urged members of his mosque and other Shi`a not to cooperate with the Israeli authorities.⁶⁴ In March 1983, the Israelis arrested him. He had not heeded their warning and, instead, turned his local mosque into the resistance headquarters for the area.⁶⁵ In February 1984, Harb was assassinated in his village of Jibsheet; the culprits were widely believed to be the Israeli security services.⁶⁶ His death was used as another rallying point for the Shi`i resistance. His picture appeared throughout Shi`i neighborhoods as a martyr for their cause (see figure 4.1). For anyone looking at the poster and reading the caption, it was obvious that Harb's death provided a rallying focus for the cause of resistance in the Shi`i community in Lebanon.

> The turning point for most Shi`a in Lebanon was the incident in Nabatiyah, described at the beginning of this book. In their minds, the belief that the Israelis would perpetrate a direct assault on one of the most important symbols

Figure 4.1. Poster of Ragheb Harb. Translation: "Hail to thee, oh leader (lit: shaykh) of the martyrs, who are worthy of following." (These martyrs are, literally, "the wellsprings of the path.") Trans. Nathan Toronto. Reproduced by permission of American University of Beirut Libraries, Archives and Special Collections.

of their religion helped to further radicalize the community in Lebanon.[67] The ideological foundations of Hezbullah flourished. Pictures of Ayatollah Khomeini appeared in villages in the South announcing the arrival of a movement that derived more of its influence from Iran rather than the more secular Amal.[68] The more the Israelis attempted to suppress the violence in South Lebanon, the more the Shi`i resistance flourished.[69]

The United States and other Western powers did not escape the wrath of the resistance. Groups such as Hezbullah viewed the multinational force sent into Lebanon as supporting the Israeli occupation. In September 1983, when the American troops supported the Lebanese army against Shi`a and Druze forces in the Shouf Mountains, their neutrality was unquestionably lost.[70] In October 1983, Shi`i radical groups targeted the French and American troops with suicide attacks similar to the ones that had taken place in South Lebanon.

In summary, the Israeli invasion of Lebanon in 1982 helped to focus the energy of the Shi`a and further radicalize portions of the community toward armed resistance and political empowerment. The Shi`a viewed America as complicit with the Israeli invasion because America failed to stop the Israeli onslaught, and because many American policymakers openly supported Israel. Israel showed very little consideration for the Shi`a plight in Lebanon and did not support changing the Christian-dominated government in Lebanon. The Iranian Revolutionary Guard's support further helped to radicalize the Shi`a of Lebanon and supported their resistance against the Israelis and the Multinational Force. The English-language press and media's representation of the Shi`a of Lebanon during this time failed to convey many of the notions previously outlined.

THE ENGLISH-LANGUAGE PRESS PRIOR TO THE ISRAELI INVASION OF LEBANON

In *Fateful Triangle: The United States, Israel, and the Palestinians*, Noam Chomsky, world-renowned linguist, scholar, and political commentator, devotes a substantive chapter on the Israeli invasion of Lebanon.[71] Chronicling the lack of coverage of Israeli attacks in South Lebanon by the American press prior to the invasion, Chomsky outlined how the American press ignored Israeli designs on Lebanon prior to the invasion.[72] In fact, Israel had long supported the Christian Maronites in Lebanon as a buffer against the Palestinians and Syrians. Prior to the invasion, Israel continued its by then very public support of the Christian militia groups. *New York Times* journalist David Shipler reported that Israeli Defense Minister Sharon had met with Phalange leader Bachir Gemayel early in 1982.[73] In May 1982, *Times* (London) reporter Christopher Walker revealed that the Israeli prime minister acknowledged publicly that the government of Israel had supplied up to fifty-five million British pounds' worth of aid to Christian militias in Lebanon since 1977.[74]

That investment in money and supplies supported Bachir Gemayel and the Maronite militia. However, a good portion of the aid went to Major Haddad of the Southern Lebanese Army (SLA) to fight the PLO and suppress Shi'a in South Lebanon.[75] Unfortunately, Shipler and Walker never explained what Israeli support to Christian militia groups meant for the Shi`i community: more nefarious actions by Christian militias also hurt the Lebanese Shi`a.

Prior to the Israeli invasion, with the support of Israeli money and logistics, Christian militias conducted operations against the Syrians and the Shi`a in order to maintain hegemony in Lebanon. Christian militia groups deliberately targeted Syrian forces within Lebanon by unconventional means. In February 1982 the *New York Times* recorded a series of car bombs against Syrian targets in predominantly Shi`i neighborhoods, which killed a number of civilians. The report linked Christian militias to the attack, but the *New York Times* never used the word *terrorism* to describe the incidents.[76] In contrast, later English-language press reports frequently used the word *terrorism* to describe car bombings perpetrated by suspected Shi`i resistance groups.

Almost simultaneously with the car-bomb explosions in Shi`i areas in Beirut, Palestinian militias harassed and targeted Shi`i groups. News articles and editorial coverage in the *New York Times* in April 1982 emphasized that Shi`i militia groups had gained new confidence and assertiveness in the face of the other militia groups in Lebanon, particularly the Palestinian Liberation Organization (PLO).[77] In fact, the Shi`i militia, Amal, was fighting on many fronts. In addition to the PLO, they fought Christian, communist, and leftist militias in order to assert their own power. Despite those varied conflicts, the *New York Times* focus on the Shi`a-Palestinian fight would set up the construct that the Shi`a had a natural affinity for Israel's agenda in Lebanon, the destruction of the PLO. This was not the case. The Lebanese Shi`a had a long and unpleasant memory of a previous Israeli invasion of South Lebanon.

A little more than three years earlier, the Lebanese Shi`a suffered an Israeli invasion of South Lebanon. During this earlier invasion, the *New York Times* failed to highlight the horrors that befell the Shi`a. In March 1978, one of the most compelling stories affecting the Shi`a unfolded after the initial Israeli incursion. Christian militiamen allied with the Israelis, who had been fighting Palestinian guerrillas in South Lebanon, forced a large group of Shi`i men, women, and children into a mosque in the village of Khiam. Under the eyes of Israeli officers, the Christian militia machine-gunned all of them to death.[78] Despite the horror, this story did not warrant a front-page headline in the *New York Times*; rather, it was covered on page 12, with just one small paragraph. The article's headline "Israelis Ponder Lebanon" failed to draw any major attention to the tragedy. It was not until the thirteenth paragraph of the story that the article mentioned that Christian militiamen killed seventy civilians, including women and children, in a mosque in Khiam.[79] The term *massacre* was never used when referring to the incident, nor was there any mention that the victims were Shi`a. Contrast that report to the report of newspaperman Jonathan Randal, who highlighted the tragedy in a March 27 *Washington Post* article entitled "Christian Militiamen Kill 70 in Lebanese Mosque." In the closing comment of the article, Randal emphasized that there was no equivalence in scale when it came to measuring Shi`a lives and Israeli lives: "And whatever the sense of outrage at the Palestinian commando carnage two weeks ago on the Haifa-Tel Aviv road statistically it killed less than half the number murdered in a Khiam Mosque."[80] The massacre of seventy Shi`a in Lebanon went underreported, while the death of thirty-three Israelis was cause for a massive invasion.

Despite that horrific memory of the Israeli incursion of 1978, a number of Shi`i villagers in South Lebanon hoped that the new Israeli invasion would rid the area of the Palestinian fighters and allow them to resume their more peaceful agrarian lifestyle.[81] However, not long after the invasion, Israeli actions demonstrated to most of the Shi`a that the Israelis would never be helpful in changing their situation for the better. This was not the initial sense conveyed in the *New York Times* or the American mass media.

Two months prior to the invasion, in April 1982, reports from *London Times* correspondents indicated that the strategic landscape was changing. Israeli president Menachem Begin's second administration was preparing to act forcefully against in the PLO in Lebanon in order to change the status quo.[82] However, in the Israeli preparation for the invasion, the Lebanese Shi`a did not factor into his invasion calculation.[83] In South Lebanon the Shi`a had a different sense of the situation. In a report in early May 1982, *Times* (London) reporters captured Lebanese Shi`i preparation for the coming conflict, noting that Amal militia members were providing weapons training to young Shi`i children in South Lebanon. The report restated that Amal had fought on many different sides during the Lebanese conflict.[84] Reporter Robert Fisk also sent detailed reports to the paper concerning the mood and the condition of the Shi`a in South Lebanon. In one such report, Fisk stated, "stirred by the disappearance of Imam Moussa Sadr, their most vociferous clerical leader, the Shia militias—now combined under the name of Amal—demanded political power insisting that the Lebanese authorities in Beirut pay more attention to their traditionally neglected sect."[85] Fisk captured the voice of the Shi`a, reflecting that the community would no longer be quiet when unfairly treated and ignored by the Lebanese government or others in Lebanese society. His report also reflected that the Lebanese Shi`a were prepared to use force to defend and assert their rights.

However, few in the Western media were able to extrapolate that report to the fiery resistance that Shi`i fighters would unleash against the IDF during its invasion and occupation.

COVERING THE INVASION IN THE ENGLISH-LANGUAGE PRESS AND MEDIA

The *New York Times* and the American media as a whole provided extensive coverage of the 1982 Israeli invasion. *New York Times* editorial writer William Safire hailed the invasion as "The Liberation of Lebanon."[86] Yet the Shi`i community in Lebanon perceived that Israeli actions were not meant to be a quick operation. Early reports of the invasion by the *New York Times* suggested that Amal (the Shi`i militia) and the Israelis were working in cooperation against the Palestinian guerrillas.[87] Although Nabih Berri, the leader of Amal, initially told his fighters not to resist the Israelis, not all members of his group heeded his instructions. As covered previously, fighting by Amal members against Israeli forces during their approach to Beirut was intense, but the *New York Times* did not cover it.[88]

Of all the representations of the Lebanese Shi`a during the initial invasion, Robert Fisk and the *Times* (London) provided the most accurate. In reporting on the Shi`i resistance against the Israelis, Fisk recorded that hundreds of Palestinian guerrillas and Shi`i militiamen had died resisting Israeli attacks on Beirut.[89] Fisk commented that only the PLO and the Shi`i Amal militia had put up a serious fight against the Israelis. The American press corps, who wrote about the cooperation of the Israelis and the Amal militia, did not cover that fact.[90] Having spent a good amount of time in Lebanon, Fisk was aware that the Shi`a would become problematic for the Israelis, although many Western media outlets were not reporting these problems during the initial stages of the conflict.

The *New York Times* coverage of the war focused on the forces of the PLO, Syrians, and the Israelis. Casualties mounted, particularly among civilians, as the Israelis advanced toward the major cities in Lebanon. In particular, the Israeli siege of the city of Beirut and Yasir Arafat's PLO headquarters drew considerable attention from the *New York Times* and American media outlets. As the siege continued and the death toll of innocent civilians mounted, considerable controversy arose about the *New York Times* negative image of the Israeli invasion.[91] American Jewish lobbyists and Israeli supporters were adamant that the *New York Times* and other American media outlets were not presenting an accurate view of the fight in Lebanon.[92] However, no corresponding voice in the American press and media pointed out the lack of Lebanese Shi`a coverage or that the *New York Times* either ignored or distorted their image. The Shi`i population suffered dearly in the southern suburbs of Beirut, but they had no significant lobby in America to focus the media's attention on their issues.

After the invasion, it did not take long for a new, more virulent form of resistance to spring up among most of the Shi'i population. In part, Nabih Berri's tacit willingness to deal with the invaders was responsible: Amal's initial agreement to participate in the reconciliation process in Lebanon and its offer to discuss a peace treaty with Israel induced a number of religiously indoctrinated members of Amal to leave the organization. Hussein Musawi, a key member of Amal's executive committee, abruptly left a meeting in June 1982 because of Nabih Berri's willingness to participate in the American-sponsored National Salvation Council.[93] He and other members of the council immediately set up the group Islamic Amal, the precursor to Hezbullah. The group moved its headquarters to Baalbek and joined with a cadre of Iranian Revolutionary Guard members for training and indoctrination in resistance against the Israeli occupation.[94]

The changes in the Shi`i community should have been apparent to observers of the situation in Lebanon. However, only Fisk's *Pity the Nation* (1990) captured the seismic shift that the formation of Islamic Amal caused in the landscape of the Lebanese Shi`a. Fisk and an Associated Press reporter traveled to Baalbek and witnessed the buildup of the Iranian Revolutionary Guard forces and their indoctrination of Lebanese Shi`i fighters.[95] After American military involvement in Lebanon, Fisk would comment that there should have been no illusions by the Americans that they had no enemies in Lebanon. Placards and banners in Baalbek denounced Israeli and American imperialism and exhorted the Lebanese to find salvation through martyrdom.[96] However, Fisk did not record his observation as to what was happening in Baalbek until he later revealed it in his book.

In August 1982, Hussein Musawi (one of the founders of Islamic Amal) traveled to Iran to obtain the blessing and support of Ayatollah Khomeini for his movement. An Iranian Republic News Agency (IRNA)[97] dispatch from Tehran covered the meeting and became available through the BBC *Summary of World* broadcast later that month.[98] Yet the British press and media were unable to ascertain the significance of this event for the Lebanese Shi'a and the Western world. Soon after the blessing was received from Khomeini, Islamic Amal sent cadre members to South Lebanon to link up with spontaneous resistance groups.[99] Even though Fisk witnessed the hallmarks of the resistance movement, not even he could predict the fury that this resistance would unleash.

As discussed previously, a segment of the Southern Lebanese Shi`a expressed initial euphoria at the prospect that the Israeli invasion would rid the area of Palestinian fighters. However, this was short lived. The Shi`a soon recognized that the Israelis showed no intention of leaving the area. In July 1982, the *Guardian* reported that all was not well in South Lebanon after the

Israeli invasion. The Lebanese Shi`a, who the *Guardian* reported had fought hardest against the Israeli invasion, were uneasy about Israel's ultimate intentions in Lebanon.[100] As the Israelis attempted to incorporate these Shi`a into the militia of Saad Haddad (as a buffer against the Palestinians), an even stronger backlash to the Israeli occupation occurred. Islamic Amal instigated this reaction because of their belief that Israel and America were their mortal enemies. Unfortunately, the English-language media were unable to discern or interpret these trends in the Shi`i community. Instead, the papers chose to cover the supposed benefits of the Israeli occupation.

In October 1982, the *Times* (London) reported some of the economic consequences of the War between Lebanon and Israel. The paper related that Israeli goods were flooding Lebanese markets, especially in the southern region. Despite a contradictory article in August about Lebanese complaints about the dumping of Israeli goods into their fragile economic market, the October article contended that this economic development was a positive result of the invasion.[101] The article did not report that the dumping of cheap Israeli goods into the Lebanese market was having disastrous economic effects for poor Shi`i farmers. They could no longer sell their agricultural goods in Lebanon for a profit and were prohibited from exporting any of their goods into Israel. As a result, antagonism grew between the Shi`i community in South Lebanon and the Israelis.

More indications of Shi`a discontent and resistance appeared in the British media and press. In November 1982, the *Times* (London) reported that five hundred well-armed Muslims, seeking an Islamic government, seized a Lebanese government building in Baalbek in the Bekaa Valley. Although the report linked the group takeover to the Amal militia and supporters of Ayatollah Khomeini, it did not differentiate this group as "Islamic Amal," an organization quite different in orientation and methodology.[102] Islamic Amal had already perpetrated one of its most successful martyrdom operations (and its first) against the Israelis. Earlier that month, an Islamic Amal operative blew up an Israeli military headquarters in Tyre, Lebanon. Ironically, the same *Times* (London) article that discussed the building takeover in Baalbek reported that an Israeli military inquiry had mistakenly established that the explosion, which destroyed the Tyre headquarters, resulted from faulty construction. It would take the Israelis several months to conclude, or to admit, that the explosion was the work of Shi`i resistance fighters.

At the same time, the *New York Times* finally began to focus seriously on the new Shi`i resistance organization's growing power in Lebanon. It also covered the seizure of the town hall of Baalbek, Lebanon, by members of Islamic Amal.[103] The article went on to report that five hundred Iranian troops stationed in the area had come to Lebanon to assist the Syrian Army and the Palestinian Liberation Organization to defend eastern Lebanon from the Israeli army. In fact, a cadre of Iranian Revolutionary Guard was there to train and, to a lesser extent, participate in the Shi`i resistance movement against the Israelis.[104] Ten days prior to the report, the *New York Times* covered the blast at Israeli headquarters that killed 141 people, over 90 of them Israeli.[105] Like the British report, the initial coverage in the *New York Times* did not categorize this as a Shi`a or Islamic Amal attack. The article suspected that a new group called the Lebanese Resistance might have been the culprit but quoted an Israeli military spokesman saying that the PLO was suspected of the attack.[106] By November 22, the *New York Times* joined the British press in quoting an Israeli military official attributing the explosion to a leaking bottle of gas that ignited. This was not the case. The explosion was the first martyrdom operation for Islamic Amal. It was perpetrated by a seventeen-year-old Shi`i villager, Ahmad Qassir, who sped into the Israeli military installation and exploded at the headquarters of the Israeli forces in South Lebanon. Islamic Amal was willing to forgo acknowledging responsibility for the attack based upon security considerations.[107]

The *New York Times* failed to query the veracity of the Israeli investigation and, as such, the paper missed an opportunity to gain greater insight into the Shi`i resistance movement in Lebanon. Five months later, a Shi`i organization would claim credit for another attack—this time against an American target. Although Shi`i resistance groups focused their ire on Israeli and American targets, Britain's military involvement in Lebanon after the Israeli invasion ensured continued media interest in the area.

In December 1982, Great Britain agreed to send a small contingent of military peacekeepers to join the Multinational Force (MNF) in Lebanon.[108] Yet a foreboding article appeared in the British press regarding the American presence. Robert Fisk sensed the peril for American involvement. That same month he penned an article for the *Times* (London) explaining that American involvement in Lebanon looked more open-ended and potentially more dangerous.[109] Two months later, in a February 7, 1983, article, Fisk warned again of the danger of America's involvement with the Israeli occupation of Lebanon.[110] On April 18, 1983, as if responding to Fisk's admonition, a truck laden with explosives pulled up alongside the American Embassy. The ensuing blast killed a number of Americans and Lebanese. Of particular consequence for the Americans was that the entire CIA Middle East contingent was meeting in the facility. They were all killed.[111] Hours later, a phone call to a Lebanese newspaper claimed that Islamic Jihad—the military arm of Islamic Amal, the group formed by Musawi in response to the Israeli invasion—had perpetrated the attack.

In covering the bombing of the American embassy, the *New York Times* reported that Islamic Jihad claimed responsibility for the bombing.[112] The paper then traced Islamic Jihad to the faction Islamic Amal, which the paper said was created eight years prior by Imam Musa al-Sadr and a disciple of Ayatollah Khomeini.[113] This statement is false. Musa al-Sadr had founded

Amal, not Islamic Amal. The groups were entirely different entities and, while its agenda was in line with the teachings of Khomeini, Islamic Amal consisted of disaffected members of Amal. Perpetrated by an Islamic Jihad suicide bomber, the attack against the embassy sent a distinct message to America that a faction of Lebanese Shi`a was committed to driving out all Western participation in Lebanon. After eight years of covering Lebanon, the *New York Times* was only now beginning to understand how this community had transformed from a quietist group to an activist, militant population willing to act decisively and violently against those who it perceived acted against its interest.

One of the US goals in Lebanon was to establish strong central governmental institutions. This included the Lebanese Army. However, the Shi`a in Lebanon viewed the Lebanese Army as an instrument of the Christian power used to exert control over them and inhibit their drive for civil rights. As the revamped, American-trained Lebanese army tried to take control of areas predominantly inhabited by Lebanese Shi`a in West Beirut, members of the Shi`i militia reacted fiercely. Thomas Friedman captured the resentment that had built up against the government of Amin Gemayel. In his report he stated:

> The fact that Shiite militiamen would attack the army was also a reflection of mounting discontent and resentment among West Beirut's Sunni and Shiite Moslems. They have increasingly come to feel the President Amin Gemayel's government has been applying laws and imposing security measures on the predominantly Moslem western half of the capital that it is not doing on the Christian eastern half, where Phalangist militia still operates freely.[114]

What Friedman failed to recognize was that there was no "mounting discontent."[115] The discontent with the Lebanese government had peaked within the Shi`i community. With the influx of trained Lebanese Shi`i militia from Iranian Revolutionary Guard, they were better able to act in response to that discontent with force.

Although Friedman captured the discontent of the Shi`a in the previous article, *New York Times* reporting on the mood of the Lebanese Shi`i was inconsistent. On September 2, 1983, an article appeared in the *New York Times* voicing concerns about threats to US Marines and the Multinational Force.[116] The article quoted Amal leader Nabih Berri saying that the Marines had turned into a fighting force against Muslims in Lebanon.[117] This statement held ominous connotations for the Marines. Yet, four days later a report by E. J. Dionne Jr. in the *New York Times* praised the Shi`i militia Amal for not fighting the Lebanese army, being supported by the Marines and American Special Forces, in a poor, predominantly Muslim town just outside of Beirut.[118] Dionne saw this move as a possible indicator of a settlement in the Lebanese Civil War.[119] His predictions about a settlement based upon Shi'i actions proved inaccurate.

By the end of September 1983, it became clearer to *New York Times* reporters that all was not well in the Shi'i areas around Beirut. Instead of transforming the situation in Lebanon into a stable peaceful environment, the Israeli invasion had unleashed a number of destructive forces within the country. Their backing of the government of Amin Gemayel, which opposed any real political reform, forced the Shi'a to resist.[120] The Shi'i town that reporter E. J. Dionne had praised for its restraint was now engulfed in a fierce battle pitting Lebanese troops against the Amal militia.[121] There were multiple factions involved in the fighting in Lebanon. *New York Times* reporter Thomas Friedman summed up the situation in the following manner.

> The gun battles in the southern suburbs illustrated how complicated and explosive the Lebanese conflict has become. At one point Friday night the Lebanese Army was fighting with the Shiites, who were being supported with artillery fire by Druse militiamen dug into Shuweifat, adjacent to the battlefield. Christian Phalangist militiamen then joined the battle against the Amal forces and the Druse, and the Syrians started lobbing shells and rockets into the area.[122]

On September 25, 1983, a *New York Times* editorial by Fouad Ajami offered another ominous warning to Americans and American policymakers. The editorial entitled "America Can't Bring Sense to Lebanon" warned that unless the government of Amin Gemayel made accommodations with the Shi'a, Druse, and the Palestinians, it was wishful thinking that American military presence offered anything more than a temporary lease on the long history of violence in the country.[123] This was one of the rare instances of clarity in the American press regarding Lebanon and the Shi'a. Ajami highlighted warning signs to his readers, yet—despite his caution about the bombing of the embassy in April 1983 and the other violent incidents—few in the American government or media were interpreting these events correctly.

Shi'i resistance coverage grew more prominent in the British press and media after the explosion of the American embassy. In October 1983 the *Economist* focused an article on the rise of the Shi'a in the Levant. The article acknowledged that the Shi'a composed the largest community in Lebanon and that Amal played a significant role in Lebanon's political stability.[124] The *Economist* article outlined the split that occurred within the Amal militia group, and that the more radical group, Islamic Amal, supported the notion of an Islamic government in Lebanon. This group, the article stated, was more supportive of the ideals of Iran and Ayatollah Khomeini, as opposed to Amal, a strictly Lebanese Shi'i movement. More violence came to the Shi'i community in mid-October: this time an incident perpetrated by the IDF galvanized almost all Shi'a in resisting the Israeli occupation. However, the difference in the Nabatiyah incident's coverage by the British press and the American press was significant.

The incident in Nabatiyah in October 1983, described in the opening of this book, was the most serious clash between the Israelis and the Shi`a of South Lebanon. Thousands of Lebanese Shi`a gathered in the town of Nabatiyah to commemorate Ashura, one of the defining events in the Shi`i religion. During the height of the ceremony, a convoy of Israeli military vehicles attempted to proceed through the ceremony. The participants, livid with rage that the Israelis would disregard their religious observance, began to throw rocks at the Israeli vehicles. The soldiers, acting with force, shot and killed two of the worshippers.

Reporter Robert Fisk actually went to Nabatiyah to investigate what happened. In the article he wrote for the *Times* (London) and later in his book *Pity the Nation*, he debunked an Israeli report on the incident and constructed a different representation of what happened. Fisk did not doubt that the townspeople had pelted the Israeli convoy with rocks: "Thousands of men and women turned on the Israelis after they tried to drive a convoy through a column of young men celebrating the Feast of Ashura."[125] Fisk actually talked to eyewitnesses of the Israeli incident and looked at film footage of what had happened. Fisk ascertained that an initial Israeli claim that no civilians were wounded by their gunfire was untrue.[126] He met and spoke with the father of Soheil Hammoura, one of the victims of Israeli fire: "He was shot in the back by the Israelis, his father said. . . . We are under occupation forces but our feeling is that of hatred for an occupation force."[127] In his reporting, Fisk captured the anger and the frustration of the Lebanese Shi`a. This Ashura incident became a turning point in the Shi`i resistance. Amal would strongly support the actions of Islamic Amal (and later Hezbullah) in resisting Israeli occupation and the intervention of all the Western forces.

In reporting the incident in Nabatiyah, the *New York Times* privileged the Israeli treatment and excluded or ignored Lebanese and Shi`a accounts of the event, although they were available. There was no attempt by the *New York Times* to follow up on the victims of the incident as Robert Fisk had in his report. On October 16, 1983, the Israeli media reported they were lifting a curfew in Nabatiyah after a noon riot broke, injuring ten residents.[128] An IDF investigation stated that those injured were hurt while fleeing and were not wounded by soldiers' shots.[129] The report characterized the Ashura commemoration as a religious festival "whose main themes are murder, revenge, blood and flagellation."[130] Nowhere in the Israeli media report were the Shi`i themes of piety, sacrifice, and devotion conveyed as hallmarks of the ceremony. Two days later, a report in the *New York Times* displayed an Associated Press photo of Shi`a in Nabatiyah running away from an Israeli vehicle (see figure 4.2). The caption of the photo highlighted that Moslems were "fleeing as worshipers clashed with an Israeli patrol."[131] Nowhere in the caption did it indicate that these were Shi`i Muslims, nor did it display Israeli troops acting against the crowd. Women and children fleeing the vehicles are visible in the picture of the crowd, but the article and the caption made no mention of these victims.

Adjacent to the Nabatiyah report, the headline focused upon the killing of a US Marine by sniper fire in southern Beirut, scores of miles away from the incident in Nabatiyah. The *New York Times* did report that one man was killed and at least seven were wounded in a clash between Israeli troops and Moslem worshippers in Nabatiyah. The paper also published the Israeli account of the incident in Nabatiyah. The report stated that Israeli troops opened fire on the worshippers only after civilians first attacked them, "probably with hand grenades but certainly by rifle fire."[132] The *New York Times* report did not cite Lebanese or Shi`i sources of information, whose narrative of the incident differed greatly. The Israelis' flagrant disregard of a sacred Shi`i ritual turned their anger to rage. Anyone supporting the Israelis was now fair game for the Lebanese Shi`i resistance—it did not take long for that to manifest itself.

On the morning of October 23, 1983, one of the most powerful conventional explosions ever recorded detonated under the headquarters of the Marine Battalion Landing Team in Beirut.[133] Another bomb detonated at the headquarters of the French multinational forces. Speculation ran wild in the *New York Times* and the American media about responsibility for the attacks. American officials and the media initially cited Syria and Iran as possible culprits for the attacks.[134] Three days later, Thomas Friedman stated that the circumstantial evidence for the attack pointed toward "a militant pro-Iranian Shiite Moslem group known both as Islamic Amal and the Party of God."[135] For the first time, the paper acknowledged that Islamic Amal was an offshoot of the main Shi`i organization, Amal. The paper also suggested that American officials did not understand the difference between Amal and Islamic Amal. The American press failed to highlight these differences to government officials and the rest of the American public. After the attack on the US Marines and the French troops, an interview conducted with Hussein Musawi, the leader of "splinter group" Islamic Amal, gave a true representation of the frustration of the Lebanese Shi`a.

In response to a query, Musawi shrugged off any fear for a proposed retaliation by the Reagan administration against his organization. He said:

> We Moslems had been slaughtered for months by the Israelis with the help of the United States, France and the Western alliance.... We have been prepared to face the Israelis and the Americans for years. We have prepared our weapons and we have prepared our shrouds. We are willing to be killed in the name of God and in the defense of our country and or our dignity.[136]

110   Chapter 4

Figure 4.2.   The *New York Times* coverage of the fighting in Nabatiyah (October 17, 1983). Reproduced by permission of the *New York Times*.

Years of frustration and humiliation at the hands of other confessional groups and national entities had brought Musawi to this point.[137] The Shi`i population of Lebanon was prepared to defend its position and rights in Lebanon with the help of other Shi`a in the transnational network. Yet the media representation of the attacks contained no indication that America's support for Israel and the Lebanese government had shown them to be an enemy of the Lebanese Shi`a. The Israeli invasion of Lebanon and its support for the government of Amin Gemayel had so radicalized the Shi`a that it became impossible for them to see the United States as a neutral party in the conflict.

The *Times* (London) and the *Guardian* had also reported explosions at the Marine Corps barracks at the Beirut airport and the French military barracks. In the British press, the culprits were thought to be connected to the Shi`i resistance movement. The *Guardian*, acknowledging that "suicide bombers" carried out the two attacks, discussed the attacks in the following manner: "Fanatic Shi`ite extremists who believe that death in battle means martyrdom and a passage to heaven have proved in the past convenient catspaws for Syrian and Iranian intelligence agents working against Western interests in Lebanon."[138] Although the *Guardian* was convinced that the attack had not been perpetrated by a pure, organic movement led by the Lebanese Shi`i resistance, reports from the *Times* put the onus of the attack on Islamic Jihad, directed by Musawi.[139] The article acknowledged that the group received support from Iran and Syria, but it also made the distinction that this group was not strictly a tool of foreign intelligence services. Later, in an exclusive interview with Hussein Musawi, reporter Robert Fisk received a denial by Musawi that his organization was involved in the attack. Yet Musawi praised the attackers and provided insight into the Shi`i resistance movement in Lebanon, saying, "the Koran permitted Muslims to defend themselves when attacked."[140] Although Fisk could not establish that the attack on the MNF was a defensive action, Musawi had long ago linked the actions of America and France to those of the Israelis.

The *Times* (London) and the *Guardian* continued to report the Shi`i resistance movement's escalating violence. The Israelis attempted to impose a blockade of occupied South Lebanon in November 1983, which further exacerbated the situation in the Shi`i community. In the fall of 1983 the *Times* reported that the Shi`i Muslim population in the Israeli-occupied south were infuriated by the blockade and threatened a general strike against the Israelis.[141] After the Israelis ended the blockade, another resistance operation occurred against an Israeli military headquarters in Tyre. The Israelis, believing that the attack was conducted by Shi`i fighters, mounted an air attack against what the *Times* (London) said were "two camps used by Muslim extremist in Lebanon's Bekaa Valley."[142] The attacks on Islamic Amal were, according to a Lebanese government statement, intended to avenge the death of American Marines and French paratroopers killed in the October bombings. Despite Israeli and American denial that this was the case, the statement by the Lebanese government further codified in the minds of the Shi`i resistance that they were fighting Israel, America, and France.[143]

Coverage of the Lebanese Shi`a resistance to the Israeli invasion and occupation continued in the British press and media. As attacks against the Israeli occupation increased, so did Israel's efforts to suppress the movement. Part of that suppression included locating and neutralizing the movement's leadership. Imam Ragheb Harb, a prominent member of the resistance movement in South Lebanon, was targeted by the Israelis in an attempt to break the resistance.[144] On February 23, 1984, the *Times* (London) reported that unknown gunmen had killed Harb. Much of the speculation over the killing fell on Israel. Reporter Christopher Walker actually interviewed Shi`i villagers in the aftermath of the attack. Harb's cousin, a French teacher in the region, told Walker the following: "No one has caught the killers but everyone is convinced they were militiamen who cooperate with the Israelis. They think that this will stop the resistance to them but it will only increase it. The people here are angry even more than they are sad."[145] An interview Walker conducted with Muhammad Ghaddar, the spokesman for the Amal militia in South Lebanon, revealed the depth of the Shi`i resistance and resentment of the Israelis. Ghaddar told Walker that new recruits for Amal were being trained as men prepared to die for the Islamic cause: "We do not take everyone. We have plenty of places in Lebanon to test whether they really are prepared to die or not."[146] Although chilling, the statement by members of the Shi`i community and the resistance offered, in their own words, a revealing representation of the commitment and the passion of the resistance.

The British press and media covered the back-and-forth retaliation between the Israelis and the Lebanese resistance movement for the next two years. As the Israelis struggled to contend with the resistance movement, they instituted their "Iron Fist" strategy of retaliating fiercely against any Shi`a attack on Israeli troops. The *Times* (London) and the *Guardian* reported on the aftermath of these harsh reprisals on Shi`i villages. Correspondents reported on the storming of the Shi`i village of Jibehit, where witnesses claimed that tanks fired into a crowd of stone-throwing demonstrators, killing at least six.[147] *Guardian* correspondent Julie Flint reported on an Israeli attack on Syr, where several villagers were shot dead in a single sweep.[148]

Ian Black, another *Guardian* correspondent, captured more of the horror of the occupation in an article. Entering a Shi`i village after an IDF raid, reporters found thirty-four corpses and a wall covered with giant slogans in Arabic saying: "This is the revenge of the Israeli Defense Force."[149] The raid, which reporter Black speculated may have been in response to a suicide bomb that killed twelve Israeli soldiers, continued to fuel the animosity of the Shi`i populace. Black stated, "While the politicians in Jerusalem argue about the pace of the three-stage withdrawal and insist that they will not be dictated to by terrorists, the withdrawal is turning into a nightmare of which the only certainty is the promise of more deaths and more vengeance."[150]

The prolonged occupation of Lebanon had a demoralizing effect on the Israelis. As Black stated in his commentary, by the middle of 1985 the Israelis had decided to withdraw to a small buffer strip north of the border. While the casualties and harshness of the occupation hurt the Lebanese Shi`i community, it also strengthened their resolve to resist. The British press reported on this strengthened resistance and recorded a new Shi`i assertiveness. The Shi`i resistance at that point expanded its influence into Christian areas of East Beirut and fought the PLO's attempts to reestablish itself in South Lebanon.[151] This new, empowered Shi`i community now constituted a major force to be reckoned with, both within Lebanon and for those entities outside of Lebanon attempting to thwart their drive toward civil rights.

From the end of 1982 through 1985, the *New York Times* and the rest of the American media tried to present a more detailed and balanced picture of the Shi`a. One such example occurred on the *CBS Evening News* report of January 7, 1984. Larry Pintak, reporting from Beirut, featured two Shi`i men, a Shi`i militia member, and a student at American University in the city. The report was one of the first on American television media that allowed Lebanese Shi`i men to express themselves on their motivation to fight—or on what they aspired to gain from a Western-style education.[152] Another report on *ABC Evening New*s dealt specifically with the Lebanese Shi`a and featured an interview with British correspondent Robert Fisk. During the report, Fisk conveyed the notion that the Lebanese Shi`a, and particularly the Khomeini supporters, were more anticommunist than the most ardent anticommunists in the Reagan administration.[153] This had not been the predominant view in American media, where leftists and communists were often conflated with the Shi`i movement in Lebanon.

The *New York Times* reports on the Lebanese Shi`a and the violence that affected their community also changed. As Shi`i resistance to the Israeli invasion and occupation of Lebanon continued, *New York Times* reporters attempted to ascertain the reason for such tough opposition. On January 20, 1985, Thomas Friedman discussed what he termed was a "Shiite-Israeli War."[154] Covering the violence, he stated that the "Shi`ites have exhibited a degree of bravery and cunning that the Israelis do not like to attribute to their Arab foes."[155] *Brave* had not been an adjective used to describe Shi'i actions in prior *New York Times* coverage. Another development was the scrutiny now given to Israeli military reports on raids on Lebanese Shi`i villages. On March 21, 1985, *New York Times* Friedman questioned the veracity of an Israeli Army spokesman's statement that a raid on a Shi`i town killed 21 terrorists.[156] Writing about the original Israeli Army report, Friedman stated:

> But it was not clear from the original spokesman's statement who the 21 "terrorists" were or how so many men including some who the Israeli spokesman indicated were unarmed, were killed during the searches and arrests. The Israeli operation did not appear to have met much resistance.[157]

Such reporting was not as forthcoming ten years prior to Friedman's account when reporter Juan de Onis had information to contradict Israeli reports on their raids on a Lebanese Shi`i village but never highlighted those discrepancies as Friedman did in his report.

By the spring of 1985, the *New York Times* and a number of American media outlets covered the Lebanese Shi`a very closely. Through investigative reporting, the *Washington Post* and the *New York Times* uncovered an attempted assassination of Shi`i cleric Sayyid Hussein Fadlallah in Beirut by CIA and Lebanese government intelligence operatives.[158] The attack killed over eighty people and wounded close to two hundred but failed to hit its intended target. Yet, even in its coverage of the terrorist attack against Fadlallah, the *New York Times* distorted his role and the narrative of the Lebanese Shi`a. In discussing Lebanon and the explosion's aftermath, the paper said:

> Much of the new terrorism is believed to be abetted from Iran, where a kind of Shiite International is in touch with local agents who propagate Ayatollah Ruhollah Khomeini's Islamic revolution. Iran has supported a Shiite group in Iraq known as Al Dawa. Iraqi and Lebanese members of Al Dawa were sentenced to death in Kuwait for their part in the bombing, which damaged the American and French Embassy.[159]

The article focused on terrorist acts committed by Shi`a instead of the terrorist act conducted by clients of the CIA. The term *Shiite International* intentionally conjures in mind the term *Communist International* (*Comintern*), whose role was to enact polices toward a worldwide socialist revolution. Although a transnational connection of Shi`i communities throughout the region existed, as previously outlined, in no way did it function as "Shiite International." The relationships within the Shi`i community were much more complex than alluded to in the article. However, throughout the American press titles like "Understanding Lebanon: The Shiite Question" and "Hostages in Lebanon; Lebanese Shiites: Once Downtrodden, now Potent," appeared in the paper attempting to explain and represent the Lebanese Shi`a.[160] The media's interest in accurately representing the Lebanese Shi`a was ten years too late. The Lebanese Shi`a community had transformed before the eyes of the Western world, but only now did they recognize the dramatic changes that shaped the community.

In conclusion, several factors stand out in the English-language prestige-press coverage of the Shi`a during and after the Israeli invasion of Lebanon.

The American prestige press and media, particularly the *New York Times*, focused on the Israeli conflict with the Palestinians in Lebanon. Despite years of violence between the predominantly Shi`a population of South Lebanon and the Israeli military, the paper disregarded how the initial invasion affected this community. As the casualties and the violence mounted, the American press was pressured by the Israeli lobby to change its coverage of the Israeli violence against the Lebanese. In *American Orientalism*, Douglas Little describes how Israel's supporters attempted to divert American media's attention by comparing the massacre at the Sabra and Chatila refugee camps in Lebanon with the destruction of the Syrian city of Hama in 1980 by President Hafez al-Assad.[161] Despite the horrendous causalities in Hama, the incident had nothing to do with the massacre in Lebanon. It was solely an attempt to divert negative coverage away from the Israeli actions by ascribing a greater evil to the Arab regime in Syria.[162] As the initial invasion continued into an occupation, the American media and press gradually began to cover some of the violence inflicted on the Shi`a and their corresponding reaction. Yet, in the end, the coverage lacked adequate comprehensiveness to provide a true appreciation for the long-term impact the Israeli invasion had on the Shi`a community.

Strong evidence exists to support that the British press and media, particularly the *Times* and the *Guardian,* constructed a representation of the Lebanese Shi`i narrative different from the American press and media and also uncovered the tensions and the buildup of forces in South Lebanon prior to the Israeli invasion of 1982. British reporters even chronicled the military training of Shi`a youth prior to the invasion. Once the invasion started, *Times* and *Guardian* reporters captured the Shi`i militia groups' resistance to the Israeli attacks. Of particular note was the reporting of *Times* correspondent Robert Fisk, whose initial reports provided a clearer representation of the Shi`a and the effects of the Israeli invasion on their community than reports in the American press and media. As the Israeli occupation of Lebanon continued, the British press provided key information on the occupation's disastrous consequences on Israeli troops and the Shi`a of Lebanon. This portrayal gave those reading British press reports a better understanding of the reality of the Israeli invasion and its aftermath.

For ten years, the narratives of the Lebanese Shi`a were crafted through the work of Musa al-Sadr and other clerics, the tragedy of Nab`a, the triumph of the Iranian Revolution and finally the Israeli invasion and occupation of 1982. The community transformation was profound, yet by the conclusion of 1985 the English-language media still unsuccessfully attempted to make sense and properly represent the story of the Lebanese Shi`a. The misfortune was that readers and viewers of these representations were never able to obtain an accurate picture of the Shi`i community in Lebanon.

NOTES

1. Rodger Shanahan, *The Shi`a of Lebanon: Clans, Parties, and Clerics* (New York: I. B. Tauris, 2005), 112.
2. Ibid.
3. Ze'ev Schiff and Ehud Ya'ari, *Israel's Lebanon War* (New York: Simon and Schuster, 1984).
4. Robert Fisk, *Pity the Nation: The Abduction of Lebanon* (New York: Thunder Mountain Press, 1990), 160–493.
5. Among the host of books by journalists who covered Lebanon during the Israeli invasion, the most prominent are Lawrence Pintak, *Seeds of Hate: How America's Flawed Middle East Policy Ignited Jihad* (London: Pluto Press, 2003); Robin Wright, *Sacred Rage: The Wrath of Militant Islam* (New York: Simon & Schuster, 1985); Selim Nassib and Caroline Tisdall, *Beirut: Frontline Story* (New York: Pluto Press, 1983); and Thomas Friedman, *From Beirut to Jerusalem* (New York: Anchor Books, 1989).
6. Fisk, *Pity the Nation*, 300.
7. Helena Cobban, *The Making of Modern Lebanon* (Boulder, CO: Westview Press, 1985), 176.
8. Fawwaz Traboulsi, *A History of Modern Lebanon* (London: Pluto Press, 2007), 206.
9. "Lebanon: The War of All against All," *Economist*, December 27, 1980.
10. Augustus Richard Norton, *Amal and the Shi`a: Struggle for the Soul of Lebanon* (Austin: University of Texas Press, 1987), 51.
11. "Voice of Hope Carries Haddad Speech to Lebanese," trans. Foreign Broadcast Information Service (Lebanon), March 9, 1981.
12. Ibid.
13. Norton, *Amal and the Shi`a*, 50.
14. Ibid., 51.
15. Raymond Tanter, *Who's at the Helm? Lessons of Lebanon* (Boulder, CO: Westview Press, 1990), 14.
16. Ibid., 26.
17. The crisis that brought Phillip Habib to Lebanon involved fighting between the Christian militia and Syria around the town of Zahle in March 1981. His efforts to solve that problem eventually led to his negotiation for a Palestinian and Israeli cease-fire. This will be covered in further depth in the American and British coverage of the Shi`a in Lebanon.
18. Schiff and Ya'ari, *Israel's Lebanon War*, 60.
19. Ibid., 37.
20. Ibid., 99.
21. Ibid., 98.
22. Schiff and Ya'ari, *Israel's Lebanon War*, 106.
23. Lawrence Pintak, *Beirut Outtakes* (Lexington, MA: Lexington Books, 1988), 22.
24. Sankari, *Fadlallah*, 192.
25. Ibid.
26. John Boykin, *Cursed Is the Peacemaker: The American Diplomat versus the Israeli General, Beirut 1982* (Belmont, CA: Applegate Press, 2002), 78.
27. Schiff and Ya'ari, *Israel's Lebanon War*, 42.
28. Norton, *Amal and the Shi`a*, 107.
29. Ibid.
30. The Pasdaran (Persian for "guardians") were a cadre of the Iranian Revolutionary Guard initially set up as a highly motivated, religiously indoctrinated military group with the role of protecting the Iranian Revolution and spreading its precepts.
31. Chehabi, *Distant Relations*, 212.
32. Amal Saad-Ghorayeb. *Hizbu`llah: Politics and Religion* (New York: Pluto Press, 2002), 10–11.
33. Hala Jaber, *Hezbollah: Born with a Vengeance* (New York: Columbia University Press, 1997), 57.
34. Ibid., 58.

35. Boykin, *Cursed Is the Peacemaker*, 93, 249.
36. "National Salvation Body Fails to Meet," trans. Foreign Broadcast Information System (Lebanon), June 15, 1982.
37. Saad-Ghorayeb, *Hizbu'llah*, 14–15.
38. Nicholas Noe, ed., *Voice of Hezbollah: The Statements of Sayyed Hassan Nasrallah* (New York: Verso, 2007), 5.
39. Saad-Ghorayeb, *Hizbu'llah*, 15.
40. "Amal Leaders Meeting with Iranian President," BBC *Summary of World* broadcast, August 4, 1982, Islamic Republic News Agency (English).
41. Saad-Ghorayeb, *Hizbu'llah*, 113.
42. Sankari, *Fadlallah*, 197.
43. Ibid., 194.
44. Norton, *Amal and the Shi`a*, 110.
45. Saad-Ghorayeb, *Hizbu'llah*, 11.
46. "Birri Says Shi`ites Becoming Israel's 'Enemies,'" trans. Foreign Broadcast Information Service (Lebanon), July 2, 1982.
47. Ibid.
48. President Reagan's statements on the massacre of Palestinians in West Beirut, September 18, 1982, obtained from *The Arab-Israeli Conflict*, vol. IV, *The Difficult Search for Peace (1975–1988)*, ed. Jon Norton Moore (Princeton, NJ: Princeton University Press, 1991), 1179.
49. Boykin, *Cursed Is the Peacemaker*, 266.
50. Charles D. Smith, *Palestine and the Arab–Israeli Conflict: A History with Documents*, 6th ed. (New York: Bedford/St. Martin's, 2007), 382.
51. Friedman, *From Beirut to Jerusalem*, 159.
52. Boykin, *Cursed Is the Peacemaker*, 268.
53. The Kahan Commission was an official panel commissioned by the Israeli cabinet on September 28, 1982, to ascertain all the facts and factors connected with the atrocities carried out by a unit of the Lebanese forces against the civilian population in the Shatilla and Sabra camps. The panel issued a report known as "The Commission of Inquiry into the Events at the Refugee Camps in Beirut" on February 7, 1983.
54. Kahan Commission, *The Beirut Massacre* (New York: Karz-Cohl Publishing, 1983), xiii.
55. Naim Qassem, *Hizbullah: The Story from Within* (London: SAQI, 2005), 89.
56. Jaber, *Hezbollah*, 77.
57. Anthony McDermott and Kjell Skjelsbaek, *The Multinational Force in Beirut, 1982–1984* (Miami: Florida International Press, 1991), 12.
58. Norton, *Amal and the Shi`a*, 10–11. See also account by William E. Farrell, "Lebanese Moslems Are Leery of Peace Talks and the Future," *New York Times*, January 3, 1983.
59. Ibid.
60. Jaber, *Hezbollah*, 18.
61. Ibid.
62. Schiff and Ya'ari, *Israel's Lebanon War*, 284.
63. Fisk, *Pity the Nation*, 552.
64. Ibid.
65. Jaber, *Hezbollah*, 21.
66. Fisk, *Pity the Nation*, 552.
67. Jaber, *Hezbollah*, 18.
68. Ibid., 19.
69. Ibid.
70. Sandra Mackey, *Lebanon: A House Divided* (New York: W. W. Norton Company, 1989), 208–9.
71. Noam Chomsky, *Fateful Triangle: The United States, Israel, and the Palestinians* (Cambridge, MA: South End Press, 1999).
72. Ibid., 181–84.
73. David K. Shipler, "Israel Is Said to Weigh an Invasion of Lebanon If PLO Raids Go On," *New York Times*, February 10, 1982.

74. Christopher Walker, "Israelis Mass on Lebanon Border," *Times* (London), May 15, 1982.
75. Norton, *Amal and the Shi`a*, 116.
76. "7 Killed and 60 Hurt by 2 Car Explosions at Market in Beirut," *New York Times*, February 24, 1982; and "Beirut Car Bomb Kills 8 and Leaves 20 Wounded," *New York Times*, February 28, 1982.
77. John Kifner's article "Shiite Moslem and Leftist Fighting Spreads in Lebanon," along with Augustus Richard Norton's editorial "Lebanon Shiites" and Terence Wong's editorial "At Last Lebanon's Shiites Take a Stand" all occurred in April 1982. They gave some keen insights on the Lebanese Shi`a, but they were often drowned out by other editorials such as one in May by A. J. Abraham ("Lebanese Sects United against Foreign Foes," *New York Times*, May 24, 1982), who said incorrectly that the Shi`ites supported the forces of Major Saad Haddad and had been traditional allies of the Christians.
78. Fisk, *Pity the Nation*, 137. There is also an account of this incident in Beate Hamizrachi's *The Emergence of the South Lebanon Security Belt: Major Saad Haddad and the Ties with Israel, 1975–1978* (New York: Praeger, 1988), 167–68. Beate Hamizrachi served as an Israeli journalist and a liaison officer between Haddad's forces and the international press. Her account of the incident claims that an Israeli officer turned over a small group of Shi`i civilians to Haddad's men. While acknowledging that unarmed civilians were killed by Haddad's forces, she alleges that less then seventy were killed. She does acknowledge that no reporter was allowed in Khiam after the massacre.
79. William F. Farrell, "Israelis Ponder Lebanon," *New York Times*, March 30, 1978.
80. Jonathan C. Randal, "Christian Militiamen Kill 70 in Lebanese Mosque," *Washington Post*, March 27, 1978.
81. Jaber, *Hezbollah*, 14.
82. Christopher Walker, "Israelis Mass on Lebanon Border," *Times* (London), May 15, 1982.
83. C. Smith, *Palestine and the Arab–Israeli Conflict*, 379.
84. "Lebanon's Warring Factions," *Times* (London), May 10, 1982.
85. Robert Fisk, "United Nations in Lebanon: Fighting a Losing Battle," *Times* (London), May 7, 1982.
86. William Safire, "The Liberation of Lebanon," *New York Times*, June 11, 1982.
87. "Shiite Group to Aid Israelis," *New York Times*, June 30, 1982.
88. Norton, *Amal and the Shi`a*, 86.
89. Robert Fisk, "How Lebanon Could Yet Humiliate the Israelis," *Times* (London), June 15, 1982.
90. See "America, the Shi`a and the Israeli Invasion of 1982" earlier in this chapter.
91. Lundrum R. Bolling, *Reporters under Fire: US Media Coverage of Conflicts in Lebanon and Central America* (Boulder, CO: Westview Press, 1985), 17.
92. Eytan Gilboa, *American Public Opinion toward Israel and the Arab–Israeli Conflict* (Lexington, MA: Lexington Books, 1987) has an entire chapter in which he asserts that much of the American media coverage of the war was biased in favor of the Palestinians and Syrians.
93. Wright, *Sacred Rage*, 61.
94. Norton, *Amal and the Shi`a*, 88.
95. Fisk, *Pity the Nation*, 468.
96. Ibid.
97. IRNA is a state-controlled news agency of the Islamic Republic of Iran. It provides radio, television, and print information for domestic and foreign audiences.
98. "Amal Leader's Meeting with Iranian President," BBC *Summary of World*, August 4, 1982.
99. Ahmad Nizar Hamzeh, *In the Path of Hizbullah* (Syracuse, NY: Syracuse University Press, 2004); and Chehabi, *Distant Relations*, 217.
100. James MacManus, "Strange New Bedfellows in South Lebanon," *Guardian*, July 15, 1982.

101. Christopher Walker, "Trade Invasion of Lebanon Denied," *Times* (London), August 31, 1982; Christopher Walker, "Israelis Find New Market in Lebanon," *Times* (London), October 9, 1982.
102. "Gunmen Demand Islamic Rule in Lebanon," *Times* (London), November 22, 1982.
103. James F. Clarity, "Shiites Seize a Lebanese City in Protest," *New York Times*, November 22, 1982.
104. Qassem, *Hizbullah*, 67.
105. Jaber, *Hezbollah*, 75.
106. James F. Clarity, "15 Israelis Killed in Blast in South Lebanon," *New York Times*, November, 12, 1982.
107. Qassem, *Hizbollah*, 78.
108. McDermott and Skjelbaek, *The Multinational Force in Beirut*, 159. Although the British military contingent was relatively modest (approximately 120 men at its height), this force confronted a newly energized Shi`i community. The British contingent was based in southeastern Beirut, an area in close proximity to the Amal militia that al-Sadr had founded over ten years previous.
109. Robert Fisk, "America Getting Trapped in the Peril of Lebanon," *Times* (London), December 4, 1982.
110. Robert Fisk, "Lebanon: The Stakes Get Higher," *Times* (London), February 7, 1983.
111. Eric Hammel, *The Root: The Marines in Beirut, August 1982–February 1984* (St. Paul, MN: Zenith Press, 2005), 78.
112. Ihsan A. Hijazi, "Islamic Attackers Seen as Pro-Iran," *New York Times*, April 19, 1983.
113. Ibid.
114. Ibid.
115. Thomas Friedman, "Lebanon Troops Battle Moslems in West Beirut," *New York Times*, July 16, 1983.
116. "Threat to Marines Voiced," *New York Times*, September 2, 1983.
117. Ibid.
118. United States Special Forces troops were also training and assisting Lebanese forces during this time period. A report on *NBC Evening News* on July 16, 1983, by reporter Jessica Savage credits American Green Berets (Special Forces) for the success of the Lebanese Army's fighting against Shi`i militiamen during the army's attempt to evict Shi`ite squatters in the old Jewish Quarter of Beirut. Report obtained from Vanderbilt Television Archives.
119. E. J. Dionne Jr., "One Hopeful Sign in Beirut Suburb: Shiites Remain Peaceful and Man Checkpoints instead of Battling the Army," *New York Times*, September 6, 1983.
120. McDermott and Skjelsbaek, *The Multinational Force in Beirut*, 86.
121. Thomas L. Friedman, "Lebanon's Troops Battle the Shiites in a Beirut Suburb," *New York Times*, September 25, 1983.
122. Ibid.
123. Fouad Ajami, "America Can't Bring Sense to Lebanon," *New York Times*, September 25, 1983.
124. "The Rise and Rise of the Shias," *Economist*, October 1, 1983, 48.
125. Robert Fisk, "Muslim Festival," *Times* (London), October 17, 1983.
126. Robert Fisk, "Gunshot Victims Belie Israeli Claims after Nabatiya Rioting," *Times* (London), October 18, 1983.
127. Fisk, *Pity the Nation,* 558.
128. "Curfew Imposed in An-Nabatiyah after Riot Lifted," trans. Foreign Broadcast Information Service, Jerusalem Domestic Service, October 17, 1983.
129. Ibid.
130. Ibid.
131. Thomas Friedman, "Snipers in Beirut Kill Marine and Wound 3 Others," *New York Times*, October 17, 1983.
132. Thomas Friedman, "Snipers in Beirut Kill Marine and Wound 3 Others," *New York Times*, October 17, 1983.
133. Wright, *Sacred Rage*, 70.

134. Francis X. Clines, "Attack Is Assailed: U.S. Says Terrorists Tied to Iran May Have Set Off the Lethal Blast," *New York Times*, October 24, 1983.

135. Thomas L. Friedman, "Suspicion in Beirut Is Now Focused on a Shiite Splinter Group," *New York Times*, October 27, 1983.

136. R. W. Apple, "Shiite Denies Role in Beirut Blasts," *New York Times*, October 28, 1983.

137. Robert Baer, *The Devil We Know: Dealing with the New Iranian Superpower* (New York: Crown Publishers, 2008), 61–62.

138. James McManus, "Suicide Bombers Kill 170 Troops," *Guardian*, October 24, 1983.

139. Robert Fisk, "US Blames Blast on Shia Splinter Group," *Times* (London), October 26, 1983.

140. Robert Fisk, "Shia Leader Praises Beirut Massacre," *Times* (London), October 28, 1983.

141. Christopher Walker, "South Lebanon Blockade Lifted after 72 Hours," *Times* (London), November 8, 1983.

142. Robert Fisk, "Israelis Avenge Suicide Bombing as Jets Strafe Muslim Camps," *Times* (London), November 17, 1983.

143. Ibid.

144. Fisk, *Pity the Nation*, 552. See also "America, the Shi`a and the Israeli Invasion of 1982" earlier in this chapter.

145. Christopher Walker, "Shaikh's Murder Fuels Shia Resentment over Israeli Occupation," *Times* (London), February 23, 1984.

146. Ibid.

147. "Israelis Storm Shia Village," *Times* (London), March 29, 1984.

148. Julie Flint, "A Visit from the Iron Fist: Israeli Military Activity in South Lebanon," *Guardian*, February 26, 1985.

149. Ian Black, "Slogans Spell Out Israel's Revenge: Shi`ite Muslim Attacks on Israel Occupation Forces in Lebanon," *Guardian*, March 13, 1985.

150. Ibid.

151. Robert Fisk, "Shia Fighters Invade Christian Beirut," *Times* (London), May 8, 1985; Robert Fisk, "Shia Militia Attack PLO in Beirut Camps to Stifle Arafat's Influence," *Times* (London), May 21, 1985.

152. *CBS Evening News*, January 7, 1984, Vanderbilt Television News Archives.

153. *ABC Evening News*, February 22, 1984, Vanderbilt Television News Archives.

154. Thomas Friedman, "Israel's Dilemma: Living with a Dirty War," *New York Times*, January 20, 1985.

155. Ibid.

156. Thomas Friedman, "Israelis Offer Little Insight into the 21 Slain 'Terrorists,'" *New York Times*, March 22, 1985.

157. Ibid.

158. "CIA Linked to Beirut Bomb," *New York Times*, May 12, 1985.

159. John Kifner, "Bombing in Beirut Has Troubling Echoes," *New York Times*, May 19, 1985.

160. Helena Cobban, "Understanding Lebanon: The Shiite Question," *Christian Science Monitor*, January 7, 1985; Ihasan Hijazi, "Hostages in Lebanon; Lebanese Shiites: Once Downtrodden, Now Potent," *New York Times*, June 18, 1985.

161. The destruction of the city of Hama by Syrian troops in February 1982 was ordered by Syrian president al-Assad. He violently suppressed a revolt against his regime by members of the Muslim Brotherhood. No exact figures are available, but thousands were killed and included a number of noncombatants. Much of the city was totally destroyed. See Friedman, *From Beirut to Jerusalem*, 76–105.

162. Douglas Little, *American Orientalism: The United States in the Middle East since 1945* (Chapel Hill: University of North Carolina Press, 2002), 37.

Chapter Five

Epilogue

The Lebanese Shi`a narrative constructed by the English language press and media from 1975 to 1985 still resonates with Western journalists in the twenty-first century. Despite modern communications technology and advances in social media that allow almost anyone to post pictures and videos and "tweet" their feelings via the worldwide web, images, videos, and tweets still need interpretations and context to frame narratives.[1] Correspondents are still vitally important to how the English language audience understands and decodes what happens in the Middle East, particularly regarding the Lebanese Shi`a. Stories of Musa al-Sadr, Muhammad Hussein Fadlallah, Hezbollah, and the Lebanese Shi`a connection to Iran are critical in understanding the conflicts that plague portions of the Middle East. Any brief review of stories emanating from the region in the second decade of the twenty-first century will uncover names and places that were prominent in the news narrative described in the ten years between 1975 and 1985. For example, the name of Musa al-Sadr still echoes in the English-language press.

In the autumn of 2011, rebel groups, with the help of military intervention from Western nations, were poised to topple President Muammar Qaddafi of Libya. As Qaddafi's hold on power weakened, many in the Lebanese Shi`a community were interested in finding the underlying cause of Musa al-Sadr's disappearance in the country in 1978. The *Guardian* printed accounts of the Lebanese foreign minister saying, "Lebanon has never abandoned efforts for one moment to determine his fate and that of his companions and there is a chance now to discover new things."[2] In a *Time Magazine* article, written just prior to Qaddafi's ouster, reporter Nicholas Blanford provided important context to understanding how Musa al-Sadr's disappearance in Libya in 1978 continues to resonate with the Lebanese Shi`a. Blanford stated that "Sadr's disappearance caused a rift between Lebanon and the Qaddafi regime that has never healed."³ Relations were so poor that Qaddafi's appearance at an Arab League summit in Beirut in March 2002 was canceled because of threats to his life from members of the Shi`i community.⁴ In that same article Blanford discussed how a former commander of Amal, the Lebanese Shi`a militia group, was still ready to sacrifice his life, and those of his sons and his entire family, to understand the fate of Musa al-Sadr. That is just one small demonstration of the continued veneration and allegiance to Musa al-Sadr by members of the Lebanese Shi`a community. So powerful is the narrative and story of Musa al-Sadr that assigning blame or responsibility to whomever was responsible for his disappearance is often used as a wedge issue to foment rifts within the Lebanese Shi`i community.

The rumors that Muammar Qaddafi had Sadr killed on behalf of Palestinian leader Yasser Arafat or that Ayatollah Khomeini convinced Qaddafi to have Sadr killed so that he would not be a rival to his accession to power in Iran are discussed in Blanford's article. Yet, Blanford fails to contextualize how this narrative continues to be used to shape and drive divisions in the Lebanese Shi`a community. Any confirmation that Yasser Arafat and the Palestinians orchestrated the death of Musa al-Sadr would weaken the traditional support groups like Hezbollah have for the Palestinians today. Any implications that Ayatollah Khomeini had participated in causing Sadr's death would also cause a rift between the Lebanese Shi`a and their Iranian supporters. Andrew Cooper's, *The Fall of Heaven: The Pahlavis and the Final Days of Imperial Iran*, written in August 2016, suggested that Khomeini was concerned about reconciliation between the Shah and Sadr and, because of that, had him killed. Despite that claim, considerable evidence outlined in previous chapters refutes that new assertion.⁵ Sadr openly supported opposition groups in Lebanon fighting the Shah's rule. Sadr's loyalty to the downtrodden transnational Shi`a community would mitigate any reconciliation with the Shah.

When authors and government officials dispute the evidence of Musa al-Sadr's disappearance, there are other agendas at stake. It is incumbent upon journalists to decode the evidence and put it in the proper perspective for their audiences. The fate of Musa al-Sadr remains an important issue today, as competition continues in the Middle East between Iran and Saudi Arabia, Sunni and Shi`a, Israeli and Arab. Understanding the importance of Musa al-Sadr to the Lebanese Shi`a narrative is essential, just as the life of Muhammad Hussein Fadlallah and his time in Nab`a remain critical to the Lebanese Shi`i narrative.

On July 4, 2010, the *New York Times* printed an obituary of Grand Ayatollah Mohammed Hussein Fadlallah. The obituary stated, "Fadlallah, the top Shiite cleric in Lebanon, whose writings and preaching inspired the *Dawa* Party of Iraq and a generation of militants including the founders of Hezbollah, died Sunday morning in Beirut. He was 75."⁶ Although the biography extolled Fadlallah's virtue as a learned Shi`i scholar, it emphasized his role in justifying suicide bombing or "other tactics of asymmetrical warfare."[7] Not once in his obituary did the *Times* mention the siege of Nab`a, or how Fadlallah wrote *Islam and the Logic of Power* while under bombardment in that Shi`i enclave. It was this experience that profoundly changed Fadlallah and convinced him that the Shi`a required strength and force to establish justice on earth.[8] Immediately after Fadlallah's death a major Western media outlet, CNN, was immersed in a controversy over a comment by one of its employees. Career journalist and Senior Middle Eastern Affairs Editor, Octavia Nasr, was fired for using social media to tweet, "Sad to hear of the passing of Sayyed Mohammad Hussein Fadlallah. One of Hezbollah giants I respect a lot..#Lebanon."[9] The pressure on CNN to fire Nasr came from outside right-wing groups who casted Fadlallah as "an Evil Hezbollah Terrorist."[10] Fadlallah never claimed to be a member of Hezbollah. Despite that, and based on questionable sources, the American intelligence agency linked him to the 1983 bombing of the Marine Barracks in Beirut. In a failed attempt to assassinate him in 1985, a CIA-trained and Saudi-financed Lebanese counterterrorist force detonated a car bomb that blew up outside his residence in Beirut.[11] The attempt resulted in the death of over eighty civilians and the wounding or more than two hundred.[12] Since the siege of Nab`a, Fadlallah maintained that the Shi`a had the responsibility to defend themselves, by violence if necessary. The assassination attempt just reinforced his commitment to self-defense. Nasr was well aware of the complex story of Fadlallah; however, silencing her voice at a major Western news outlet stunted the ability of others to understand the complexity of the narrative behind Fadlallah and how his theological opinions shaped the Lebanese Shi`a and other Shi`i communities throughout the world. The experience of Nab`a continues to resonate in the Lebanese Shi`a in the writing of Muhammad Fadlallah along with the aftermath of the 1982 Israeli invasion and the birth of Hezbollah.

Thirty-six years after Israel's invasion of Lebanon, purportedly to rid itself of the threat of the Palestinian Liberation Organization, Israel continues to view Hezbollah as a major threat. Yet when reporters discuss Hezbollah today, it is essential to recount that Hezbollah was a reaction to the Israeli invasion. Members of the Lebanese Shi`a community felt it necessary to form a more religiously indoctrinated resistance group than Amal to counter the Israeli occupation. Islamic Amal morphed into Hezbullah. Today the United States government lists Hezbollah as a terrorist organization. Hezbollah operators actively support armed groups in Iraq, Yemen, and, significantly, the Syrian government of Bashar al-Assad.

In the spring of 2016 a comprehensive study in the *Journal of Middle East Media* examined the media's framing of Lebanese Hezbollah. Using the *New York Times*, *Agence France-Presse*, *Lebanese Daily Star*, and the *Times*

(London), the paper quantitatively coded how the organization was portrayed to their readers.[13] The paper focused on the complexity of a group such as Hezbollah, which is multidimensional and has aspects of political, humanitarian, and military activities within the organization. Understanding how news organizations frame this group provided key insights into the current construction of news narratives. Within the study, the authors were able to capture the fact that although Hezbollah has continued to evolve from its origins as a resistance group, news organizations continued their static frame of the organization.[14] "In particular the *New York Times* merely decreased its use of terrorism frames of Hezbullah without increasing its political frames of the organization over time."[15] Hezbollah is only one segment of the Lebanese Shi`a society; however, events in the region have once again propelled it to prominence. Currently, there is no more critical factor in understanding the importance of Hezbollah than the Syrian Civil War. The Lebanese Shi`a inserted themselves into the turmoil of the Syrian Civil War that commenced in 2011. The images of violence in Syria, broadcast sometimes live, and press releases reaching Western media outlets still need interpreters. This is why the manner in which those images and words are interpreted remains vital.

In an April 2013 *New York Times* editorial, David Pollock, a senior fellow at the Washington Institute, discussed the growing conflict in Syria and the potential for violent clashes between the Israelis and Hezbollah. Pollock intimated that rumored Israeli attempts to create a proxy force of Syrian Druze along its Northern border with Syria would be a bad idea. Pollock said, "that would be very much like what happened in Lebanon, with disastrous long term consequences."[16] The evolution of those proxy forces set-up by Israel in Lebanon fostered the growth of the Shi`a resistance and the birth of Hezbollah. Such astute analysis of this history and narrative is vital to the consumers of the media to make sense of the growing conflict in the region. However, for every instance the media demonstrates a nuanced, thoughtful, understanding of the vital role of the Lebanese Shi`a, media reporting and commentary that does not appreciate this narrative continues.

On June 4, 2013, Bret Stephens, a political commentator and regular contributor to the *Wall Street Journal*, wrote an opinion piece entitled, "The Muslim Civil War." In the article, Stephens attempted to paint the civil war in Syria as a sectarian conflict between the Sunnis and the Shi`a. His advocacy for a larger American involvement in the conflict posits that a similar conflict between Sunni and Shi`a occurred during the Iran and Iraq War in the 1980s which brought us, "the hostage taking in Lebanon, and the birth of Hezbollah, with suicide bombing of the U.S. marine barracks and embassy in Beirut."[17] Stephens either inadvertently or deliberately leaves out an accurate representation of the Lebanese Shi`a and their own narrative regarding the formation of Hezbollah. Throughout the opinion piece, he never mentioned

Israel's invasion of Lebanon in 1982 and the formation of Hezbollah as a resistance movement directly opposed to the Israeli occupation of Lebanon. Hezbollah was never set up to fight or oppose Sunni religious groups. In fact one of the earliest supports of Hezbollah, Muhammad Shams al-Din, stated that jihad (struggle) against other Muslims is illegitimate.[18]

To understand fully Hezbollah's role in Lebanese society, it is vital for the English language media to provide a nuanced representation of the group. Essential in the construction of the current narrative of Hezbollah is how members of the Lebanese government view the organization. In the fall of 2017, an interview with the Lebanese President, Michel Auon, prior to his speech before the UN General Assembly, shed some light on the relationship between Hezbollah and Lebanese society. Auon stated, "Hezbollah, you know, is a Lebanese organization that was founded to liberate our territory from the Israeli occupation. It was created for that in 1985"[19] He went on to relate that he attempted to sign a memorandum with Hezbollah to disarm in the summer of 2006. However, after the Israeli attack in 2006, Auon said, you cannot tell Hezbollah, "We have to dismantle your organization, since Israel is provoking Lebanon and it is attacking."[20] Recent Western media outlets such as the Public Broadcasting System and an article in the *New York Times* have begun to demonstrate some of the nuance required to understand the group and its connection with Iran.

On June 13, 2017, the Public Broadcasting System (PBS) aired a television program on the *PBS New Hour* covering the growing influence of Hezbollah in the Middle East. Although the broadcast briefly described the group's origins outlined in this book, it continued to emphasize Hezbollah's original charter that calls for the destruction of Israel.[21] The media's narrative of Hezbollah's threat to Israel is pervasive throughout the English language press and media. However, other narratives of this group deserve attention. The program briefly covered Hezbollah's larger public and social works program. As Andrew Exum, a former top Middle East policy expert in the Obama administration stated, it is important to recognize that the social services that Hezbollah provides are services that the Lebanese government is not providing for the Shi`a community in Lebanon.[22] It is unreasonable to believe that Lebanese Shi`a or others in their orbit would turn away from healthcare services, pensions and rehabilitation for Hezbollah resistance fighters, food aid, and jobs for those without means. This lack of social services and protections between 1975 and 1985 is the very origin of the movement of the deprived covered in this book. However, one of the most prominent links presented in the PBS documentary was the connection between Iran and the Lebanese Shi`a community, particularly through Hezbollah.

Iran is an important nation in the world today. The Islamic government of Iran, formed in 1979, remains intact and resurgent despite the many obstacles it faced. Iran fought a long and costly war with its neighbor Iraq in the 1980s, survived internal unrest, and outlasted major sanctions from the international community over its nuclear program. The support of Lebanese Shi`i scholars and Amal fighters during the Iranian revolution is often overlooked by reporters who see the relationship between Iran and the Lebanese Shi`a as strictly a one-sided affair. This relationship has been cemented over hundreds of years not just the latest revelations and timelines given in the press.

Current news headlines tout the connection between Iran and Lebanese Shi`a, and, with Iran as a potential adversary to the West, these headlines are of major concern to the consumers. The *New York Times* headline, "Iran Out to Remake Mideast with Arab Enforcer: Hezbollah," immediately grabs the attention of their readers.[23] However, the sensational headlines belie the necessity for a deeper, more important understanding of the ancient connection between the Lebanese Shi`a and the country of Iran. The referenced *Times* article, by Ben Hubbard, is a comprehensive look at the relationship between Iran and Hezbollah. However, despite Hubbard's extensive research into this complex relationship, he was unable to accurately depict the long, enduring, historic connections between the Lebanese Shi`a and Iran. In describing the alignment between the Lebanese Shi`a and Iran as it relates to the Syrian Civil War, Hubbard outlined how these two groups were able to enlist Shi`a fighters from throughout the Middle East to help in the battle of Aleppo. "The roots of that network go back to the American invasion of Iraq in 2003, when Iran called on Hezbollah to help organize Iraqi Shiite militias that in the coming years killed hundreds of Americans."[24] As previously presented, the Shi`i transnational network is much older than the American invasion of Iraq, and it should not come as a surprise that such a network could provide the flow of money, material, and fighters to help the Shi`i-dominated regime of Bashar al-Assad. Shi`a from Afghanistan, Pakistan, Iraq, and other countries flocked to this battlefield and were able to turn the tide in the direction of Assad.[25] English-language media consumers must also view this transnational flow of people and material in a larger context. Presently, there remains a larger competition between the Shi`a world—led by the most powerful Shi`a state, Iran—and the Sunnis. The Sunni world is dominated by wealthy Saudi Arabia and others states in the Persian Gulf. This contest for the heart and soul of Islam will continue to play out in the future. How Western journalists and reporters understand this competition, and how they recognize the role of the Lebanese Shi`a in it, is important. Iran remains adversarial to the United States and Israel, the United States's closest ally in the Middle East. Israel remains wary of Hezbollah because of their belief that it is the proxy of the Iranian government. Conflict between these groups could have devastating effects on the future of the Middle East. Before political leaders in the West and their public make a decision to confront these entities in conflict, they should be informed about the history and the narrative of people who may be their potential adversaries. It is my hope that this book has provided some of that understanding.

NOTES

1. Tweet refers to the social media platform of Twitter, which allows 140 characters to post immediately into the worldwide web to express or share any form of information or communication.
2. Saeed Kamali Dehgham. "Lebanon, Iran Urge Libyan Rebels to Probe 33-Year-Old Mystery," *Guardian,* August 24, 2011.
3. Nicholas Blanford. "As Gaddafi Teeters, Will the Mystery of Lebanon's Missing Imam Be Solved," *Time Magazine,* February 25, 2011.
4. Nicholas Blanford. "Latest Spat Leaves Qaddafi in the Cold with His Camels," *Christian Science Monitor*, January 22, 2002.
5. "Today Al-Sadr disappearance story is complete," http://libyaprospect.com/index.php/2016/01/18/today-al-sadr-disappearance-story-is-complete/ (accessed January 18, 2016).
6. Thanassiss Cambanis, "Grand Ayatollah Fadlallah, Shiite Cleric Dies at 75," *New York Times*, July 4, 2010.
7. Ibid.
8. Daniel Helmer, "Hezbollah's Employment of Suicide Bombing during the 1980s: The Theological, Political, and Operational Development of a New Tactic," *Military Review*, July–August 2006.
9. "Demonizing Journalist: The Corporate Media's bias against the Arab World," www.cairchicago.org/blog/2010/07/demonizing-journalist-the-corporate-media-bias-against-the-arab-world/ (accessed October 13, 2017).
10. "Octavia Nasr's firing and what the Liberal Media allows," July 8, 2010, https://www.salon.com/2010/08/media-259/ (accessed October 13, 2017).
11. Jamal Sankari, *Fadlallah: The Making of a Radical Shi`ite Leader* (London: SAQI, 2005), 209.
12. Helmer, 78.
13. Rebekah Lynam, Maureen Taylor, and Peter Gade, "Newspaper Frames of Hizbullah: Uni-Dimensional Framing of a Multi-Dimensional Organization," *Journal of Middle East Media*, Vol. 12, Spring 2016.
14. Ibid., 83.
15. Ibid.
16. David Pollock, "Syria's Forgotten Front," *New York Times,* April 16, 2013 http://ebird.osd.mil/ebfiles/ebfiles/e20130416920453.html
17. Bret Stephens, "The Muslim Civil War," *The Wall Street Journal*, June 4, 2013.
18. Rola el-Husseini, "Resistance, Jihad and Martyrdom in Contemporary Lebanese Shi`a Discourse," *Middle East Journal* Vol. 62, No. 3, Summer 2008, 402.
19. "Auon Sees Role for Hezbollah until Threats to Lebanon Cease," *Al-Monitor*, September 21, 2017, http://www.al-monitor.com/pulseoriginals/2017/09/lebanon-president-aoun-unga-hezbolla (accessed October 5, 2017).
20. Ibid.
21. "What the Rising Power of Hezbollah Means for the Middle East," June 13, 2017, https//www.pbs.org/newshour/show/rising-power-hezbollah-means-middle-east (accessed October 24, 2017).
22. Ibid.
23. Ben Hubbard, "Iran Out to Remake Mideast with Arab Enforcer: Hezbollah," *New York Times*, August 27, 2017.
24. Ibid.
25. Ibid.

Conclusion

> There are no shortcuts in covering complex stories outside of the familiar Western cultural framework. To grasp the intricacies of political events in the Middle East and other non-Western environments, the Western media simply have to work harder and invest more in acquiring better expertise.
> — Iraj Bagherrade

Reporting and recording events about a different culture is no easy task. As the epigraph indicates, covering stories in foreign countries with dissimilar traditions and institutions requires expertise, hard work, and commitment. Yet reporters and correspondents have a professional obligation to provide accurate representations of the people, cultures, and viewpoints they cover.[1] This book examined how the English-language prestige press and media—particularly the *New York Times*, the *Times* (London), and the *Guardian*—represented the Lebanese Shi`a from 1975 to 1985. In concluding this examination, the preponderance of evidence shows that these media outlets did not accurately represent the Lebanese Shi`a—why?

The question of why offers the foundation for another academic query; however, in concluding *this* book, several things come into sharp focus. First, journalists and reporters of 1975–1985 had access to ample information to construct an accurate representation of the Lebanese Shi`a. The dominant Shi`a figure of the decade, Musa al-Sadr, was prominently represented in the Lebanese press as the leading representative of this formerly "quietist" group. The Lebanese media extensively covered his demands for fair treatment of the Shi`a and the cessation of Israeli violence against Southern Lebanese villagers. He was the darling of *Al Hayat* and *An Nahar*, the two most prominent and influential papers in Lebanon. The *Beirut Daily Star*, the Lebanese English-language daily (which was run by the owner of *Al Hayat*), also covered al-Sadr prominently.[2] Lebanese radio broadcasts afforded interested parties access to al-Sadr's statements and his involvement in peace negotiations during the early stages of the Lebanese Civil War. Throughout, this book referenced posters, pamphlets, radio broadcasts, and local news reports available to reporters during the period covered. The Foreign Broadcast Information Service and the British Broadcast Monitoring Service translated many of these reports into English. Key Shi`i officials in Lebanon were available for interviews and commentary regarding their situation, yet rarely were their voices used in Western reporting. Oftentimes, so-called Middle East experts from the West were used to speak for the Shi`i community.

Second, constructing a coherent representation of the Lebanese Shi`a required some understanding of the dominant narrative of the community. Narrative remains a key element in this process because historically grounded stories reflect a community's self-identity and experience and can explain its hopes, aspirations, and concerns.[3] How could the media cover and represent a community and give its story context if the reporters failed to understand the group's self-identity, history, and major concerns? This is, in essence, what took place in the English-language media's initial coverage and representation of the Lebanese Shi`a.

This book outlined four major events between 1975 and 1985 that shaped a dominant narrative within the Lebanese Shi'i community. In each of these events the English-language media ignored the plight of the Shi`a, conflated their civil rights movement with other Arab independence movements, or failed to record and understand the transnational linkage occurring within the community. In the end, the predominant reporting by the English-language media prevented an accurate representation of the Lebanese Shi`a. The Shi`i narrative of a civil rights struggle or their justification for armed resistance to violence and injustice against their community were largely overlooked in the narrative constructed in the Western press.

The American and British media virtually ignored the Lebanese Shi`a prior to and immediately after 1975. Despite major changes occurring throughout the Shi`i community and the horrendous violence befalling Shi`a on the Israeli–Lebanese border, they were effectively overlooked by the English-language media. Additionally, the Shi`i community's issues were often conflated with the issues of the Palestinian community in South Lebanon. Only Manchester's *Guardian* commented on the growing importance of the Lebanese Shi`i community and the key leadership role of Musa al-Sadr as early as May 1970.[4]

The rise of Musa al-Sadr and his efforts to obtain fair treatment and civil rights for the Lebanese Shi`a established the foundation of the Shi`i narrative. Al-Sadr gave voice to the needs of the Shi`i community in Lebanon. When his efforts toward a peaceful resolution to the inequality in Lebanese society failed, al-Sadr voiced the need for the Shi`i community to defend itself with armed force if necessary. "Arms are an adornment of men," he said during a large rally in Lebanon.⁵ The battle of Nab`a reinforced the Shi`a's need to protect themselves by force. Despite their cries for help and support, when a large Shi`i community was violently expelled from an area of Eastern Beirut by Christian militia, no one outside of the community itself came to its aid. The press and media coverage of this story conflated the horrors the Shi`a suffered with what was happening to the plight of Palestinians in the adjacent enclave of Tal al-Za`tar.

Noteworthy during this period was the role of another prominent Shi`i leader, Sayyid Hussein Fadlallah. Like Musa al-Sadr, Fadlallah was born outside of Lebanon; however, the transnational nature of the Shi`i networks afforded him an opportunity to rise to prominence in the Lebanese context. As previously documented, Fadlallah worked tirelessly to raise the Lebanese Shi`a's standard of living and acquire greater civil rights for the community. While under bombardment in the town of Nab`a, Fadlallah wrote *Islam and the Logic of Force* (1977). Years later, the English-language press referenced the book as the intellectual link between Shi`i fundamentalists in Lebanon and the "Iran-oriented philosophy."⁶ By this time, the Western media tainted the "Iran-oriented philosophy" with the notion of antimodernism and fanaticism. The press missed the nature of Shi`i thought and logic as a transnational phenomenon. Shi`i thought was not confined to a particular country or individual but was an intellectual discourse that spanned many different centers of Shi`i learning. Exposed to Shi`i thinking in centers of Najaf, Iraq, and Qom, Iran, Fadlallah wrote in a way that extended beyond the topic of Islam and violence. He wrote prolifically on subjects such as the nature of Islamic proselytizing and of Western secular legal thought on Islam.⁷ Not understanding this factor was key to the press's inability to capture the narrative of the Lebanese Shi`a and properly represent them.

Third, the Iranian Revolution and the Israeli invasion of Lebanon in 1982 are presented as critical events in constructing a dominant Shi`a narrative in Lebanon. The English-language press initially marginalized the Shi`i revolutionary movement in Iran. They largely ignored the connection between the Shi`i revival in Lebanon and Iranian dissidents. Business and investment news dominated the English-language press and media's early coverage of Iran. The initial coverage of the dissent in Iran focused on what the papers called an Islamic–Marxist alliance.⁸ The *New York Times* and other American media sources expended little effort in unpacking the grievances of Iran's Shi`i religious establishment against the policies and the actions of the shah, whose rapid demise proved a surprise to most in the West. The media had misinformed Westerners about the nature of the Shi`i revolution and the importance of Shi`ism to Iranian society.

After the shah's ouster and Ayatollah Khomeini's return to Iran, the American press and media coverage turned negative toward the Shi`a, as evidenced by their characterization as antimodernization and anti-Western.⁹

When Iranian students seized the American embassy, the American press and media made a more concerted effort to demonize and characterize the Shi`a as the Other. The lack of background and context to the Shi`a actions in Iran distorted the prestige press and media's representation of political dynamics at work during this period. By demeaning and demonizing the Shi`i religion, the American media and press failed to portray an accurate and unbiased picture of the large Shi`a movement for civil rights and fairness, which was also taking place in Lebanon.

Although the British press did not report on many of the early antishah activities, it proved able to exhibit distinctive reporting on the dysfunctions within his regime. At the beginning of 1975, the *Times* (London) published a series of reports covering human rights abuses emanating from the shah of Iran's secret police. Part of that regime of torture focused on Shi`i leaders and clerics who formed the religious opposition to the shah. Although the *Times* (London) and the *Guardian* did not cover the initial connection between the Lebanese Shi`a and the Iranian revolutionary movement, eventually a November 1978 *Times* (London) article discussed the importance of the religion and its effect on the Iranian Revolution.[10]

When Khomeini returned to Iran in January 1979, the British press and media uncovered a link between the Movement of the Deprived in Lebanon and the fledgling Iranian government.[11] The *Guardian* covered a number of meetings between the Lebanese Shi`a and the Khomeini regime, emphasizing that the Lebanese delegation had offered support for the new Khomeini government. Reporter Robert Fisk discovered that there was also an inspirational connection between the Iranian Revolution and the Lebanese Shi`a. In a 1980 article, Fisk recounted that the Shi`i militia in Lebanon, who were battling Palestinian, Baathist, and Christian militias, looked to the Iranian Revolution for spiritual guidance.[12] This linkage, and other reports that appeared in the British press and media, painted a different picture of the connection between the Iranian Revolution and the Lebanese Shi`a. As Shi`i militia groups in Lebanon fought for their survival and independence, the connection between the Iranian Revolution and the Lebanese Shi`a would become even closer, particularly after the Israeli invasion of Lebanon in 1982. The Iranian Revolutionary Guard was quick to answer the Lebanese Shi`a call for support to resist the Israeli invasion. The British and American press and media took a different approach in representing the Lebanese Shi`a during this time. The American media focused on the possibility of cooperation between the Shi`a and the Israelis, while the British press focused on the frictions that existed between the two communities.

Just prior to the 1982 Israeli invasion of Lebanon, the *New York Times* emphasized Amal's conflict with Palestinian militias. The paper never highlighted the fact that Amal was fighting on many different fronts, and the paper's articles even suggested the possibility of a Shi`a–Israeli alliance against the PLO.[13] The *New York Times* failed to recognize that, having suffered at the hands of the Israelis and their Christian allies in the Israeli invasion of 1978, the Lebanese Shi`a were wary of all outsiders. When Israeli troops crossed into Lebanon in the summer of 1982, Lebanese Shi`a were skeptical of Israeli intentions, despite their best hopes.

New York Times editorials hailed the initial invasion in 1982 as the liberation of Lebanon, but the Shi`a suffered tremendously in the collateral damage of the Israeli attacks.[14] The *New York Times* and other American media outlets slowly began to focus on the growing power of the Shi`i resistance in November 1982. Yet, the American media and the prestige press never quite represented the resentment and the Shi`a's hostility toward Israel and their foreign supporters. After the explosion of the Marine Barracks at Beirut's airport in October 1983, the *New York Times* and the rest of the American media finally considered the narrative of the Lebanese Shi`a.

The British press and media reports of the Israeli invasion's impact on the Lebanese Shi`a differed from that of the American press and media. The *Times* (London) had at least anticipated the potential invasion of Lebanon early in 1982.[15] Prior to the invasion, a *Times* reporter captured preparation by members of the Shi`i community for a conflict with the Israelis. The article also made the point that the Shi`a were fighting on many different fronts within Lebanon. They did not presuppose that Amal would be a great ally of the Israelis against the PLO, as Amal was prepared to defend itself against any entity that would restrict its rights or infringe on the Shi`i population. Once the invasion started, *Times* reporter Robert Fisk emerged as one of the few Western journalists to specifically acknowledge the fierce resistance that Shi`i fighters offered during the Israeli attack on Beirut.[16] After the Israeli invasion, the *Guardian* reported that the Lebanese Shi`i community in the south was growing restless and uneasy about the Israeli occupation. In November 1982 the *Times* indicated that more trouble and discontent were brewing with the Shi`a as members of Islamic Amal took over Lebanese government buildings in the Bekaa Valley. All these events indicated that the majority of the Lebanese Shi`a were dissatisfied with the results of the Israeli invasion and that they were prepared to resist the Israelis and those who supported them. By December 1982, as Fisk indicated in a *Times* article, the Americans' involvement as a peacekeeping force placed them in a dangerous position. It would not be long before his assessment proved correct as Shi`i militant groups bombed the American embassy in April 1983 and the Marine barracks in October 1983.

The bombing of the American embassy and the Marine barracks focused the British and American media and prestige-press attention on the ongoing violence between the Shi`i resistance fighters and the Israeli forces. Examples of that coverage included the assassination of Imam Ragheb Harb in February 1984, the coverage of the "Iron Fist" policy carried out by the

Israeli forces, and American and British news reports in which Lebanese Shi`a expressed their own concerns about the situation in their country. These reports helped paint a clearer picture of how the invasion affected the Shi`a in Lebanon. Ten years of Shi`a history had constituted a distinct narrative of people who were determined to chart their own destiny within Lebanese society. However, the English-language prestige press was just starting to capture a true representation of the plight of the Lebanese Shi`a. Despite a considered attempt in the British press, the English-language media proved unable to fully construct an accurate news narrative of the Lebanese Shi`a for its Western audience.

The concept of Orientalism must be operative when ascertaining why the press failed to represent the Lebanese Shi`a correctly. As observed by Edward Said and as covered in this book, Westerners frequently approach the study and coverage of the "Orient" in a specific manner, the driving element of which is a historical prejudice toward occidental power relationships over the East.[17] In covering the Lebanese Shi`a, this Orientalist view increased the media's tendency to overlook primary sources, as well as the language of the people concerned, and to privilege interpretations by so-called Middle East experts from the West. Whether exhibited through the use of terms like *Arab guerrillas* and *terrorists* to describe an entire group of people bearing the brunt of Israeli military operations in South Lebanon or made obvious in depicting the marginalization of Shi`i institutions that did not fit into a Western construct, Orientalism was alive and well in Western reporting from Lebanon.[18] This book has traced these misrepresentations through selected English-language prestige-press and media reports.

In the end, reporters and correspondents assume a unique and special duty within society. Their profession requires expertise and a skill set for accurately recording events. In the realm of international reporting, that expertise should be dedicated to the task of acting as cultural interpreters. To cover foreign events effectively, reporters and correspondents must decode the symbols of language, religion, traditions, and rites to give them appropriate meaning and context.[19] They should also compare them with domestic, national, or local cultures and explain them to their audiences. In covering the Lebanese Shi`a, the English-language prestige press and media failed to interpret, or decode, symbols born of foreign context and attach, or relate appropriate meanings. Despite the subtle differences in coverage between the American and British prestige press and media, neither fully captured the symbols of the Lebanese Shi`a. They never fully developed an accurate news narrative about the Lebanese Shi`a between 1975 and 1985, one that responsibly represented events in that community. This failure to relay a true representation of the Lebanese Shi`a narrative led to a general lack of understanding of the goals and aspirations of this group. As the largest religious group in the country with the most impactful military organization (Hezbullah), the Lebanese Shi`a are critical to the future stability of Lebanon. This failure deprived Western audiences of the contextual information necessary to truly appreciate the role and the importance of the Lebanese Shi`a.

NOTES

1. "Code of Ethics," *Society of Professional Journalists*, http://www.Columbia.edu/itc/journalism/j6075/edit/ethiccodes/SPJ.html (accessed August 17, 2012).
2. Fouad Ajami, *The Vanished Imam: Musa al-Sadr and the Shia of Lebanon* (Ithaca, NY: Cornell University Press, 1986), 136; H. E. Chehabi, *Distant Relations: Iran and Lebanon in the Last 500 Years* (London: I. B. Tauris, 2006), 173.
3. See Introduction.
4. David Hirst, "Lebanese May Ask for Troops," *Guardian*, May 26, 1970.
5. Ajami, *The Vanished Imam*, 168.
6. John Kifner, "Bombing in Beirut Has Troubling Echoes," *New York Times*, May 19, 1985.
7. Jamal Sankari, *Fadlallah: The Making of a Radical Shi`ite Leader* (London: SAQI, 2005), 106.
8. See "Iran and the American Press and Media" in chapter 3.
9. Ibid.
10. Edward Mortimer, "Iran's Brand of Islam a Religion of Opposition," *Times* (London), November 23, 1978.
11. BBC *Summary of World* broadcast, "Lebanon: In Brief; Return of Shi`i Delegation from Iran," June 20, 1980.
12. Robert Fisk, "Shia Militiamen in Beirut Clash with Palestinians," *Times* (London), May 29, 1980.
13. See "The English Language Press Prior to the Israeli Invasion of Lebanon" in chapter 4; also "Shiite Group to Aid Israelis," *New York Times*, June 30, 1982.
14. See "Covering the Invasion in the English Language press and Media" in chapter 4.
15. Ibid.
16. Ibid.
17. Edward Said, *Orientalism* (New York: Vintage Books, 1979), 273.
18. Edmund Ghareeb, *Split Vision: The Portrayal of Arabs in the American Media* (Washington, DC: American–Arab Affairs Council, 1983), 14.
19. Kai Hafez, ed., *Islam and the West in the Mass Media: Fragmented Images in a Globalizing World* (Cresskill, NJ: Hampton Press, 2000), 37.

Bibliography

Abrahamian, Ervand. "The Guerrilla Movement in Iran, 1963–1977." *The Middle East Research and Information Project Reports*, no. 86 (March–April 1980): 3–15.
———. *Khomeinism: Essays on the Islamic Republic*. Berkeley: University of California Press, 1993.
Afary, Janet, and Kevin Anderson. *Foucault and the Iranian Revolution: Gender and the Seductions of Islamism*. Chicago: University of Chicago Press, 2005.
Ajami, Fouad. *The Vanished Imam: Musa al-Sadr and the Shia of Lebanon*. Ithaca, NY: Cornell University Press, 1986.
Alagha, Joseph. "Hizbullah: The Islamic Resistance in Lebanon." Review of *Hezbollah: A Short History*, by Augustus Richard Norton. H-Net Levant. Last modified April 2008. http://www.h-net.org/reviews/showrev.php?id=1422.
Baer, Robert. *The Devil We Know: Dealing with the New Iranian Superpower*. New York: Crown, 2008.
Ball, George. *Error and Betrayal in Lebanon: An Analysis of Israel's Invasion of Lebanon and the Implications for U.S.–Israeli Relations*. Washington, DC: Foundation for Middle East Peace, 1984.
Beeman, William O. "Iran and the United States: Postmodern Culture Conflict in Action." *Anthropological Quarterly* 76, no. 4 (2003): 671–91.
Behi, Kambiz. "The Real in Resistance: Transgression of Law as Ethical Act." Unpublished manuscript, 2008.
Bill, James A. *The Eagle and the Lion: The Tragedy of American–Iranian Relations*. New Haven, CT: Yale University Press, 1988.
Bolling, Landrum R. *Reporters under Fire: US Media Coverage of Conflicts in Lebanon and Central America*. Boulder, CO: Westview Press, 1985.
Bonney, Richard. *Jihad: From Qur'an to bin Laden*. New York: Palgrave Macmillan, 2004.
Bowden, Mark. *Guest of the Ayatollah: The First Battle in America's War with Militant Islam*. New York: Grove Press, 2006.
Boykin, John. *Cursed Is the Peacemaker: The American Diplomat versus the Israeli General, Beirut 1982*. Belmont, CA: Applegate Press, 2002.
Braley, Russ. *Bad News: The Foreign Policy of the* New York Times. Chicago: Regnery Gateway, 1984.
Brinkley, Douglas. *The Reagan Diaries*. New York: Harper Collins, 2007.
Cannon, Lou. *President Reagan: The Role of a Lifetime*. New York: Public Affairs, 1991.
Chamai, Joseph G. *Days of Tragedy: Lebanon '75–'76*. London: Transaction Books, 1984.
Chehabi, H. E., ed. *Distant Relations: Iran and Lebanon in the Last 500 Years*. London: I. B. Tauris, 2006.

Chomsky, Noam. *Fateful Triangle: The United States, Israel, and the Palestinians*. Cambridge, MA: South End Press, 1999.
Cleveland, William. *A History of the Modern Middle East*. Boulder, CO: Westview Press, 2000.
Cobban, Helena. *The Making of Modern Lebanon*. Boulder, CO: Westview Press, 1985.
Cohen, Eliot A. "The Historical Mind and Military Strategy." *Orbis* (Fall 2005): 575–88.
Cole, Juan. *Sacred Space and Holy War: The Politics, Culture and History of Shi`ite Islam*. New York: I. B. Tauris & Co. Ltd., 2002.
Collelo, Thomas, ed. *Lebanon: A Country Study*. 3rd ed. Washington, DC: United States Government, 1989.
Dabashi, Hamid "Edward Said's *Orientalism*: Forty Years Later," May 3, 2018, Al Jazeera, https://www.aljazeera.com/indepth/opinion/edward-orientalism-forty-...
Davis, M. Thomas. *40 Km into Lebanon*. Washington, DC: National Defense University Press, 1987.
Deeb, Lara. *An Enchanted Modern: Gender and Public Piety in Shi'i Lebanon*. Princeton, NJ: Princeton University Press, 2006.
Deeb, Marius. *Syria's Terrorist War on Lebanon and the Peace Process*. New York: Macmillan, 2003.
Dershowitz, Toby, ed. *The Reagan Administration and Israel: Key Statements*. Washington, DC: American Israeli Public Affairs Committee, 1987.
Dolphin, Glenn E. *24 MAU: 1983 A Marine Looks Back at the Peacekeeping Mission to Beirut, Lebanon*. Baltimore, MD: Publish America, 2005.
Dorman, William A., and Mansour Farhang. *The U.S. Press and Iran: Foreign Policy and the Journalism of Deference*. Berkeley: University of California Press, 1987.
Elhadj, Elie. *The Islamic Shield: Arab Resistance to Democratic and Religious Reforms*. Boca Raton, FL: Brown Walker Press, 2008.
Enayat, Hamid. *Modern Islamic Political Thought*. Austin: University of Texas Press, 1982.
Esposito, John, ed. *The Iranian Revolution: Its Global Impact*. Miami: Florida International University Press, 1990.
Evans, Harold. *Good Times, Bad Times*. New York: Atheneum, 1983.
Fatemi, Khosrow. "The Iranian Revolution: Its Impact on Economic Relations with the United States." *International Journal of Middle East Studies* 12, no. 3 (1980): 303–17.
Fisk, Robert. *Pity the Nation: The Abduction of Lebanon*. New York: Thunder Mountain Press, 1990.
Frank, Benis M. *US Marines in Lebanon 1982–1984*. Washington, DC: History and Museums Division, Headquarters Marines, 1987.
Friedman, Thomas. *From Beirut to Jerusalem*. New York: Anchor Books, 1989.
Geraghty, Timothy J. *Peacekeepers at War: Beirut 1983, The Marine Commander Tells His Story*. Washington, DC: Potomac Books, 2009.
Ghareeb, Edmund. *Split Vision: The Portrayal of Arabs in the American Media*. Washington, DC: American–Arab Affairs Council, 1983.
Gilboa, Eytan. *American Public Opinion toward Israel and the Arab–Israeli Conflict*. Lexington, MA: Lexington Books, 1987.
Gillespie, Thomas R. *Reagan Administration Foreign Policy: Military Intervention and International Law*. Ann Arbor, MI: UMI, 1990.
Gutman, Roy. "Battle over Lebanon." *Foreign Service Journal* (June 1984): 28–33.
Hafez, Kai, ed. *Islam and the West in the Mass Media*. Cresskill, NJ: Hampton Press, 2000.
Hagerdal, Nils. "Ethnic Cleansing as Military Strategy: Lessons from Lebanon, 1975–1990." Doctoral dissertation, Harvard University, Graduate School of Arts & Sciences, 2016.
Haig, Alexander. *Caveat: Realism, Reagan and Foreign Policy*. New York: Macmillan, 1984.
Halawi, Majed. *A Lebanon Defied: Musa al-Sadr and the Shi`a Community*. Boulder, CO: Westview Press, 1992.
Hall, David K., and William J. Farrel. "Lebanon Revisited." *Selected Readings in Policy Making and Process 1*. Newport, RI: Naval War College of Distance Education, National Security Decision Making, 2005–2006.

Hamizrachi, Beate. *The Emergence of the South Lebanon Security Belt: Major Saad Haddad and the Ties with Israel, 1975–1978.* New York: Praeger, 1988.
Hammel, Eric. *The Root: The Marines in Beirut, August 1982–February 1984.* St. Paul, MN: Zenith Press, 2005.
Hamzeh, Ahmad Nizar. *In the Path of Hizbullah.* Syracuse, NY: Syracuse University Press, 2004.
Helmer, Daniel, "Hezbollah's Employment of Suicide Bombing during the 1980s: The Theological, Political, and Operational Development of a New Tactic," *Military Review* (July–August 2006).
Herrera, Gary A., and Matthew W. Quinn. "Asymmetric Warfare and the Will to Win." Master's thesis, Naval Postgraduate School, 2001.
Hodgson, Marshall G. S. *The Classical Age of Islam.* Vol. 1 of *The Venture of Islam: Conscience and History in a World Civilization.* Chicago: University of Chicago Press, 1961.
Hovsepian, Nubar, ed. *The War on Lebanon: A Reader.* Northampton, MA: Olive Branch Press, 2006.
Husseini, Rola el. "Resistance, Jihad and Martyrdom in Contemporary Lebanese Shi'a Discourse." *Middle East Journal* 62, no. 3 (Summer 2008): 399–416.
Ignatius, David. "How to Rebuild Lebanon," *Foreign Affairs* 61, no. 4 (Summer 1983): 1140–56.
Jaber, Hala. *Hezbollah: Born with a Vengeance.* New York: Columbia University Press, 1997.
Kahan Commission. *The Beirut Massacre: The Complete Kahan Commission Report.* New York: Karz-Cohl, 1983.
Kamalipour, Yahya R., ed. *The U.S. Media and the Middle East: Image and Perception.* Westport, CT: Praeger, 1995.
Keddie, Nikki R. *Modern Iran: Roots and Results of Revolution.* New Haven, CT: Yale University Press, 2006.
Kelly, John. "Lebanon: 1982–1984." RAND Corporation. http://www.rand.org/pubs/conf_proceedings/CF129.chapter 6 (accessed April 15, 2007).
Khater, Akram Fouad. *Sources in the History of the Modern Middle East.* Boston: Houghton Mifflin, 2004.
Khomeini, Ruhollah. *Islamic Government.* USA: *Studies in Islam and the Middle East,* 2004. http://majalla.org (accessed December 28, 2011).
———. "We Shall Confront the World with Our Ideology." *Middle East Research and Information Project Reports,* no. 88 (June 1980): 22–25.
Korbani, Agnes. *U.S. Intervention in Lebanon, 1958 and 1982: Presidential Decisionmaking.* New York: Praeger, 1991.
Kramer, Martin. "Sacrifice and Self-Martyrdom in Shi'ite Lebanon." *Terrorism and Political Violence* 3, no. 3 (Autumn 1991): 30–47.
LaQueur, Walter, and Barry Rubin, eds. *The Israel-Arab Reader: A Documentary History of the Middle East Conflict.* New York: Penguin, 2008.
Lindblom, Charles E., and Edward J. Woodhouse. *The Policy-Making Process,* Englewood Cliffs, NJ: Prentice Hall, 1993.
Little, Douglas. *American Orientalism: The United States in the Middle East since 1945.* Chapel Hill: University of North Carolina Press, 2002.
Lynam, Rebekah, Maureen Taylor, and Peter Gade. "Newspaper Frames of Hizbullah: Uni-Dimensional Framing of a Multi-Dimensional Organization." *Journal of Middle East Media,* Vol. 12 (Spring 2016).
Maasri, Zeina. *Off the Wall: Political Posters of the Lebanese Civil War.* London: I. B. Tauris, 2009.
Mackey, Sandra. *Lebanon: A House Divided.* New York: W. W. Norton Company, 1989.
Martin, David C., and John Walcott. *Best Laid Plans: The Inside Story of America's War against Terrorism.* London: Harper & Row, 1988.
Matar, Dina, and Farah Dakhlallah. "What It Means to Be Shiite in Lebanon: Al Manar and the Imagined Community of Resistance." *Communication and Culture* 3, no. 2 (2006): 22–40.
McDermott, Anthony, and Kjell Skjelsbaek. *The Multinational Force in Beirut, 1982–1984.* Miami: Florida International University Press, 1991.

McLaurin, R. B. *The Battle of Zahle*. Springfield, Virginia: Abbott Associates, 1986.
Mearsheimer, John J., and Stephen M. Walt. *The Israel Lobby and U.S. Foreign Policy*. New York: Farrar, Straus and Giroux, 2007.
Momen, Moojan. *An Introduction to Shi`i Islam: The History and Doctrines of Twelver Shi`ism*. New Haven, CT: Yale University Press, 1985.
Moore, John Norton, ed. *The Arab-Israeli Conflict*. Vol. IV, *The Difficult Search for Peace (1975–1988)*. Princeton, NJ: Princeton University Press, 1991.
Najjar, Alexandre. *L'ecole de la guerre*. London: Telegram Books, 2006.
Nasr, Salim, and Diane James. "Roots of the Shi`i Movement." *Middle East Research and Information Reports*, no. 133 (June 1985): 10–16.
Nasr, Vali. *The Shia Revival: How Conflicts within Islam Will Shape the Future*. New York: W. W. Norton, 2006.
Noe, Nicholas, ed. *Voice of Hezbollah: The Statements of Sayyed Hassan Nasrallah*. London: Verso, 2007.
Norton, Augustus Richard. *Amal and the Shi`a: Struggle for the Soul of Lebanon*. Austin: University of Texas Press, 1987.
———. *Hezbollah*. Princeton, NJ: Princeton University Press, 2007.
O'Ballance, Edgar. *Civil War in Lebanon, 1975–92*. New York: St. Martin's Press, 1998.
Olson, Steven P. *The Attack on U.S. Marines in Lebanon on October 23, 1983*. New York: Rosen, 2003.
Ostovar, Afshon. *Vanguard of the Imam: Religion, Politics and Iran's Revolutionary Guards*. New York: Oxford University Press, 2016.
Peterson, Scott. "In South Lebanon, Resistance from Cradle to Grave," *Christian Science Monitor*, last modified June 7, 2007. http://www.csmonitor.com/2007/0607/p14s01-wome.htm.
Petit, Michael. *Peacekeepers at War: A Marine's Account of the Beirut Catastrophe*. Winchester, MA: Faber & Faber, 1986.
Petran, Tabitha. *The Struggle over Lebanon*. New York: Monthly Review Press, 1987.
Picard, Elizabeth. *Lebanon: A Shattered Country*. New York: Holmes & Meir, 2002.
Pintak, Lawrence. *Beirut Outtakes: A TV Correspondent's Portrait of America's Encounter with Terror*. Lexington, MA: Lexington Books, 1988.
———. *Seeds of Hate: How America's Flawed Middle East Policy Ignited Jihad*. London: Pluto Press, 2003.
Poole, Elizabeth. *Reporting Islam: Media Representations of British Muslims*. London: I. B. Tauris, 2002.
Poole, H. John. *Tactics of the Crescent Moon: Militant Muslim Combat Methods*. Emerald Isle, NC: Posterity Press, 2004.
Porter, Patrick. *Military Orientalism: Eastern War through Western Eyes*. New York: Columbia University Press, 2009.
Qassem, Naim. *Hizbullah: The Story from Within*. London: SAQI, 2005.
Quandt, William B. *Peace Process: American Diplomacy and the Arab–Israeli Conflict since 1967*. Berkeley: University of California Press, 2005.
———. *Reagan's Lebanon Policy: Trial and Error*. Washington, DC: Brookings Institute, 1984.
Rabinovich, Iatmar. *The War for Lebanon, 1970–1985*. Ithaca, NY: Cornell University Press, 1984.
Randal, Jonathan. *Going All the Way: Christian Warlords, Israeli Adventurers, and the War in Lebanon*. Toronto: Vintage Books, 1984.
Rippin, Andrew. *Muslims: Their Religious Beliefs and Practices*. 2nd ed. New York: Routledge, 2001.
Rowayheb, Marwan, G. "Lebanese Militias: A New Perspective." *Middle Eastern Studies* 42, no. 2 (March 2006): 303–18.
Saad-Ghorayeb, Amal. *Hizbu'llah: Politics and Religion*. New York: Pluto Press, 2002.
Said, Edward. *Covering Islam: How the Media and the Experts Determine How We See the Rest of the World*. New York: Vintage Books, 1997.
———. *Orientalism*. New York: Vintage Books, 1979.

Salibi, Kamal. *A House of Many Mansions: The History of Lebanon Reconsidered.* Berkeley: University of California Press, 1988.
Sammii, Abbas W. "The Shah's Lebanon Policy: The Role of SAVAK." *Middle Eastern Journal* 33, no. 1 (January 1997): 66–91.
Sankari, Jamal. *Fadlallah: The Making of a Radical Shi`ite Leader.* London: SAQI, 2005.
Sasley, Brent E. *The Cold War in the Middle East 1950–1991.* Broomall, PA: Mason Crest, 2007.
Schiff, Ze'ev, and Ehud Ya'ari. *Israel's Lebanon War.* New York: Simon & Schuster, 1984.
Senellart, Michel, ed. *Michel Foucault: Security, Territory, Population: Lectures at the College De France 1977–1978.* New York: Palgrave Macmillan, 2004.
Shaery-Eisenlohr, Roschanack. *Shi`ite Lebanon: Transnational Religion and the Making of National Identities.* New York: Columbia University Press, 2008.
Shanahan, Rodger. *The Shi`a of Lebanon: Clans, Parties, and Clerics.* New York: I. B. Tauris, 2005.
Shatz, Adam. "In Search of Hezbollah." *The New York Review of Books* 51, no. 7 (April 29, 2004).
Simpson, Christopher. *National Security Directives of the Reagan and Bush Administrations: The Declassified History of U.S. Political and Military Policy, 1981–1991.* Boulder, CO: Westview Press, 1995.
Smeeta, Mishra. 2006. "Islam and Democracy: An Analysis of Representation in the United States Prestige Press from 1985–2005." PhD diss., University of Texas, Austin.
Smith, Charles D. *Palestine and the Arab–Israeli Conflict: A History with Documents.* 6th ed. New York: Bedford/St. Martin's, 2007.
Smith, Michael. *Killer Elite.* New York: St. Martin's Press, 2006.
Spitzer, Robert J. *Media and Public Policy.* Westport, CT: Praeger, 1993.
Stock, Raymond. "Prestige Press at War: The *New York Times* and *Le Monde* in Lebanon." *Middle East Journal* 39, no. 3 (Summer 1985): 317–40.
Stork, Joe. "The War of the Camps, The War of the Hostages." *Middle East Research and Information Project*, no. 133 (June, 1985): 3–7, 22.
Tanter, Raymond. *Who's at the Helm? Lessons of Lebanon.* Boulder, CO: Westview Press, 1990.
The Beirut Massacre. New York: Karz-Cohl Publishing, 1983.
Traboulsi, Fawwaz. *A History of Modern Lebanon.* London: Pluto Press, 2007.
Tueni, Nadia. *Liban Poemes d'amour et de guerre.* Syracuse, NY: Syracuse University Press, 2006.
Walker, Martin. *Powers of the Press: Twelve of the World's Influential Newspapers.* New York: Pilgrim Press, 1983.
Wenger, Martha, and Julie Denney. "Lebanon's Fifteen-Year War 1975–1990." *Middle East Report*, no. 162 (1990).
White, Hayden. *The Content of the Form: Narrative Discourse and Historical Representation.* Baltimore: Johns Hopkins University Press, 1987.
Wills, David. *The First War on Terrorism.* Toronto: Rowman & Littlefield, 2003.
Wright, Robin. *Dreams and Shadows: The Future of the Middle East.* New York: Penguin Books, 2009.
———. *Sacred Rage: The Wrath of Militant Islam.* New York: Simon & Schuster, 1985.

WASHINGTON, DC

The Library of Congress in Washington, DC, has an extensive collection of newspapers from across the Middle East that includes microfilm of Beirut's *Daily Star*, Aman's *Star*, and the *Kuwait Times*.
The National Archives in Washington, DC, has an extensive list of documents from the Reagan administration during the time frame 1981–84.
The National Security Archive at George Washington University is an online source that provides government documents obtained through a Freedom of Information Act (FOIA)

request. The Digital National Security Archives are available at http://nsarchive.chadwyck.com/marketing/index.jsp.

WESTERN NEWSPAPERS AND MAGAZINES

The Boston Globe
The Christian Science Monitor
The Economist
The Times (London)
The Los Angeles Times
The New York Times
Time
The Sunday Times
The Telegraph (London)
The Washington Post

FOREIGN NEWSPAPERS

An-Nahar
The Daily Star
L'Orient-Le Jour

Index

ABC. *See* American Broadcasting Corporation
Abu Bakr, xix, xx
Abu Dharr al-Ghifari, xix–xx
Abu Nidal Organization (ANO), 92
Abu Talib, xix–xx
administrative areas (*vilayets*), xxi
Afwaj al-Muqawama al-Lubnaniya (Amal), xiv, 63, 81–82; BLT bombing and, xv, xxvn14; communism and, 26; Fatah and, 25–26; Ghaddar of, 112; Haddad and, 91; Iran and, 76; Israeli invasion of Lebanon and, 91, 93, 94–95, 96–97, 106–107, 107, 109; Nab`a battle and, 43, 51–52; al-Sadr and, 7, 10–11, 91; South Lebanon and, 91, 95; *Times* (London) on, 101, 102. *See also* Islamic Amal
aircraft hijacking, 28–29
Ajami, Fouad: Orientalism of, 2; on al-Sadr, 2–3, 16, 31n44, 34n147
Ali (imam), xix–xx, 83n12
Amal. *See Afwaj al-Muqawama al-Lubnaniya*
America, xv, xxvn14; on Iran, 69–71, 73–75; Israeli invasion of Lebanon and, 92, 94, 95, 95–96, 99, 105–106, 116n17; kidnapping and, 90; shah and, 73–75. *See also* Central Intelligence Agency; *specific leaders*

American Broadcasting Corporation (ABC), 19, 33n112, 80, 113
American embassy: bombing of, 105–106; seizure of, 77, 77–79, 80
American Orientalism: The United States in the Middle East Since 1945 (Little), xvii, 115
American Public Opinion toward Israel and the Arab–Israeli Conflict (Gilboa), 118n92
American Special Forces, 106, 119n118
An-Nahar, 12
ANO. *See* Abu Nidal Organization
Arab guerrilla, 21
Arab-Israeli war (1948), xxiii
Arafat, Yasir, 11–12, 27, 122
Ashura, xiii–xiv, 108–109
Assad, Kamel, 23
al Assad, Ahmad Bey, xxii
al Assad, Kamel, xxii
al-Assad, Bashar, 126
al-Assad, Hafez, 6, 27, 115, 120n161
assassination, 95; by Forqan, 76; of Harb, 112
assassination attempt, 45, 114, 123
Auon, Michel, 125

Bakhtiar, Shahpur, 77, 86n97
Begin, Menachim, 13, 92
Beirut *Daily Star*, 7–8, 23

143

Berri, Nabih, 63–64; Israeli invasion of Lebanon and, 93, 95, 96–97, 103, 106
Black, Ian, 112–113
"Black–Red alliance," 70
Black September, xxiii
Blanford, Nicholas, 121–122
BLT. *See* Marine Battalion Landing Team (BLT) bombing
British military contingent, 119n108
British press and media, xv–xvi, xviii, 69. *See also Economist*; *Guardian* (Manchester); *Sunday Times*; *Times* (London)
Brotherhood Association, 41

capitalism, 85n60
Carter, Jimmy, 77, 86n97
Central Intelligence Agency (CIA): American Embassy bombing and, 105; assassination attempt by, 45, 114, 123
Chamran, Mostafa, 33n120, 43, 44, 61, 76, 93–94
Chehabi, H. E., 6, 38, 44, 57–58
Chomsky, Noam, 99
Christian Maronites, xxiii, xxiii–xxiv, xxvin54; power of, 42; al-Sadr and, 8, 12, 25, 31n44, 51
Christian militias, 96; in Nab`a battle, 42–43, 46, 48, 49, 50; *New York Times* and, 99–100; al-Sadr and, 13; *Washington Post* on, 101
Christians, xiii, xxi–xxii, xxivn3
CIA. *See* Central Intelligence Agency
clan leaders (*zuama*), xxii, 45–46
clerical class (*ulama*), xx
CNN, 123
Cobban, Helen, 37
Cody, Edward, 67, 81–82, 86n97
Cold War, 85n60, 92
communism, 26, 68, 73, 85n60
Cooper, Andrew, 122
Covering Islam: How the Media and the Experts Determine How We See the Rest of the World (Said), xviii, 65–66, 82–83
Cultural Council for South Lebanon, 13, 14

Daily Star (Lebanon), 7–8
al-Da`wa party, 60, 68, 114, 122

Dickie, James, 79
Dionne, E. J., Jr., 106–107
Distant Relations: Iran and Lebanon in the Last 500 Years (Chehabi), 6, 38, 57–58
Dodge, David, 90
dominant narrative, xxvn24
Dorman, William A., 65
Druze, xxi, xxii, 9, 99, 107, 124

economics, Iran and, 69–70
Economist, 51, 107
education, 5; Fadlallah and, 40, 59; from al-Sadr, 20–21, 33n120
Egyptian Mamluks, xx
The Emergence of the South Lebanon Security Belt: Major Saad Haddad and the Ties with Israel, 1975–1978 (Hamizrachi), 118n78
English-language press and media, xv, 57, 115; ISIL and, xvi; MERIP and, 18; narrative of, xvi; before 1975, 18–19; political communications theory and, xvi; social media and, 121, 127n1. *See also specific newspapers and media*
Esposito, John, 57–58, 58
"ethnic cleansing," 47, 48
Exum, Andrew, 125

Fadlallah, Sayyid Muhammad Hussein, xxvn24, 37, 39, 40, 52n1; assassination attempt on, 114, 123; education and, 40, 59; Hezbullah and, 52, 122–123; Iranian Revolution and, 64; *Islam and the Logic of Power* from, 41, 46, 52, 123; Lebanon relocation of, 40–41; Nab`a and, 41, 44–45, 52; *New York Times* on, 122–123; social services from, 41
Fadlallah: The Making of a Radical Shi`ite Leader (Sankari), 38, 44–45, 53n23
The Fall of Heaven: The Pahlavis and the Final Days of Imperial Iran (Cooper), 122
Farhang, Mansour, 65
Fatah, 21, 92; Amal and, 25–26
Fateful Triangle: The United States, Israel, and the Palestinians (Chomsky), 99
fatwa (religious decree), xiv, 5
fiqh (Shi`i jurisprudence), 1

Fisk, Robert, 29, 67, 69, 79, 90, 103. *See also Times* (London)
Flint, Julie, 112
Forqan, 76
Foucault, Michel, 80
France, xxi; Israeli invasion of Lebanon with, 99, 109, 111–112
French barracks bombing, 111–112
Friedman, Thomas, 106, 109; skepticism of, 113–114

Gage, Nicholas, 82, 85n79
Gandhi, Mahatma, 25, 29, 34n147
Gemayel, Bachir, 44, 51; Israeli invasion of Lebanon and, 94, 95, 95–96, 96–97, 99–100, 106; Nab`a siege and, 44
Gemayel, Pierre, xxvin54
Geraghty, Timothy J., xxvn14
Ghaddar, Muhammad, 112
Gilboa, Eytan, 118n92
government, Lebanese Civil War and, 10, 13
"government of the jurist" (*vilāyat-i faqīh*), 59–60
Guardian (Manchester), xv, 18, 115; BLT bombing in, 111; Hirst at, 18–19, 25; Iran's Shi`a in, 75–76, 79; Israeli invasion of Lebanon and, 103–104; Khomeini in, 75–76; Nab`a in, 51; reprisals in, 112–113; al-Sadr disappearance in, 29, 121; al-Sadr in, 25, 27, 29, 30, 121; "suicide bombers" in, 111
Gwertzman, Bernard, 48

Habib, Phillip, 92, 94, 95–96, 116n17
Haddad, Saad, 100, 118n77–118n78; Amal and, 91
Hagerdal, Nils, 47
Halawi, Majed, 2, 2–3
Hama destruction, 115, 120n161
Hamizrachi, Beate, 118n78
Hammoura, Soheil, xiii, xiv, 108
Harakat al Mahrumin (Movement of the Deprived), 7, 10–11, 24
Harb, Ragheb, 112; poster of, 97, 98
Hezbullah, 94; current view of, 123, 125; Fadlallah and, 52, 122–123; "Journal of Middle East Media" on, 123–124; on Nab`a, 52; *New York Times* on, 123–124, 126; PBS on, 125; proxy forces and, 124; social services from, 125; *Wall Street Journal* on, 124–125
Higher Islamic Shi`i Council (HISC), 11; al-Sadr and, 3–5, 12, 15
"Higher Islamic Shi`ite Council of Lebanon," xiv
Hirst, David, 18–19, 25
HISC. *See* Higher Islamic Shi`i Council
historical background, xix–xx, xx–xxi; clan leaders in, xxii
A History of Modern Lebanon (Traboulisi), 53n23
Hizbu`llah Politics and Region (Saad-Ghorayeb), 53n23
Hofmann, Paul, 70
Hubbard, Ben, 126
Husayn, Imam, xiii–xiv, xxivn3
Hussein (king), xxiii
Hussein, Sayyid Abdul, 1

Icarus, 2
IDF. *See* Israel Defense Force
imam, 30n1, 83n12
In Vanguard of the Imam: Religion, Politics and Iran's Revolutionary Guards (Ostovar), 62
Iran, 29, 59, 62, 65, 122; Amal and, 76; America on, 69–71, 73–75; assassination attempt and, 114; Chehabi on, 6, 38, 57–58; current position of, 125–126; economics and, 69–70; LMI of, 60; al-Sadr and, 5–6, 69
Iranian Republic News Agency (IRNA), 103, 118n97
Iranian Revolution, xviii, 2, 67, 69, 89–90; Fadlallah and, 64; Lebanese Shi`a related to, 57–58; Lebanon and Iranian resistance and, 63, 63–64; Lebanon related to, 58–60; *New York Times* on, 65, 66, 70–71, 80; *Times* (London) on, 65, 67, 68, 68–69
Iranian Revolutionary Guard, 93, 99, 116n30
The Iranian Revolution: Its Global Impact (Esposito), 57–58, 58
"Iran Out to Remake Mideast With Arab Enforcer: Hezbollah" (Hubbard), 126

Iran's Shi`a: in *Guardian*, 75–76, 79; in *New York Times*, 72–73, 76, 79, 82; in *Times* (London), 72, 75, 76, 78, 79; in *Washington Post*, 81–82
Iraq, 59, 60, 91
IRNA. *See* Iranian Republic News Agency
"Iron Fist" strategy, 112
ISIL. *See* Islamic State in the Levant
Islam, 31n44; schism within, xix; Wahhabi Movement of, 85n75. *See also specific topics*
Islam and the Logic of Power (Fadlallah), 41, 46, 52, 123
Islamic Amal, 94–95, 97, 103, 123; Musawi on, 109–111; *Times* (London) on, 111
Islamic faith (*umma*), xix–xx
Islamic Government (Khomeini), 62
Islamic State in the Levant (ISIL), xvi
Israel Defense Force (IDF), xiv, 13–15; Lebanon raids by, 5–6, 7–8, 19–20, 33n112, 33n122; revenge by, 112
"Israeli Forces Raid 2 Lebanon Villages; 6 Houses Blown Up," 33n112
Israeli invasion of Lebanon, 89–90, 90; Amal and, 91, 93, 94–95, 96–97, 106–107, 107, 109; America and, 92, 94, 95, 95–96, 99, 105–106, 116n17; Berri and, 93, 95, 96–97, 103, 106; France with, 99, 109, 111–112; Gemayel, B., and, 94, 95, 95–96, 96–97, 99–100, 106; *Guardian* and, 103–104; *New York Times* on, 99, 100–101, 102, 104–105, 105–106, 106–107, 108–109, 118n77; PLO and, 92, 93, 96, 100; refugee camps massacre and, 95–96, 97; *Times* (London) and, 99, 101–102, 102, 104, 105

Jabal Amil region, xx
Jacobson, Philip, 67
Jisr al-Basha, 47, 51
Jordan, xxiii, xxvin32
"Journal of Middle East Media," 123–124
Jumblatt, Kamal, 27, 27–28, 42

Kahan Commission, 96, 117n53
Karami, Rashid, 10, 11–12, 26–27

Karantina, 42, 47
Kfar Shuba raid, 22–23
Khalid, Hassan (Shaykh), 11, 15, 27
Khomeini, Ruhollah Ayatollah, 2, 59, 68; in *Guardian*, 75–76; Lebanon and Iranian resistance and, 62–64, 63; in *New York Times*, 72, 73–74, 79; poster of, 63; al-Sadr and, 60, 122; in *Sunday Times*, 74; in *Time* magazine, 77, 78, 80–81
"Khomeini Declares Indignant Rejection of Carter's Appeal" (Cody), 86n97
kidnappings, 29, 69, 90
King, Jerry, 49
King, Martin Luther, 24, 29, 34n146

Lebanese Civil War, xxvin54; government and, 10, 13; *New York Times and*, 23–24, 24–25, 25–26, 27–29, 30; Palestinians and, xxii–xxiv, 8–9; al-Sadr and, 7–9, 23–30; Shi`a before, 8–10; *Times* (London) and, 24, 25, 26–27, 29
Lebanese National Movement (LNM), 9, 12, 41–42
Lebanon, xxiii, 2–3, 25; Christian Maronites in, xxi–xxii, xxiii, xxiii–xxiv, xxvin54, 8, 12, 31n44, 42; clan leaders in, xxii, 45–46; IDF raids on, 5–6, 7–8, 19–20, 33n112, 33n122; Iranian Revolution related to, 58–60; Vocational High School in, 20–21, 33n120
Lebanon and Iranian resistance, 60; Iranian Revolution and, 63, 63–64; Khomeini and, 62–64, 63; networks for, 62, 64, 67, 89–90, 126; SAVAK and, 61–62
A Lebanon Defied: Musaal-Sadr and the Shi`a Community (Halawi), 2, 2–3. *See also* Halawi, Majed
leftist, term usage, 25–26
Levant, xvi, xviii, xxvin32
Lewis, Anthony, 74
Liberation Movement of Iran (LMI), 60
Libya, 15, 16, 28, 91; Gadhafi of, 121–122
Little, Douglas, xvii, 115
LMI. *See* Liberation Movement of Iran
LNM. *See* Lebanese National Movement
Los Angeles Times, 28

Manchester Guardian. See Guardian
Mandela, Nelson, 29
Marine Battalion Landing Team (BLT) bombing, 123; Amal and, xv, xxvn14; in *Guardian*, 111; *New York Times* on, 109; *Times* (London) on, 111; *Wall Street Journal* on, 124
Markham, James, 48
Marsden, Eric, 19
Martin, Paul, 25. *See also Times* (London)
martyrdom, 79, 97, 98, 105, 111, 112
"Marxist-Muslims," 68, 70
massacres, 13, 68, 100–101, 118n78; Nab`a battle and, 46, 49, 51; of refugee camps, 95–96, 97, 115
"Media Coverage of the Middle East: Perception and Foreign Policy" (Shaheen), 33n122
MERIP. *See* Middle East Research and Information Project
metanarrative, xviii–xxi, xxvin33
Middle East Research and Information Project (MERIP), 18
Military Orientalism: Eastern War through Western Eyes (Porter), xvii–xviii
MLT. *See* Marine Battalion Landing Team (MLT) bombing
MNF. *See* Multinational Force
Moqaddem, Farouk, 27
Mortimer, Edward, 72
"The Moslem World Rekindles Its Militancy" (Wren), 70–71
Motahari, Ayatollah Moretez, 76
Motashami, Ali Akbar, 62
Movement of the Deprived (*Harakat al Mahrumin*), 7, 10–11, 24
Mu'awiya, xx
Muhammad (Prophet), xix–xx, 37, 52n1
Multinational Force (MNF), 105, 106
Musawi, Hussein, 109–111
Muslim Brotherhood, 120n161

Nab`a, 38, 39, 42, 50, 53n23; alliances within, 41–42; Christian Maronites and, 42; *Economist* and, 51; Fadlallah and, 41, 44–45, 52; in *Guardian*, 51; Hezbullah on, 52; *New York Times* and, 46, 48–49, 50; Norton on, 37–38; omissions about, 46–51; Syria and, 41–42; Talal-Za`tar compared to, 44; *Times* (London) and, 47–48, 51; *Washington Post* and, 47
Nab`a battle, 47; Amal and, 43, 51–52; Christian militias in, 42–43, 46, 48, 49, 50; Jisr al-Basha and, 47, 51; massacres and, 46, 49, 51; Palestinians in, 43–44, 44; al-Sadr and, 43, 51; Syria and, 42–43, 43
Nab`a expulsion, xxvn24, 37–38, 51, 53n23, 54n71; origins of, 41–42; al-Sadr and, 44, 45; truths after, 45–46
Nab`a siege, 28; Gemayel, B., and, 44; al-Sadr and, 44; Shams ad-Din and, 44
Nabatiya incident, xiv–xv, 97–99, 108; *New York Times* on, 108–109, 110; *Times* (London) on, 108
narrative, xv–xvi, xxiv; dominant, xxvn24; metanarrative, xviii–xxi, xxvin33
Nasr, Octavia, 123
Nasr, Vali, 64
National Security Agency, xxvn14
National Security Council (NSC), xxvn19
National Security Policy Group (NSPG), xxvn19
Nazis, xxvin54
NBC Evening News, 49, 54n70, 119n118
"news narrative," xvi
New York Times, xv, xxvn20, 17–18, 85n79; assassination attempt in, 114; balance in, 113–114, 115; on BLT bombing, 109; Christian militias and, 99–100; without context, 71; on Fadlallah, 122–123; on Hezbullah, 123–124, 126; on Iranian Revolution, 65, 66, 70–71, 80; Iran's Shi`a in, 72–73, 76, 79, 82; on Israeli invasion of Lebanon, 99, 100–101, 102, 104–105, 105–106, 106–107, 108–109, 118n77; on Kfar Shuba raid, 22–23; Khomeini in, 72, 73–74, 79; Lebanese Civil War and, 23–24, 24–25, 25–26, 27–29, 30; Nab`a in, 46, 48–49, 50; on Nabatiya incident, 108–109, 110; Orientalism in, 72, 75, 83; al-Sadr disappearance and, 28; al-Sadr in, 22–23, 23–24, 24, 24–25, 25–26, 27–29, 30, 35n172; shah in, 72, 73–74; *Shi`ite conservatism* in, 70, 71; on South Lebanon raids, 19,

20–21, 21; Tal al-Za`tar in, 46
The New York Times Index 1975, 34n130
Norton, Richard August, xxvn24, 5, 9, 34n146, 44; on Nab`a, 37–38
NSC. *See* National Security Council
NSPG. *See* National Security Policy Group

O'Ballance, Edgar, xxiii
Onis, Juan de, 18, 20–21, 22, 23. *See also New York Times*
Orientalism, xvii–xviii, 115; of Ajami, 2; in *New York Times*, 72, 75, 83
Orientalism (Said), xvii, xviii
Ostovar, Afshon, 62
Ottomans, xx–xxi

Pace, Eric, 72
Pahlavi, Reza (shah), 28, 45, 58–59, 60, 66; America and, 73–75; in *New York Times*, 72, 73–74; opposition to, 59, 72, 122; al-Sadr and, 61–62
Palestinian Liberation Army (PLA), 42
Palestinian Liberation Organization (PLO), xxiii, 8, 12–13; Arafat and, 11–12, 27, 122; Israeli invasion of Lebanon and, 92, 93, 96, 100; Nab`a and, 41–42; al-Sadr and, 13
Palestinians: Lebanese Civil War and, xxii–xxiv, 8–9; in Nab`a battle, 43–44, 44; al-Sadr, Musa and, 5–6, 14–15, 31n44
Pan-Islamism/Arabism, 31n44
Parker, Richard, 15
PBS. *See* Public Broadcast System
persecutions, xx–xxi, 6–7. *See also* massacres
Phalange, xxii, xxvin54, 12, 28, 46, 93, 96
Pintak, Larry, 113
Pity the Nation: The Abduction of Lebanon (Fisk), 29, 67, 90, 103
PLA. *See* Palestinian Liberation Army
PLO. *See* Palestinian Liberation Organization
political communications theory, xvi
Pollock, David, 124
Popular Resistance Militia, 27
Porter, Patrick, xvii–xviii
posters, xviii–xix; of Cultural Council for South Lebanon, 13, 14; of Harb, 97, 98; of Khomeini, 63; of al-Sadr, 3, 4, 16, 17
Powers of the Press: Twelve of the World's Influential Newspapers (Walker, M.), 65
prestige press, xxvn20, 21
Progressive Socialist Party (PSP), 9, 27–28
protest, 68; al-Sadr disappearance related to, 15–16, 29
proxy forces, 124
PSP. *See* Progressive Socialist Party
Public Broadcasting System (PBS), 125

el Qaddafi, Muammar, 15, 16, 91, 121–122

Rabinovich, Itamar, xxiv
Randall, Jonathan, 47, 85n79, 101
refugee camps massacre: Hama destruction compared to, 115; Israeli invasion of Lebanon and, 95–96, 97
religious cleansing, 48
religious decree (*fatwa*), xiv, 5
religious militants, 70
resistance, 13, 14; violence conflated with, 19–20, 20–21, 22, 22–23. *See also Afwaj al-Muqawama al-Lubnaniya*; Lebanon and Iranian resistance
rituals, xiv, 109

Saad-Ghorayeb, Amal, 53n23
Sadek, Habib, 23
al-Sadr, Baqr, 82, 91; al-Da`wa party and, 60, 68; Khomeini and, 60, 122
al-Sadr, Musa, xxii, xxvn24, 121; aircraft hijacking and, 28–29; Ajami on, 2–3, 16, 31n44, 34n147; `Alawites and, 6; Amal and, 7, 10–11, 91; background of, 1, 3, 59; balance of, 8, 9–10; Bekaa Valley speech by, 6; Berri after, 63–64; Chamran and, 44, 61; Christian Maronites and, 8, 12, 25, 31n44, 51; Christian militias and, 13; description of, 2, 3, 4, 34n147; disappearance of, xxiv, 15–17, 17, 28–29, 69, 91, 121–122; disappearance protest regarding, 15–16, 29; education from, 20–21, 33n120; fast of, 10, 25; Gandhi compared to, 25, 29, 34n147; government and, 13; in *Guardian* (Manchester), 25, 27, 29, 30, 121;

Halawi on, 2, 2–3; HISC and, 3–5, 12, 15; image of, 24–25; Iran and, 5–6, 69; Jumblatt and, 27, 27–28; King, M. L., compared to, 24, 29, 34n146; Lebanese civil war and, 7–9, 23–30; Movement of the Deprived from, 7, 10–11, 24; Nab`a battle and, 43, 51; Nab`a expulsion and, 44, 45; Nab`a siege and, 44; in *New York Times*, 22–23, 23–24, 24–25, 25–26, 27–29, 30, 35n172; Palestinians and, 5–6, 14–15, 31n44; Pan-Islamism/Arabism and, 31n44; PLO and, 13; posters of, 3, 4, 16, 17; pragmatism of, 10–11, 16–17; reconciliation and, 8, 10, 15, 25, 27, 28; role of, 3; shah and, 61–62; social services from, 5; Syria and, 6, 12–13, 27; in Taibe, 21; *Times* (London) on, 21–22, 24, 25, 26–27, 29; violence and, 20–23; Vocational High School and, 20–21, 33n120

Said, Edward, xviii, 65–66, 82–83; *Orientalism* from, xvii, xviii

Salam, Saeb, 27

Salibi, Kamal, xix

Salim I (sultan), xx–xxi

Sankari, Jamal, 38, 44–45, 53n23

Sarkis, Ilyas, 13

Saudi Arabia, 70–71, 85n75, 122, 126

Savage, Jessica, 119n118

Sazeman-i Ettela' at Va Amniyat Kishvar (SAVAK), 61–62, 67, 74

Shaery-Eisenlohr, Roschanack, xx, 3, 16–17, 60, 63, 65

shah. *See* Pahlavi, Reza

Shaheen, Jack G., 33n122

Shams ad-Din, Shaykh Muhammad Mahdi, xiv, 44, 59

Shanahan, Rodger, xxvn24, 9

Shariati, Ali, 68

Sharon, Ariel, 92–93, 93, 97

Shi`a, xxiv, xxvn16, 83n12. *See also* specific topics

The Shi`a of Lebanon: Clans, Parties, and Clerics (Shanahan), 9

The Shi`a Revival: How Conflicts within Islam Will Shape the Future (Nasr, V.), 64

Shi`i jurisprudence (*fiqh*), 1

Shi`i learning centers, 59–60

Shi`ite conservatism, 70, 71

Shiite International, 114

Shi`ite Lebanon: Transnational Religion and the Making of National Identities (Shaery-Eisenlohr), 3, 16–17

Shi`ite Revolutionary Organization, 45

Shipler, David, 99

Smith, Hendrick, 85n79

Smith, Howard K., 19, 33n112

social media, 121, 127n1

social services: from Fadlallah, 41; from Hezbullah, 125; from al-Sadr, 5

source materials, xviii

South Lebanon: Amal and, 91, 95; resistance in, 97–99; Taibe in, 20–21

South Lebanon raids, 93; *New York Times* on, 19, 20–21; *Times* (London) on, 19–20, 21–22. *See also* Israeli invasion of Lebanon

Soviet Union, 13, 92

Stempel, G. H., xxvn20

Stephens, Bret, 124–125

suicide bombers, 106, 111, 122–123, 124

Sunday Times, 77–79; Khomeini in, 74; on torture, 67

Sunni sect, xix, 126

Sunni Wahhabis, 70–71

Syria, xxi; al-Assad, H., of, 6, 27, 115, 120n161; Hama destruction in, 115, 120n161; Nab`a and, 41–42; Nab`a battle and, 42–43, 43; PLA of, 42; al-Sadr and, 6, 12–13, 27

Syrian Civil War, 124, 126

Taibe, South Lebanon, 20–21

Tal al-Za`tar, 42–43, 49, 54n70; Nab`a compared to, 44; in *New York Times*, 46

Tanner, Henry, 49

terrorism, 100; aircraft hijacking, 28–29; suicide bombers, 106, 111, 122–123, 124

terrorists, 21, 33n122, 89

text organization, xvi–xvii

Time magazine: Gadhafi in, 121–122; Khomeini in, 77, 78, 80–81

Times (London), xv, 18, 90, 115; on Amal, 101, 102; on blockade, 111; on BLT bombing, 111; on Iranian Revolution,

65, 67, 68, 68–69; Iran's Shi`a in, 72, 75, 76, 78, 79; on Islamic Amal, 111; Israeli invasion of Lebanon and, 99, 101–102, 102, 104, 105; Lebanese Civil War and, 24, 25, 26–27, 29; on Nab`a, 47–48, 51; on Nabatiya incident, 108; on reprisals, 112; on al-Sadr, 21–22, 24, 25, 26–27, 29; on South Lebanon raids, 19–20, 21–22
torture, 61, 67, 132
Traboulisi, Fawwaz, xxi, xxiv, 37, 53n23
Twelver Shi`a, xx, xxvn16, 6, 30n1
Twitter (tweets), 121, 127n1
Tyre, Lebanon, 20–21, 33n120

ulama (clerical class), xx
umma (Islamic faith), xix–xx
United Nations Commission, 47
United Nations General Assembly, 125
United Nations Resolution 425, 94
The U.S. Press and Iran: Foreign Policy and the Journalism of Deference (Dorman and Farhang), 65
Uthman (third caliphate), xx

Vanderbilt University, 54n70–54n71

The Vanished Imam (Ajami), 2–3, 16, 31n44, 34n147
vilāyat-i faqīh ("government of the jurist"), 59–60
vilayets (administrative areas), xxi
violence, 89; resistance conflated with, 19–20, 20–21, 22, 22–23; al-Sadr and, 20–23
visual materials, xviii–xix. *See also* posters
Vocational High School (Tyre, Lebanon), 20–21, 33n120

Wahhabi Movement of Islam, 85n75
Walker, Christopher, 99, 112
Walker, Martin, 65
Wall Street Journal, 124–125
Washington Post, 28, 86n97; assassination attempt in, 114; on Christian militia, 101; Iran's Shi`a in, 81–82; Nab`a and, 47
al-Wazzan, Shafiq, xiv
World War I, xxi
Wren, Christopher, 70–71

Yazid I (caliphate), xiii

zuama (clan leaders), xxii, 45–46

About the Author

Robert Tomlinson is associate professor in the National Security Affairs (NSA) department of the Naval War College at the Naval Postgraduate School, Monterey, California. He received his BA from the College of the Holy Cross in Worcester, MA. He holds masters degrees from Golden Gate University, San Francisco, in Public Administration, and from California State University, Northridge in Modern Middle Eastern History. He earned his PhD in Modern Middle Eastern History and National Security Policy from Claremont Graduate University, Claremont, CA. Prior to his academic career Bob served twenty-six years in the Air Force, retiring as a colonel. His area of study is Shi`a representation in Lebanon.

Lightning Source UK Ltd.
Milton Keynes UK
UKHW030733201020
371752UK00017B/144